VOICES

— FROM THE —

WORKHOUSE

PETER HIGGINBOTHAM

The
History
Press

First published 2012
Reprinted 2013

The History Press
The Mill, Brimscombe Port
Stroud, Gloucestershire, GL5 2QG
www.thehistorypress.co.uk

British Library Cataloguing in Publication Data.
A catalogue record for this book is available from the British Library.

ISBN 978 0 7524 6749 8

Typesetting and origination by The History Press
Printed and bound in Great Britain by
Marston Book Services Limited, Didcot

CONTENTS

ACKNOWLEDGEMENTS

RATEFUL THANKS ARE DUE to the following: Chris Jones and the *Carmarthenshire Historian* digitisation project (carmarthenshirehistorian.org) for the extracts from *Workhouse Days Remembered* by E.V. Jones; Hertfordshire Record Publications for extracts from *The Diary of Benjamin Woodcock*; The London Record Society for extracts from *Richard Hutton's Complaints Book*; Professor Tim Hitchcock for his transcription of the Kearney appeals; Delia Campbell for the memoirs and picture of her father Charles Burgess; PAC Holdings for permission to include the extract from *My Autobiography* by Charles Chaplin; Random House Group and University of Reading, Special Collections for the Rutherford letter. The Chell workhouse image is courtesy of The Potteries Museum & Art Gallery, Stoke-on-Trent, with special thanks to Sam Richardson. The image of Thomas Hartley's letter (MH 12/14019/195) is reproduced by courtesy of The National Archives. The text of Hartley's correspondence is Crown copyright and reproduced under the Open Government Licence (www.nationalarchives.gov. uk/doc/open-government-licence). All other illustrations are from the author's own collection.

INTRODUCTION

OVER THE PAST couple of decades, a great deal has been written about the workhouse and, more generally, about the wider poor relief system of which it formed a pivotal part. In addition to general surveys of the system,[1] some authors have focused on particular political or economic developments, charting the evolution of policy at a national level and exploring the huge body of statistical data and other information accumulated in official reports and archives.[2] Other writers have been more concerned with examining the poor relief system at a more local level, with studies of a particular region or comparing administration in different areas.[3] Still others have considered particular themes such as the treatment of groups such as children or the sick, or the evolution of institutional architecture or diet.[4]

What is common to virtually all this body of literature, and also to the great majority of previous writing on the subject over the past three or four centuries, is that it has been generated in the main by those who have had no first-hand experience of the institution they are discussing. The present-day limits on human longevity inevitably mean that writing about any event that took place more than about ninety years or so ago will not be based on direct personal testimony or recollections but on other accounts which themselves may often be second-hand.

That is not, of course, to say that such studies are any the worse for that. An absence of personal involvement and the perspective offered by the passage of time can make for a more measured appraisal of past events. A dispassionate tracking of, say, the annual statistics for expenditure on workhouse accommodation for different categories of inmate, or examining the public pronouncements or private correspondence of politicians of the day, can undoubtedly inform our understanding of how and why particular policies were pursued, compromises made, and events unfolded in the way that they did.

On the other hand, hearing from those who – in a variety of roles – passed through the doors of a workhouse and experienced conditions there for themselves, can provide a different yet equally valuable insight into the operation of the workhouse system.

Although it is workhouse inmates that perhaps most readily spring to mind as the source of personal testimony, accounts of life 'inside' are relatively few, particularly bearing in mind the numbers who, over the years, resorted to 'the house'. The reasons for this may include the often basic literacy of those concerned, a lack of opportunity or incentive to record such matters, and the limited audience for such accounts. Apart from the pauper inmates, however, many others had a first-hand acquaintance with the institution – visitors of various sorts, workhouse staff and their families, local administrators, official inspectors, reformers, journalists, 'social explorers', or even just the plain curious. The words of these individuals come down to us in a variety of forms – letters, songs, poems, autobiographies, newspaper articles, and official reports and inquiries. In more recent times, the activities of local historians have preserved a wealth of informal reminiscences via the medium of oral history projects and collections.

While many authors have drawn upon such accounts, for example to support or illustrate a particular argument, their quotations are usually brief. Where longer extracts have occasionally made an appearance, they have generally been limited to a specific individual, theme or time period. The aim, in compiling the present volume, has been to provide a diverse and wide-ranging collection of fifty different workhouse voices, covering a period of almost 300 years, and – within the limits of space available – to include rather more than the usual one or two sentence 'sound-bite'.

Those writing or speaking about their experience of or involvement with the workhouse can often provide us with valuable insights into how an institution was run, the character or behaviour of inmates and staff, or small details of its operation which may not be recorded elsewhere. Their own reactions and feelings about the establishment can also add much to our understanding. Personal testimony should not, however, be assumed always to be truthful or unbiased. The authors of many of the examples included in this book were pursuing particular agendas, with their words intended to evoke sympathy for themselves, to entertain, to shock, to substantiate a complaint or grudge, to obtain a better salary, to reprimand, to evade, to bring about reform, or to sell newspapers.

In modern times, the workhouse is often portrayed as an unremittingly grim institution, with its inmates routinely subjugated, abused and 'dehumanised'. However, as several of the examples in this book illustrate, this is a rather distorted picture. Workhouses could indeed be badly run, with inmates – particularly in the mid-nineteenth century – being poorly treated and accommodated in far from wholesome conditions. However, conditions did gradually change, with improved medical care, more varied and better quality food, and a relaxation of petty regulations. Inmates too, were not always passive and submissive but were quite capable of 'playing the system' to their own advantage, as is made clear in several of the pieces included here.

For a small and shrinking group of individuals, the existence of the workhouse is still within living memory. I've had the pleasure of talking to several such people and some of their recollections are included in this volume. A question I'm often asked in this regard is 'when did the last workhouse close?' My reply usually begins with the words, 'well, it all depends…' One candidate for marking the end of the workhouse is 1 April 1930 when legislation came into effect abolishing the Poor Law Unions and their Boards of Guardians who had administered the poor relief system for the best part of a century. On that date, responsibility for 'public assistance' passed to county and borough councils. Under the new regime, some workhouses were closed but the majority continued in operation rebranded as Public Assistance Institutions (PAIs). However, since PAIs inherited existing workhouse buildings, staff and inmates, there was usually little to distinguish them from what had gone before. Indeed, PAIs invariably continued to be referred to locally as 'the workhouse'. During the 1930s, some former workhouse infirmaries, particularly those in urban areas, were 'appropriated' by local councils as municipal hospitals with new facilities such as maternity units being added. Others languished as largely neglected homes for the elderly or chronic sick. The inauguration of Britain's National Health Service in 1948 saw the end of PAIs, with some premises being disposed of, while others were incorporated into the new system as hospitals, elderly care homes, or other more specialised establishments. However, the adamant refusal of many elderly people to enter a hospital or old people's home located in a former workhouse continued for very many years afterwards.

Author's Note

Many of the selections included in this volume have been abridged to varying degrees. This has been to reduce the extracts to a manageable length, taking out material which I considered to be less interesting or less relevant to the main thrust of each piece, or which would be better appreciated within the context of the whole work. In order to assist readability, such excisions are generally not indicated in the text.

Peter Higginbotham, 2012

A WORKHOUSE TIMELINE

THIS BOOK DOES NOT aim to be a comprehensive history of the workhouse system. However, for those not familiar with its development, here is a brief timeline of some major events:

1601   The Poor Relief Act is the basis of what becomes known as the Old Poor Law. Parishes become responsible for relieving their own poor funded by a local property tax – the poor rate. The poor rate can be spent on 'out-relief' (handouts to individuals) or accommodation for the 'impotent' poor – the elderly, lame or blind.

1630s   Workhouses gradually evolve to house the poor, with labour required from the able-bodied. Prototype workhouses include Reading, Abingdon, Sheffield, Newark and Newbury.

1698   Bristol's parishes promote a local Act of Parliament allowing them to jointly administer poor relief and run workhouses.

1723   Knatchbull's Act allows parishes to establish workhouses. Parishes can dispense with out-relief and offer relief claimants only the workhouse – a 'test' that they are truly destitute. Workhouse operation can be handed over to private contractors, the practice becoming known as 'farming the poor'.

1777   Around 2,000 workhouses are in operation, covering about 20 per cent of parishes. Out-relief is still the dominant form of provision, however.

1782   Gilbert's Act allows groups of parishes to form 'unions' and run joint workhouses to house non-able-bodied paupers.

1818   The national poor relief bill reaches an all-time high, having risen fivefold over the previous forty years.

1834   The Poor Law Amendment Act (the New Poor Law) establishes a new national system of poor relief administration, run by the central Poor Law Commissioners, based on groupings of parishes called Poor Law Unions. Each union is run by a locally elected Board of Guardians and has to provide a central union workhouse.

1837   Charles Dickens' *Oliver Twist* begins publication.

1838   A total of 584 Poor Law Unions are now operative in England and Wales. The Poor Relief (Ireland) Act establishes a union workhouse system in Ireland.

1845   The Poor Law (Scotland) Act introduces a new poor relief system in Scotland, with poorhouse provision as an option.

1847   The Poor Law Board replaces the Poor Law Commissioners.

1867   The Metropolitan Poor Act improves medical care for London's poor, with the new Metropolitan Asylums Board to deal with infectious and mental conditions.

1872   The Local Government Board replaces the Poor Law Board.

1900   A major overhaul of workhouse food allows more varied and flexible menus.

1905   A Royal Commission begins a major review of the poor relief system. Its report, published in 1909, recommends abolition of Boards of Guardians, replacement of workhouses by more specialised institutions, removal of children from workhouses, and the provision of old age pensions, health insurance and unemployment support.

1913   Updated official regulations now refer to 'poor law institutions' rather than 'workhouses', and 'poor persons' rather than 'paupers'. Inmate uniforms are now described as 'suitable and sufficient clothing'.

1915   Children aged over three are no longer allowed to reside in workhouses.

1930   Boards of Guardians are abolished. The administration of poor relief, now known as 'public assistance', passes to county and borough councils.

1948   The National Health Service is inaugurated.

ONE

INMATES

OVER THE CENTURIES, the numbers of individuals passing through the gates of the workhouse ran into millions. Yet first-hand accounts of their experiences by workhouse inmates are relatively few and far between. Many paupers would, of course, have had a limited degree of literacy. For those who would have been able to record a written account of their encounter with the institution, there was probably little incentive to do so. Anyone struggling to regain their independence outside the workhouse was likely to have rather more pressing concerns, such as providing a roof over their head and putting food on the table. Besides, who would be interested in hearing about an experience which was both commonplace and also widely regarded as deeply shameful? It is perhaps not surprising then, that such accounts as do survive are often anonymous or never intended for publication. One source of workhouse memoirs that did reach a wider audience comes from those who ultimately made a success of their lives and were then happy to reveal their humble origins to an interested audience.

Whatever a person's life story, or the reasons for their words coming down to us, their views of the workhouse have always to be viewed in the context in which they were recorded. Recollections of the time spent in a workhouse can often create an unbalanced view of the institution as they inevitably tend to focus on the most memorable or distressing aspects of the experience. Conditions inside the workhouse and the treatment received by inmates also have to be measured by the contemporary standards typically experienced by those outside the establishment. Workhouse food may have been plain and repetitive, but certainly no worse than the diet of many independent labourers and their families. The flogging of boys in workhouse schools may seem barbaric, but this was the norm in many Victorian children's institutions.

This collection begins with two of the earliest surviving workhouse 'voices'. In both cases, although the words recorded were spoken (or sung) by workhouse inmates, they were composed by others. Nonetheless, each provides an interesting insight into the workhouse experience in the seventeenth and early eighteenth centuries when children often featured prominently in workhouse populations.

London Corporation Workhouse
Poor Out-Cast Children's Song and Cry

The London Corporation of the Poor was first established in 1647 under *An Ordinance for the Relief and Employment of the Poor, and the Punishment of Vagrants and other Disorderly Persons*, whose provisions included the erection of 'work-houses' – one of the first pieces of legislation to employ the word. The Corporation was given two confiscated royal properties – Heiden (or Heydon) House in the Minories, and the Wardrobe building in Vintry – in which it established workhouses. By 1655, up to a hundred children and 1,000 adults were receiving relief via the establishment although residence was not a prerequisite. Adults could perform out-work in their own homes, or carry it out each day at one of the workhouses. As well as basic literacy, children in Corporation care were taught singing. A verse of one of their songs, very much a propaganda piece for the Corporation, paints a very rosy picture of their treatment:

> In filthy Rags we clothed were;
> In good warm Raiments now appear
> from Dunghils to Kings Palaces transferr'd,
> Where Education, wholesom Food,
> Meat, Drink and Lodging, all that's good
> For Soul and Body, are so well prepared.[5]

Lack of funds hindered the Corporation's activities and a later verse of the song makes an explicit appeal to the parliamentary legislators who in the mid-1650s were prevaricating on a scheme to expand England's fishing industry to the detriment of other nations such as the Dutch and Danes:

> Grave Senators, that sit on high,
> Let not Poor English Children die,
> and droop on Dunghils with lamenting notes:
> An Act for Poor's Relief, they say,
> Is coming forth; why's this delay?
> O let not Dutch, Danes, Devils stop those Votes!

The Corporation's activities came to a halt with the Restoration in 1660 when Charles II reclaimed his properties.

John Trusty
Dinner Speech at the Bishopsgate Workhouse

In 1698, the newly revived City of London Corporation established a workhouse on Bishopsgate Street, on what is now the site of Liverpool Street station. In 1720, the workhouse was said to be 'a very strong and useful Building, and of large Dimensions, containing (besides other Apartments) three long Rooms or Galleries, one over another, for Workhouses, which are all filled with Boys and Girls at Work, some Knitting, most Spinning of Wool; and a convenient Number of Women and Men teaching and overseeing them; Fires burning in the Chimneys in the Winter time, to keep the Rooms and the Children warm.'[6] The children, up to 400 in number, were taught to read and write, and given work to do until they could be put out to be apprentices, sent to sea, or 'otherwise disposed'. The youngsters all wore clothing made from 'Russit Cloth'[7], with a round badge worn on the breast representing a poor boy and a sheep with the motto 'God's Providence is our Inheritance'.

On 29 October 1702, John Trusty, an eleven-year-old boy from the workhouse, was selected to make an address to Queen Anne at the Lord Mayor's Day dinner in the Guildhall. Although clearly penned by someone else, his words – possibly the earliest on record spoken by an identifiable workhouse inmate – conjure up a rather charming scene:

The front entrance of the city of London's Bishopsgate Street workhouse.

May it please Your Most Excellent Majesty: To Pardon this great Presumption in Us poor Children, who throw our Selves at your Royal Feet, among the Rest of your Glad Subjects, who here in Crowds appear to behold Your Sacred Majesty.

We, MADAM, have no Fathers, no Mothers, no Friends; or, which is next to none, those who through their Extreme Poverty cannot help us. God's Providence is our Inheritance. (*Pointing to the motto on his breast.*) All the Support we have is from the Unexhausted Charities of Your Loyal Citizens of London, and other Your Good Subjects, and the Pious Care of our Governors, who are now teaching our little Hands to Work, and our Fingers to Spin.

These Threads, MADAM, (*Holding some yarn in his hands*) are some of the Early Fruits of our Industry. We are all daily employed on the Staple Manufacture of England, learning betimes to be useful to the World. And there seemed nothing wanting to compleat our Happiness, but the Opportunity which this Day affords us, of being the Objects of Your Tender Pitty and Compassion. One Gracious Smile from YOUR MAJESTY on this New Foundation will make us Live, – and Live to call You Blessed.

And may God Almighty long Preserve YOUR MAJESTY for the Good of these Your Kingdoms, and Your Royal Consort the PRINCE. So Pray We, Your Little Children: And let All Your People say, AMEN.[8]

Paul Patrick Kearney
London Pauper Farms

In the eighteenth century, parishes in the city of London increasingly moved away from running their own workhouses and instead used the services of private contractors who operated 'pauper farms', often located outside the city boundaries.

One inmate of such an establishment was Paul Patrick Kearney, a colourful and disreputable character who was finally reduced to claiming poor relief from the City parish of St Dionis Backchurch where he had legal settlement.[9] In 1764, after his initial requests for relief were turned down by two of the churchwardens, Kearney – as was every applicant's right – took his case to the Lord Mayor of London who, like local justices of the peace elsewhere, could overrule such decisions. Churchwarden William Kippax then agreed to offer Kearney relief which, to Kearney's horror, consisted not of the anticipated handout but of a note of admission to the parish's pauper farm – or 'mock workhouse' as Kearney referred to it. The note, as Kearney later related, was addressed to the farm's proprietor:

One Richard Birch in Rose Lane in the parish of Christ church Spitalfields in the county of Middlesex not only out of the said parish of Saint Dionys but also out of the city of London and Jurisdiction of the Lord Mayor which written note instead of being an order for this informants relief was a warrant of commitment of this informants body to imprisonment labour or work in an infected filthy dungeon called a work house kept by the said Richard Birch containing near one hundred poor victims to parish cruelty but not capacious enough healthily to hold forty persons, and therein the said Birch grossly insulted and abused and ordered [me] to work at emptying the soil out of vaults that pass in drains or sewers through under or in the said mock work house which so overcame [me, that I] fainted and fell sick and was in that condition forced into a nasty bed where [I] was swarmed with lice and got the Itch mange and a malignant or pocky leprosy.[10]

Although conditions on pauper farms had a poor reputation, the woeful picture painted by Kearney is clearly one whose intent is primarily to provoke sympathy for his claim for out-relief.

For several years afterwards, Kearney managed to extract relief from the parish in various forms including cash, lodging, clothing and medicine. In February 1771, by which time the parish was housing paupers with a contractor at Hoxton, Kearney was again petitioning the Lord Mayor. On this occasion, his pleas were heard by a sitting of aldermen who:

Sent me into prison to be bodily & unlawfully punished & mentally tortured in a Slaughter house for poor human bodies unlawfully kept by John Hughes & Wm Phillips & their accomplices at Hogsden [Hoxton].[11]

At a subsequent inspection of the Hoxton workhouse by the St Dionis churchwardens, Kearney complained:

I was perishing of cold for want of clean warm apparel & lodging ill of a complication of distemper occasioned by the cruelties exercised on me at Birches &c and that I could not eat half the victuals allowed me because of my illness & their being cold & not warm victuals fit for an ailing person, nor any spoon meat not even Sage tea & but 3 pints of small beer which occasion'd my drinking more water there than beer daily, and that I was insulted tormented vexed & otherwise constantly abused in so much that my life was a burthen to me there.[12]

Soon afterwards, Kearney proposed that in return for a one-off payment of forty shillings, he would agree never again to claim relief from the parish. The money was to allow him to take up a post as secretary to a Captain Scot who was embarking on several years of travels abroad. Although it is not clear if the money was paid, Kearney was not heard from again.

Ann Candler
Reflections on My Own Situation

Ann Candler was born in 1740 at Yoxford in Suffolk, the daughter of glover William More and his wife. As a child, Ann displayed a 'fondness for reading', her favourites being travel books, plays and romances, though not poetry. Despite this, her first efforts after learning to write were in verse.[13]

In 1762, she married a man named Candler, a cottager from the nearby village of Sproughton. Candler's heavy drinking, coupled with his service in the militia from 1763 to 1766, kept Ann and her growing family destitute. When Candler re-enlisted in 1777, Ann was ill for eleven weeks and was forced to put four of her six children into the Tattingstone workhouse. In 1780, she took refuge in the workhouse herself, where she gave birth to twin sons, an event which became the subject of one of her poems. Sadly, both twins died after a few weeks. Following Candler's military discharge in 1783, the two of them entered the workhouse. Six months later, Candler departed – the last Ann ever saw of him. Remaining in the workhouse, she began writing more poetry, some of which was published by the *Ipswich Journal*. She gained several literary patrons, including the poet Elizabeth Cobbold, and in 1802 advance subscriptions for a small volume of her poems, *Poetical Attempts*, enabled Ann to take furnished lodgings near her married daughter Lucy.

The Tattingstone House of Industry was erected in 1768 to house 300 paupers, later becoming the Samford Union workhouse and now converted to residential use.

The poem 'Reflections on my own Situtation, Written in T–tt–ngst–ne House of Industry, February 1802' expresses her feelings about the 'niggard alms' of the institution. However, having acquired 'a friend indeed' outside the workhouse – presumably Mrs Cobbold – salvation is at hand. Here is the first part of the poem:

> How many years are past and gone,
>   How alter'd I appear,
> How many strange events have known,
>   Since first I enter'd here!
>
> Within these dreary walls confin'd,
>   A lone recluse, I live,
> And, with the dregs of human kind,
>   A niggard alms receive.
>
> Uncultivated, void of sense,
>   Unsocial, insincere,
> Their rude behaviour gives offence,
>   Their language wounds the ear.
>
> Disgusting objects swarm around,
>   Throughout confusions reign;
> Where feuds and discontent abound,
>   Remonstrance proves in vain.
>
> No sympathising friend I find,
>   Unknown is friendship here;
> Not one to soothe, or calm the mind,
>   When overwhelm'd with care:
>
> Peace, peace, my heart, thy duty calls,
>   With cautious steps proceed:
> Beyond these melancholy walls,
>   I've found a friend indeed!

Charles Shaw
When I Was a Child

Charles Shaw was born in 1832 at Piccadilly Street, Tunstall, in the Staffordshire Potteries. He was the sixth of eight children of Enoch Shaw, a painter and gilder, and Ann, *née* Mawdesley. After attending a dame school[14] in Tunstall, he began work as a mould runner to an apprentice muffin maker,[15] earning a shilling a week. When he was eight, he moved to another factory as a handle maker. In 1842 his father lost his job after participating in a strike and for a few weeks the family were forced into Wolstanton and Burslem Union workhouse at Chell.

Shaw later became a minister, a mill owner, and a writer. His book, *When I Was a Child*, was published in 1903[16] under the pen name of 'An Old Potter':

We went by the field road to Chell, so as to escape as much observation as possible. One child had to be carried as she was too young to walk. The morning was dull and cheerless. I had been through those fields in sunshine, and when the singing of birds made the whole scene very pleasant. Now, when the silence was broken, it was only by deep agonising sobs. If we could have seen what was driving us so reluctantly up that hill to the workhouse ('Bastile', as it was bitterly called then), we should have seen two stern and terrible figures – Tyranny and Starvation. No other powers could have so relentlessly hounded us along. None of us wanted to go, but we must go, and so we came to our big home for the time. The very vastness of it chilled us. Our reception was more chilling still. Everybody we saw and spoke to looked metallic, as if worked from within by a hidden machinery. Their voices were metallic, and sounded harsh and imperative. The younger ones huddled more closely to their parents, as if from fear of these stern officials. Doors were unlocked by keys belonging to bunches, and the sound of keys and locks and bars, and doors banging, froze the blood within us. It was all so unusual and strange, and so unhomelike. We finally landed in a cellar, clean and bare, and as grim as I have since seen in prison cells. We were told this was the place where we should have to be washed and put on our workhouse attire. Nobody asked us if we were tired, or if we had had any breakfast. We might have committed some unnameable crime, or carried some dreaded infection. We youngsters were roughly disrobed, roughly and coldly washed, and roughly attired in rough clothes, our under garments being all covered up by a rough linen pinafore. Then we parted amid bitter cries, the young ones being taken one way and the parents (separated too) taken as well to different regions in that merciful establishment which the statesmanship of England had provided for those who were driven there by its gross selfishness and unspeakable crassness.

I was ushered or shoved into a large room which I found was both dining and schoolroom. There were many guests assembled, and on the principle, 'The more the merrier', we ought to have dined merrily. But I saw no merriment, not even in that company of boys, at whose age Heaven usually endows them with almost irrepressible fun. I saw hungry-looking lads, with furtive glances, searching everything and everybody, and speaking in subdued whispers. I saw a stern, military, cadaverous-looking man, who was said to be the schoolmaster.

I noticed his chilling glances, carrying menace in every look. When dinner was ready this stony-looking individual bent his head a few seconds and mumbled something. I suppose it was grace he was saying before meat, but as far as I could see there was no grace in anything he did. I noticed he did not join us in our repast, and I know now he was a wise man for not doing so. He had asked God's blessing on what we were to eat; but he would have cursed it had he had to eat it himself. It was a fine piece of mockery, though I did not know it then, or I should have admired his acting. I was hungry, but that bread! that greasy water! those few lumps of something which would have made a tiger's teeth ache to break the fibres of! The strangeness, the repulsiveness, and the loneliness, made my heart turn over, and I turned over what I could not eat to those near me, who devoured voraciously all I could spare. It was the first great dinner I ever attended, and I didn't like it. I have been at other big dinners where there were many courses, and flowers, and gleaming silver, glass, and other amenities. But this big dinner was simply coarse, and looked only coarse even for a poor lad who had not been too daintily fed. In the afternoon we had our school work to do, and as I could read well I had no trouble with such lessons as were given. But if some of the other lads had had heads made of leather stuffed with hay they could not have got more knocks. It was a brutal place for the 'dull boy'. However hard he worked, and however patiently he strove, he got nothing but blows. Tea and supper by a wise economy were joined together. The New Poor Law was to be economical if anything, even to the least quantity of food a growing boy's stomach could do with. But supper time came. What would it bring? That was the question for me. It brought a hunch of bread and a jug of skilly. I had heard of workhouse skilly but had never before seen it. I had had poor food before this, but never any so offensively poor as this. By what rare culinary-making nausea and bottomless fatuousness it could be made so sickening I never could make out. Simple meal and water, however small the amount of meal, honestly boiled, would be palatable. But this decoction of meal and water and mustiness and fustiness was most revolting to any healthy taste. It might have been boiled in old clothes, which had been worn upon sweating bodies for three-score years and ten. That workhouse skilly was the vilest compound I ever tasted, unutterably insipid, and it might never have been made in a country where either sugar or salt was known.

Our bedroom was a long, narrow room, with the beds in rows on each side of the room. Down the middle of the room was a long, narrow passage. The bed clothing was scant enough, and the beds hard enough for athletic discipline. At the end of the room, near the staircase, was a wide, shallow tub. There were boys there as cruel as neglect and badness could make them. They soon found out the timid ones, and would 'walk the midnight air' to frighten all they could by ghostly appearances. A poor lad, seeking the tub at night, would sometimes shriek through some brutal attempt to frighten him. By sheer weariness some would soon drop off to sleep, while others, alive with fears, would have to listen to the most harrowing stories of ghosts, boggarts and murders. Every new boy had to sing a song or tell a tale – the other boys wanted a taste of his quality – the first night, and pitied was that poor boy to be who could neither sing nor tell a tale. He was bullied, was pulled out of bed, and scarified by pitiless mockery such as that of 'a schoolboy ere he's learned to pity'.

Feverishly and restlessly I spent that first night. Hunger and terror were about my bed. A lively imagination made real and present some of the characters in the tales which had been told by the boys who were now asleep. I saw the ghosts they had spoken of. I saw the murderers, red-handed, rushing through the room. I heard their footsteps, and only found out too late that the footsteps were those of the poor little fellows who were visiting the tub at the end of the room. Sanitation was an angel undreamed of in the workhouses in those days, as well as in England generally. That tub, too, had to be carried down the stairs every morning before breakfast by two small boys in turn.

This first day's experience of the Bastile was like most others, and the night's too. On the Sunday, I remember, we were taken to church in the morning. After the church the clergyman came to our 'dining-room', but, like the schoolmaster, not to dine with us. He was to say 'grace before meat' in place of the schoolmaster as it was a most sacred day. He also gave us a preliminary homily as long as the sermon he had given in church. We stood up while this was given. We were told on that and other Sundays, as I well remember, of the great mercies we enjoyed, of the good food provided, of the comfortable clothing we had, and how we were cared for by those about us. All this was said while before us on the table lay a small hunk of bread, a small plate with a small slice of thin, very thin cheese, and some jugs of water. This was our Sunday dinner, and for such a dinner 'that good man, the clergyman', was brought to say grace. It was a dinner we liked, nevertheless, because of the bit of cheese with its appetising taste, and its power, as was said in those days, 'to eat a lot of bread'. And because we liked it we disliked the parson for keeping us so long from enjoying it. However, the homily and the grace came to an end at last and the parson departed, but not to a dinner, however sumptuous, that he relished more than we did that bit of cheese. This was the one bit of food that reminded us of home.

Sunday afternoon brought an hour of unspeakable joy. The children who had mothers were permitted to go to the women's room. It can easily be imagined what happened then. Bedlam was let loose for an hour. Wild joy, frantic exclamations, every conceivable form of speech possible to such people under such circumstances were employed. Love went mad in many cases. But all did not give way to the wild revelry of passion. Some mothers and children hung together in quiet, intense endearments. These were conveyed more by soft pressures of hands, embraces, and lips, than by words. Even among the poor many stand worlds apart. This was the one sweet merciful relief in the harsh discipline of the workhouse.

There was one 'case of discipline' while I was at the Bastile to which I must refer. It was a conspicuous case, and therefore had 'to be made an example of'. So ran the official cant. Discipline was administered with unfailing regularity every day. Hardly a boy escaped some form of it, and it was usually a merciless form. It seemed to be a standing regulation that this treatment was as necessary for the soul as skilly was for the body. No distinction was made, the same cuts and slashes and cuffs were aimed at the mobile and sensitive boy as were aimed at the sluggish and dull boy. The one boy would writhe and sob, and the other maintained a stolid silence. The case I am now going to refer to was that of a boy of lively temperament and unflagging energy. His activity was always bringing him into trouble. The theory formed by the officials seemed to be that his activity was essentially vicious, and so, instead of trying to guide it into wise and useful developments, it must be sternly repressed. Such a policy goaded the lad. He became defiant and reckless. Punish him they might, but he could not be repressed. One day, after being unusually provoked and punished, he scaled the workhouse wall, and bolted. Soon a hue and cry was raised, searchers were sent out, and after a few hours the lad was captured and brought back. This incident made an awful flutter in our little dove-cote. All were sorry for the lad, for he had made no enemies among us. All sorts of punishment were imagined as likely to be inflicted, but the boys who had been longest in the workhouse said he would be flogged in the presence of the other boys with a pickled birch rod – that is a rod which has been kept soaking in salt water. After the usual skilly supper that night we were all told to remain in the room. None were to go out on any account. The long table was cleared, and a smaller square table was brought in and placed in the middle of the room. The knowing ones whispered that the flogging would take place on this table, and this news made us all curious, eager, yet fearful. Several persons came in whom we did not usually see. Then the governor came in. To us poor lads he was the incarnation of every dread power which a mortal could possess. He was to us the Bastile in its most repulsive embodiment. Personally, he may have been an amiable man, I don't know. He never gave one look or touch which led me to feel he was a man. He was only 'the governor', and as such, in those days, when the New Poor Laws meant making a workhouse a dread and a horror to be avoided, he was perhaps only acting the part he felt to be due to his office. His functions, and any outward compassion, were as wide asunder as the poles. He may have had compassion. He may have been inwardly tortured by the necessity for outward callousness. May Heaven forgive me if I do him any wrong, but word or act of kindliness from him I never heard or saw towards myself or anyone else. Now, however, the governor was in the room, and his presence seemed to fill it with an awful shadow. We were duly informed by him what was to take place, the

A view of the Wolstanton and Burslem Union workhouse at Chell in Staffordshire, where Charles Shaw and his family spent time in 1842.

bad qualities of the runaway were ponderously and slowly described, and we were exhorted in menacing tones to take warning by his 'awful example'. This homily was enough of itself to make us shiver, and shiver most of us did with fear of those present and fear of the sight we were about to witness. When the solemn harangue was finished, the poor boy was pushed into the room like a sheep for the slaughter. He had a wild, eager look. His eyes flashed, and searched the room and all present with rapid glances. His body was stripped down to his waist, and in the yellow and sickly candlelight of the room his heart could be seen beating rapidly against his poor thin ribs. To punish such a boy as that, half nourished, and trembling with fear, was a monstrous cruelty. However, discipline was sacred, and could do no wrong in a Bastile sixty years ago. The boy was lifted upon the table, and four of the biggest boys were called out to hold each a leg or an arm. The boy was laid flat on the table, his breeches well pushed down, so as to give as much play as possible for the birch rod. The lad struggled and screamed. Swish went the pickled birch on his back, administered by the schoolmaster, who was too flinty to show any emotion. Thin red stripes were seen across the poor lad's back after the first stroke. They then increased in number and thickness as blow after blow fell on his back. Then there were seen tiny red tricklings following the course of the stripes, and ultimately his back was a red inflamed surface, contrasting strongly with the skin on his sides. How long the flogging went on I cannot say, but screaming became less and less piercing, and at last the boy was taken out, giving vent only to heavy sobs at intervals. If he was conscious, I should think only partially so. The common rumour was that he would have his back washed with salt water. Of this I don't know. I do know there had been cruelty enough. A living horror, hateful in every aspect, had been put before the eyes of the boys present.

There was little sleep in our room for some boys, all their pulses were alive with fear and terror. The night bore on slowly and wearily. The broken whispers told of restlessness and sleeplessness. But the morning came, and the skilly, and the room where we had witnessed the bleeding back of the boy. The boy didn't come, however. Where he was none of us knew. I never saw him again.[17]

Some of the events that Shaw recounted were incorporated by Arnold Bennett into his 1910 novel *Clayhanger*.

James Reynolds Withers
Written from Newmarket Union

Withers was an unsuccessful shoemaker from the village of Weston Colville in Cambridgeshire. He and his family became inmates in the Newmarket workhouse where, in 1846, he composed a verse letter to his sister. He bemoans the monotonous food and lack of beer, the ill-fitting workhouse uniform, and the irreligious behaviour of his fellow inmates. The usual workhouse labour − turning a capstan-operated corn-mill − does not appear to have been too arduous, however:

Since I cannot, dear sister, with you hold communion,
I'll give you a sketch of our life in the Union.
But how to begin I don't know, I declare:
Let me see; well, the first is our grand bill of fare.
We've skilley for breakfast; at night bread and cheese,
And we eat it and then go to bed if you please.
Two days in the week we've puddings for dinner,
And two we have broth, so like water, but thinner;
Two meat and potatoes, of this none to spare;
One day, bread and cheese − and this is our fare.

And now then my clothes I will try to pourtray;
They're made of coarse cloth, and the colour is grey,
My jacket and waistcoat don't fit me at all;
My shirt is too short, or else I am too tall;
My shoes are not pairs, though of course I have two,
They are down at heel and my stockings are blue.

The entrance archway of the Newmarket Union workhouse. This view, from the interior of the premises, would have been a familiar sight to James Withers.

But what shall I say of the things they call breeches?
Why mine are so large they'd have fitted John Fitches.
John Fitches, you'll say, well, pray who was he?
Why one of the fattest men I ever did see.
To be well understood, dear, they ought to be seen;
Neither breeches nor trowsers, but something between;
And though they're so large, you'll remember, I beg;
They're low on the waist and high on the leg.

And no braces allowed me – oh dear, oh dear!
We are each other's glass, so I know I look queer.
A sort of Scotch bonnet we wear on our heads;
And I sleep in a room where there're just fourteen beds:
Some are sleeping, some snoring, some talking, some playing,
Some fighting, some swearing, but very few praying.

Here are nine at a time who work on the mill;
We take it by turns so it never stands still:
A half hour each gang, 'tis not very hard,
And when we are off we can walk in the yard.
We have nurseries here, where the children are crying;
And hospitals too for the sick and the dying.

But I must not forget to record in my verse,
All who die here are honor'd to ride in a hearse.
I sometimes look up at the bit of blue sky
High over my head, with a tear in my eye,
Surrounded by walls that are too high to climb,
Confin'd like a felon without any crime;
Not a field nor a house nor a hedge can I see –
Not a plant, not a flower, nor a bush nor a tree,
Except a geranium or two that appear
At the governor's window, to smile even here.

But I find I am got too pathetic by half,
And my object was only to cause you to laugh;
So my love to yourself, your husband and daughter,
I'll drink to your health with a tin of cold water:
Of course, we've no wine, no porter nor beer,
So you see that we all are teetotallers here.[18]

Reynolds later came to the attention of literary society and was fashionable for a while, but he eventually died in poverty.

Thomas Hartley
Letters of Complaint to the Poor Law Commissioners

Those who felt sufficiently aggrieved about their treatment in a Union workhouse occasionally wrote directly to the central authorities to present their complaints. A typical example is the letter sent to the Poor Law Commissioners (recently superseded by the Poor Law Board) in April 1848 by Thomas Hartley, an inmate of the Kidderminster Union workhouse in Worcestershire. Hartley's complaints covered the infrequent washing of inmates' stockings, favouritism in the provision of tea and butter to the elderly, the incorrect classification of disabled elderly men as able-bodied, the sending of an eighty-year-old man to work in the stone yard, and the housing of 'idiots' in subterranean accommodation:

Kidderminster Union
Apl 17th 1848
Gentlemen, I make my address to you being an inmate of the above mentioned Union which statement is as follows, 1st several weeks ago I made a complaint to the Governer about wearing my stockings 3 weeks without Washing some time after I wrote to the Bord of Gardians stateing the above with other

A page from Thomas Hartley's letter, now preserved in the National Archives' vast collection of Poor Law Correspondence. Part of this important resource has now been digitised. (Image reproduced by courtesy of The National Archives) representations, also I told them I was ready to answer them any Questions they Chus'd to put to me, they have put none at all to me, it lies quite dark to me that some has wore stockings 2 months without washing but since my letter to the Gardians some little alterations have been made but our stockings are not changed yet Weekly, 2nd Concerning men 60 years of age & upwards to get Tea & Butter if thought requisite, there are men at 80 who wish for it do not get, plainly speaking it should be if thought favourites, 3rd Men above 60 years of age Ruptured, to hard labour by breaking of stones, according to a piece of a report I have picked who were falsely return'd, Disabled then were return's able Boddyed it may be the case now, 4th Concerning an Old man which is 80 years of age or upwards forc'd to the stone some times carried upon a mans back some times Weeld down in a Weelbarrow look at this iniquity if I let this pass in silence should I be any then a Cristian, 5th Sick men mixt among well, 6th Idiots in places below the earth I have enough to inform you gentlemen that place wants much investigation, I wish an inquiry before I procede father. I conclude for the Present yours Respectfully Thomas Hartley an inmate of Kidderminster Union[19]

Hartley's letter is annotated by comments from John Thomas Graves, the Poor Law Inspector responsible for Kidderminster, saying that he will visit Kidderminster and inquire into the complaints. He also notes that 'there has long been discontent in this workhouse'. However, a separate unsigned internal memo (in a different hand) contends that since most of the many such complaints were proved to lack foundation, they should not be acknowledged as this only encouraged the senders. Graves clearly did pursue the matter as revealed by a subsequent letter from Hartley who (confirming the memo-writer's prediction) expanded upon his grievances at length. Hartley's new missive concluded with the suggestion that only a surprise visit by the authorities would reveal the true state of affairs at the workhouse since any prior warning resulted in a rapid cleaning-up exercise:

Kidderminster Union

May 1st 1848

Gentlemen I send you my letter of thanks for your kind endeavours in regard of my last to you & I have Confidence to say that every inmate who is a rational man is thankful for the same, what it as Produc'd and what the Future Result may likely be the Commishoner who came to Kidd' I imagine could not help witnessing that I was rather annoy'd in the Room with the gardians, The governer said he wore stockings 3 weeks himself, I answer'd more shame for you to say so, I was then called to Order by one of the gdn's, another said he wore stockings 3 weeks to, so they acknoleg'd themselves to be dirty, you I expect herd one say to me why dont you go out if you dont like it, the Clerk in his examination refer'd to What stockings I wore when out, which was quite out of the question I was aware this was done to Confuse me, when you

No. 1.—DIETARY for ABLE-BODIED MEN and WOMEN.

		BREAKFAST.		DINNER.				SUPPER.		
		Bread.	Gruel.	Cooked Meat.	Potatoes.	Soup.	Suet, or Rice Pudding.	Bread.	Cheese.	Broth.
		oz.	pints.	oz.	lbs.	pints.	oz.	oz.	oz.	pints.
Sunday	Men	6	1½	5	½	..	..	6	..	1½
	Women	5	1½	5	½	..	..	5	..	1½
Monday	Men	6	1½	..	..	1½	..	6	2	—
	Women	5	1½	..	..	1½	..	5	2	—
Tuesday	Men	6	1½	5	½	..	..	6	..	1½
	Women	5	1½	5	½	..	..	5	..	1½
Wednesday	Men	6	1½	..	..	1½	..	6	2	—
	Women	5	1½	..	..	1½	..	5	2	—
Thursday	Men	6	1½	5	½	..	..	6	..	1½
	Women	5	1½	5	½	..	..	5	..	1½
Friday	Men	6	1½	..	..	..	14	6	2	—
	Women	5	1½	..	..	..	12	5	2	—
Saturday	Men	6	1½	..	..	1½	..	6	2	—
	Women	5	1½	..	..	1½	..	5	2	—

Old people of sixty years of age and upwards may be allowed one ounce of tea, five ounces of butter, and seven ounces of sugar per week, in lieu of gruel for breakfast, if deemed expedient to make this change.

Children under nine years of age to be dieted at discretion; above nine, to be allowed the same quantities as women.

Sick to be dieted as directed by the medical officer.

The 'No. 1 Dietary for Able-Bodied Men and Women', one of six alternative menu-plans issued to union workhouses in 1835. It notes that the elderly could be permitted to forego their breakfast gruel in exchange for a weekly allowance of tea, butter and sugar.

alude to going up to the Union, I was better sattisfy'd, the Reverend Fletcher said as I was about to retire to the governor how is he employ'd the answer at the stone block, then keep him to it was the answer which I considered a clandestical threten, This was the language from a Minnister of the gospel of Christ view it in a morral light view it in spiritual you will find it is neither morral or spiritual I shall next procede to the Case of a madman who came from Droit Wich Assilem into this Union, the name of this man is Bates, he has sometimes been a little governable sometimes strapt down, quite in a derang'd state for months, This man his own close were put on him the gate opened and let out by himself, this was on Easter monday Returned on wednesday 26ᵗʰ apˡ, Raskally us'd on the 27ᵗʰ by an inmate William Smith commonly called Callis, the man Bates came out of his place in his Shirt in the Publick yard, Smith went behind him and expos'd his nakedness bates turned round to him He Smith then struck him two severe blows on the sides of his head I informd the mistress on Friday Morning Riseing from my bed I came into the room I heard the governer in an ajoining partment have loud words with the men, he came in up to me and said Mʳ Hartley you may Report that to the Commishoners if you like, I said should that which was right fear nobody & keep enemies at arms length, the governer Returning down stairs said I will look after you, which I considers a threatening, On Friday last Mr Duncomb one of the gardians came up Inquirey being made who had any thing to say

must go to the Committee, I went I stated the Case of the madman going out in state of insanity, how the governor had accosted me also making making inquirey what was meant by the Rev[d] Fletchers speech leaving the Bord Room, the answer was not decidely answerd as M[r] Duncom of Corse could not tell anothers mistecal meaning, the governer said he had no animosity towards me, I shall next procede to a case of defraud or intent to defraud Concerning old men allow'd and Receiving butter, it appears on Friday last Tho[s] Simmons and others made a Complaint to Mr Duncomb, That being allowd 5 oz of Butter per Week being enquir'd into their only receiving 4 oz for a number of Weeks, on Saturday being their butter day it was altered to 5 oz again, Gower is the only man who Receives butter in our Room, I ask'd him how many Weeks he had been on the reduc'd allowance of butter he said 5 Weeks if not more, Now the number of Weeks deficient is Robery or defraud, Thomas Simmonds told me after they made the Complaint that the governer came into the Room and told them they should have no butter at all, this is to give you an insight into on these kind of places When you come to these kind places the best way is to come on an unexpected way if they have the least notice they will be prepard for it if taken on a sudden you will find its General state, the general way of this place when any one in Authority comes is sweep the place put clean bedquilts on those beds there put clean sheets there change those beds which are dirtyd through & those among the Idiots, such running in all quarters like as if an Enemy was come at the same same as its friend I hope this may be useful for your information I am gentlemen yours with the greatest Respect and thankfulness
Thomas Hartley
inmate of Kidderminster Union[20]

A subsequent report from John Graves made a number of recommendations – that the Kidderminster Guardians be asked as to whether the allegation of fraud relating to butter had been pursued; that the workhouse medical officer make a list of those entitled to receive an allowance of butter and tea; and that inmates' complaints should be investigated by the Guardians in a more regular manner.

Anonymous
An Unemployed London Carpenter

In 1849 and 1850 the journalist and social researcher Henry Mayhew wrote a series of 'letters' for the *Morning Chronicle* based on hundreds of interviews he had conducted with the 'street folk' of London. These articles formed the basis of the three-volume work entitled *London Labour and the London Poor* published in 1851.

Mayhew's work was notable for its richly detailed descriptions of his subjects, their work and their domestic lives. It covered a diverse range of occupations at the lower end of the social scale including street-sellers, street-musicians, crossing-sweepers, coal-heavers, sweeps, scavengers, mudlarks, sewer-hunters and rat-catchers. Many of these people lived a life that was economically precarious with the workhouse an ever-present threat when times were bad. A typical report looked at the situation of carpenters and joiners whose trade was increasingly being mechanised with the introduction of equipment such as steam-operated saws and planes. For one unnamed carpenter, the workhouse provided temporary help through its labour yard, while in winter his whole family were forced into 'the house':

I am a jobbing carpenter, and in very great distress. All my tools are gone – sold or pawned. I have no means of living but by parish relief, and picking up what I can in little odd jobs along the waterside. Sometimes I get a job at painting, glazing, or whitewashing, now that I have lost my own work; sometimes I get a day's work at the London or St Katherine Docks – anywhere I can get anything to do. And when I can't find any other employment I go to the workhouse yard and get a job there at wheeling the barrows and breaking stones. Sometimes I go to the yard four days in the week, sometimes only one day, and sometimes the whole of the week, according as I can get work. At the workhouse yard I get 1s 6d when I'm paid by the day; and when I'm at work on the stones I get 2d a bushel for all I break, and the most I can do is six bushel in a day. Some men does 9 and 10 bushel, but then they're stronger men than me. I have got a wife and three children to keep out of my earnings, such as they are. My wife does nothing. She has a young child six months old to take care on, so it all lays on my hands. My eldest is a boy of 13 years. He got a place at a glass polisher's, and gets 5s a week. He lives with his uncle. I've only the two others to look to. On Saturday my wife has a loaf and a shilling given to her from the parish, and that, with the shilling I earn at the yard, is all we has to keep and pay rent for the four of us, from Saturday till Monday. We can't go to work at the yard till Tuesday morning, for on Mondays we has the day to look after a job at some other place. Taking one week with another, I reckon I get, with parish allowance and all, from 5s to 6s, and out of that I pays 1s 6d a week rent for one room – a first floor back, in an alley. It's my own things that's in it, and I'm obliged to scrape up 2d and 3d at a time to raise the rent, and give it 'em at the end of the week. I reckon we has generally from 4s to 4s 6d a week at the outside to live upon – all the four. Sometimes it arn't that, for I go down to the docks to look after some work, and lose my day. We live upon bread and butter and coffee or tea, and maybe we manage sometimes to have a herring or two; and if we do have a taste of meat, why it's a bit of bacon – twopennyworth – which I buys instead of butter. Perhaps, if I've been very lucky in the week, I picks up a pound of bits at 4*d* on the Saturday night, and we makes a hash on it, with a few taturs, for Sunday. My wife does the washing at home, and the things is dried in the room we live and sleep in. In the winter we all of us goes into the house (the union), because we can't afford to pay for firing outside. I leaves my things, such as they are, with my brother-in-law. To people like myself the cheapening of food has been the greatest of good. I don't know who brought it about, but I'm sure whoever it was, he has blessings for it. It was said that the bread was to be brought down to 4*d* a loaf, but it's never been less than 5*d* round about us. It's mostly bread that keeps us alive. Sometimes we has a pennyworth of taturs, but that's not our usual food. Half-a-quartern loaf will last us to the next day, and when I goes to work I puts a bit of bread in my hat, and that's my dinner, and all I have until night, when I go home and get a cup of tea. We have a halfpenny candle of an evening and a quarter of a pound of soap on a Saturday. My wife buys 14lbs of coals for 2*d* about twice a week, and that serves for boiling our kettle and such like. That's how we live.[21]

H.M. Stanley (John Rowlands)
Autobiography

In 1847, the fatherless five-year-old John Rowlands became an inmate of the St Asaph Union workhouse in North Wales. In later life in the USA, Rowlands adopted the name Henry Morton Stanley and, as a journalist for the *New York Herald*, tracked down the missing explorer Dr David Livingstone, greeting him with the famous words 'Dr Livingstone, I presume?'

Stanley had been placed in the workhouse by his foster parents Richard and Jenny Price after his uncles had refused to pay them an increase in the boy's maintenance. Stanley's autobiography recalls his time at the St Asaph workhouse:

Dick Price [the Price's own son] took me by the hand one day, Saturday, February 10th, 1847, and, under the pretence that we were going to Aunt Mary at Fynnon Beuno, induced me to accompany him on a long journey.

The way seemed interminable and tedious, but he did his best to relieve my fatigue with false cajolings and treacherous endearments. At last Dick set me down from his shoulders before an immense stone building, and, passing through tall iron gates, he pulled at a bell, which I could hear clanging noisily in the distant interior. A sombre-faced stranger appeared at the door, who, despite my remonstrances, seized me by the hand, and drew me within, while Dick tried to sooth my fears with glib promises that he was only going to bring Aunt Mary to me. The door closed on him, and, with the echoing sound, I experienced for the first time the awful feeling of utter desolateness.

The great building with the iron gates and innumerable windows, into which I had been so treacherously taken, was the St Asaph Union Workhouse. It is an institution to which the aged poor and superfluous children of that parish are taken, to relieve the respectabilities of the obnoxious sight of extreme poverty, and because civilisation knows no better method of disposing of the infirm and helpless than by imprisoning them within its walls.

Once within, the aged are subjected to stern rules and useless tasks, while the children are chastised and disciplined in a manner that is contrary to justice and charity. To the aged it is a house of slow death, to the young it is a house of torture. Paupers are the failures of society, and the doom of such is that they shall be taken to eke out the rest of their miserable existence within the walls of the Workhouse, to pick oakum.[22]

The sexes are lodged in separate wards enclosed by high walls, and every door is locked, and barred, and guarded, to preserve that austere morality for which these institutions are famous. That the piteous condition of these unfortunates may not arouse any sympathy in the casual visitor, the outcasts are clad in fustian suits, or striped cotton dresses, in which uniform garb they become undistinguishable, and excite no interest. Their only fault was that they had become old, or so enfeebled by toil and sickness that they could no longer sustain themselves, and this is so heinous and grave in Christian England that it is punished by the loss of their liberty, and they are made slaves.

At one time in English history such wretches were left to die by the wayside; at another time, they incurred the suspicion of being witches, and were either drowned or burnt; but in the reign of Queen Victoria the dull-witted nation has conceived it to be more humane to confine them in a prison, separate husband from wife, parent from child, and mete out to each inmate a daily task, and keep old and young under the strictest surveillance. At six in the morning they are all roused from sleep; and at 8 o'clock at night they are penned up in their dormitories. Bread, gruel, rice, and potatoes compose principally their fare, after being nicely weighed and measured. On Saturdays each person must undergo a thorough scrubbing, and on Sundays they must submit to two sermons, which treat of things never practised, and patiently kneel during a prayer as long as a sermon, in the evening.[23]

The scourge of St Asaph workhouse was the schoolmaster, James Francis, whose cruelty seemed to know no bounds. Francis had previously been a collier until losing his left hand in an accident. Stanley recalls his first flogging from Francis, one Sunday evening in 1849. Having read the Old Testament story of Joseph being sold as a slave into Egypt, Francis tested the boys' attention by suddenly asking Stanley who it was that had interpreted the dream of the King:

With a proud confidence I promptly replied, –

'Jophes, sir.'

'Who?'

'Jophes, sir.'

'Joseph, you mean.'

'Yes, sir, Jophes.'

Despite his repeated stern shouts of 'Joseph', I as often replied 'Jophes', wondering more and more at his rising wrath, and wherein lay the difference between the two names.

He grew tired at last, and laying hold of a new birch rod he ordered me to unbreech, upon which I turned marble-white, and for a moment was as one that is palsied, for my mind was struggling between astonishment, terror, and doubt as to whether my ears had heard aright, and why I was chosen to be the victim of his anger. This hesitation increased his wrath, and while I was still inwardly in a turmoil he advanced upon me, and rudely tore down my nether garment and administered a forceful shower of blows, with such thrilling effect that I was bruised and bloodied all over, and could not stand for a time. During the hour that followed I remained as much perplexed at the difference between 'Jophes' and 'Joseph' as at the peculiar character of the agonising pains I suffered. For some weeks I was under the impression that the scourging was less due to my error than to some mysterious connection it might have with Genesis.

With such a passionate teacher it may be imagined that we children increased his displeasure times without number. The restlessness of childhood, and nature's infirmities, contributed endless causes for correction. The unquiet feet, the lively tongues, defects of memory, listlessness, the effects of the climate, all sufficed to provoke his irritation, and to cause us to be summarily castigated with birch or stick, or pummelled without mercy.

Day after day little wretches would be flung down on the stone floor in writhing heaps, or stood, with blinking eyes and humped backs, to receive the shock of the ebony ruler, or were sent pirouetting across the school from a ruffianly kick, while the rest suffered from a sympathetic terror during such exhibitions, for none knew what moment he might be called to endure the like. Every hour of our lives we lived and breathed in mortal fear of the cruel hand and blighting glare of one so easily frenzied.

Francis later appeared to have been implicated in the death of a classmate of Stanley called Willie Roberts. On hearing of Willie's death, Stanley and several other boys sneaked into the workhouse mortuary and discovered his body covered in scores of weals. Stanley's growing hatred of Francis led to a violent showdown:

Above The entrance block of St Asaph Union workhouse in Flintshire, North Wales. In 1959, the site was renamed the H.M. Stanley Hospital in commemoration of its illustrious former inmate.

Left Stanley's link with St Asaph was also marked by a plaque on the building.

In May, 1856, a new deal table had been ordered for the school, and some heedless urchin had dented its surface by standing on it, which so provoked Francis that he fell into a furious rage, and uttered terrific threats with the air of one resolved on massacre. He seized a birch which, as yet, had not been bloodied, and, striding furiously up to the first class, he demanded to know the culprit. It was a question that most of us would have preferred to answer straight off; but we were all absolutely ignorant that any damage had been made, and probably the author of it was equally unaware of it. No one could remember to have seen anyone standing on the table, and in what other manner mere dents had been impressed in the soft deal wood was inexplicable. We all answered accordingly.

'Very well, then,' said he, 'the entire class will be flogged, and, if confession is not made, I will proceed with the second, and afterwards with the third. Unbutton.'

He commenced at the foot of the class, and there was the usual yelling, and writhing, and shedding of showers of tears. One or two of David's oaken fibre submitted to the lacerating strokes with a silent squirm or two, and now it was fast approaching my turn; but instead of the old timidity and other symptoms of terror, I felt myself hardening for resistance. He stood before me vindictively glaring, his spectacles intensifying the gleam of his eyes.

'How is this?' he cried savagely. 'Not ready yet? Strip, sir, this minute; I mean to stop this abominable and barefaced lying.'

'I did not lie, sir. I know nothing of it.'

'Silence, sir. Down with your clothes.'

'Never again,' I shouted, marvelling at my own audacity.

The words had scarcely escaped me ere I found myself swung upward into the air by the collar of my jacket, and flung into a nerveless heap on the bench. Then the passionate brute pummelled me in the stomach until I fell backward, gasping for breath. Again I was lifted, and dashed on the bench with a shock that almost broke my spine. What little sense was left in me after these repeated shocks made me aware that I was smitten on the checks, right and left, and that soon nothing would be left of me but a mass of shattered nerves and bruised muscles.

Recovering my breath, finally, from the pounding in the stomach, I aimed a vigorous kick at the cruel Master as he stooped to me, and, by chance, the booted foot smashed his glasses, and almost blinded him with their splinters. Starting backward with the excruciating pain, he contrived to stumble over a bench, and the back of his head struck the stone floor; but, as he was in the act of falling, I had bounded to my feet, and possessed myself of his blackthorn. Armed with this, I rushed at the prostrate form, and struck him at random over his body, until I was called to a sense of what I was doing by the stirless way he received the thrashing.

I was exceedingly puzzled what to do now. My rage had vanished, and, instead of triumph, there came a feeling that, perhaps, I ought to have endured, instead of resisting. Someone suggested that he had better be carried to his study, and we accordingly dragged him along the floor to the Master's private room, and I remember well how some of the infants in the fourth room commenced to howl with unreasoning terror.[24]

Terrified of the consequences of his actions, Stanley absconded over the workhouse wall and subsequently ran away to sea.

Richard Gibson
Neglect at St Giles's Workhouse

In February 1865, Richard Gibson, aged forty, a patient in the St Giles's workhouse infirmary, asked fellow inmate Felix John Magee to write a letter on his behalf to local magistrate Sir Thomas Henry:

Sir, I wish to bring under your notice the case of a pauper named Richard Gibson, at present an inmate of St Giles's Workhouse, 47 Ward. His disease is scurvy, and through weakness he has been unable to wait on himself, and therefore has been inhumanly neglected. On Sunday morning he asked me to wash his face, and he would give me twopence, I took it, for it enabled me to write. I washed him, and such a sight of suffering may I never see again. He was covered from the crown of the head to the soles of the feet with scabs and sores. He had sores on the back, and his legs are in a shocking state from neglect. I have never seen them dressed since I have been in the ward, and I can say on oath that they have not, and so will others. The bed he lies on has not been made for five nights. It is an iron bedstead, with wood laths for the bottom, with no mattress, in a dark corner of this underground ward, and it is only through part of the day that you can discern his features. On Sunday when I washed him I took out of his head a half-pint of scabs. His hair is unusually long, and was matted from constantly lying in bed, and his hands were as it were enamelled with his own soil. It was an eighth of an inch thick on the palm of his hand and fingers, for I see no night-stool and bed-pan in this ward. Sir, I hope you will send an officer as soon as you can, for should he die, the ends of justice would be evaded. If the officer keeps the object of his visit a secret I will be able to get the under nurse and helper to own to it themselves. He is now delirious, and cannot last long, and if he dies the proof of guilt will be removed.

I remain, your obedient servant, Felix John Magee.[25]

Gibson died two days later. A post-mortem examination found his body to be extremely emaciated, with the hair of his head matted together, his nostrils closed up with dirt, his beard a mass of filth, and vermin swarming over his face, chest and neck.

At the end of a lengthy inquest, the jury essentially concurred with the claims in Magee's letter. Their verdict was that Gibson's death from 'serum on the brain' had been greatly accelerated by the neglect of all the officials in the workhouse, and that the ward in which he had died should be closed as improper for the reception of sick paupers. They also considered that the neglect of the nurses to change the linen of the deceased 'was highly reprehensible.'

Casual Ward Inmates
Workhouse Graffiti

In 1865, Poor Law Board Inspector Andrew Doyle recorded some of the graffiti left by the tramps and vagrants who frequented the casual wards of the workhouses he visited.[26] The casuals, who were allowed an overnight stay in return for a spell of work such as stone-breaking, used the workhouse walls as an informal notice-board for leaving messages and passing on news – rather in the style of present-day social networking.

First, a selection of 'notices':

'Private notice.–Saucy Harry and his moll will be at Chester to eat their Christmas dinner, when they hope Saucer and the fraternity will meet them at the union.–14th November 1865.'

'Notice to our pals.–Bristol Jack and Burslem was here on the 15th of April, bound for Montgomeryshire for the summer season.'

'Notice to Long Cockney, or Cambridge, or any of the fraternity.–Harry the Mark was here from Carmarthen, and if anybody of the Yorkshire tramps wishes to find him he is to be found in South Wales for the next three months. –17th August 1865.'

'Spanish Jim, the b– fool who robbed two poor b– tramps in Clatterbridge union, was here on the – find it out.'

'Taffy, the Sanctus, was here on the 28th of November 1865.'

'Yankey Ben, with Hungerford Tom and Stockport Ginger. The oakum was tried to be burned here on 28th October by Messers John Whittington, Joseph Walker, Thos. Pickering, Jas. Hawthornwaite.'

'The Flying Dutchman off to Brum for a summer cruise at the back doors or any other door.'

'Cockney Harry and Lambeth bound for Brum for jolly rags.'

'Beware of the Cheshire tramps, Spanish Jem, Kildare Jem, Dublin Pick, Navvy Jack, Dick Graven, the shrewd Cheshire tramps.'

'Wild Scoty the celebrated king of the cadgers, is in Newgate in London, going to be hanged by the neck till he is dead; this is a great fact.–Written by his mate.'

'Never be ashamed of cadging. I was worth five hundred pounds once, and now I am glad to cadge for a penny or a piece of bread.–Lanky Tom.'

'The Governor of Chester Castle orders all subalterns to meet at Stourbridge.'

'If ragtailed Soph stays here (Shiffnal) come on to Stafford.'

'The York Spinner, Dick Blazeanvy, Lancashire Crab, Dublin Smasher, and Bob Curly called for one night on their road for the tip at Birmingham.'

'Bow Street, Long Macclesfield, Welsh Ned, Sailor Jack, the Islington Kid, Wakefield Charley, and an Irish cabinet maker were located here 10th September 1865.'

The graffiti often included complaints or comments on the character of the relief afforded in different unions. The 'bare-boards' of some vagrant wards were carefully distinguished from the 'good padding' of others, and warnings given about the treatment of 'tear-ups' – those deliberately tearing up their clothing in the hope of being given a better replacement suit. The character of the Congleton workhouse (near Sandbach) was recorded thus:

Oh Sandbach, thou art no catch,
For like heavy bread, a damned bad batch,
A nice new suit for all tear-ups,
And stones to crack for refractory pups.

Elsewhere:

Beware of Ludlow–bare boards, no chuck.

Bishop's Castle Union Workhouse is a good place to be down in, but a damned bad lot of paupers about it.

Bow Street and two other raggamuffins slept here on the night of 12th April, and was quite shocked at the clownish impudence of the old pauper at the lodge. The thundering old thief denied us a drink of water. So help me Bob.

This bloody hole is lousey.

This is a rum place for a fellow to come to for a night's lodging; you will never catch me here again.–Old Bob Bridley, Ok!

An 1887 illustration of
the interior of a London
men's casual ward, with
the inmates in their
workhouse nightshirts.

The workhouse of the Seisdon Union (at Trysull) had a rather better reputation:

> Dry bread in the morning, ditto at night,
> Keep up your pecker and make it all right.
> Certainly the meals are paltry and mean,
> But the beds are nice and clean;
> Men, don't tear the beds, sheets, or rugs,
> For there are neither lice, fleas, or bugs
> At this little clean union at Trysull.
> But still at this place there is a drawback,
> And now I will put you on the right track,
> For I would as soon lodge here as in Piccadilly
> If along with the bread they gave a drop of skilly,
> At this little clean union at Trysull.
> So I tell you again, treat this place with respect,
> And instead of abusing, pray do it protect,
> For to lodge here one night is certainly a treat,
> At this little clean union at Trysull. –Bow Street.

Some of the inmates had definite poetic talents:

A little power, a little sway,
A sunbeam on a winter's day
Is all the rich and mighty have,
Between the cradle and the grave. –Yankey Ben.

My unfortunate friends, pray look around,
And tell me for what is this place renowned;
The room is large, but the windows are small,
But that don't much matter at all at all.
A pint of skilly for your supper to drink;
But of sleep you cannot get a wink.
You may lay on the boards or the chilly floor,
About as warm as a North American shore.
The old bed is full of fleas all alive:
I killed in number about five times five.
They are not poor, but all thorough-bred,
And before morning you will wish they were all dead;
And by this and by that it plainly is clear,
This is the worst relief in all Staffordshire. –Bow Street.

Inspector Doyle described 'Bow Street' as the 'laureate of cadgers'. Here are some of his other compositions:

Mickleham Mick, the wandering jockey,
Laid his nob on these boards the other night,
He is not now half so cockey
As when with Ben Anson's dumplins he did fight. –Bow Street.

Stafford, land of wax and capstones,
Heel balls, wax, and leather,
Where the broth is made of bones,
Where the cobblers face all weather,
Where the stove is seldom lighted,
Where the rugs are daily boxed,
Where the tramps are daily righted,
And out of their grub are foxed. –Bow Street.

It's an ill dog that don't deserve a crust
Is a maxim true and just,
So we must be dogs of the very worst breed,
When we don't receive what we greatly need;
For it's very unkind, nay, further cruel,

To give here merely a drop of thin gruel.
But let them keep it, we can do without it,
And I mean to let half the town know about it. –Bow Street.

Before you close your eyes to sleep, boys, pray for fine weather,
For human hearts need sun as well as corn and oats;
For this rain of late, and at present too, is to had altogether,
Considering the state of our old shoes and the thinness of our coats.
In this place there is a stove, but it is very seldom lighted,
In fact to make you comfortable they don't intend to try,
And the clerk of the weather office must surely be short-sighted,
Or he would see the benefit of sunny days as well as you or I.
    –Bow Street, 16th August 1865.

'W.H.R.'
The Autobiography of a Pauper Boy

In the Local Government Board's Report for 1874, a section on the education of pauper children in the Metropolitan District by Mr E. Carleton Tufnell includes a number of accounts from those who had experienced the system first-hand. One particularly striking contribution, written by 'W.H.R.', is introduced as 'the autobiography of a pauper boy, showing his ascent from the condition of a street Arab to competence and respectability.' It provides a rare insider's view of life at a union workhouse in the 1850s.

Few clues are provided as to the identity of W.H.R. – he once refers to himself as 'Billy', has a younger sister in the same workhouse, and later became workhouse schoolmaster. My own research has identified the writer as William Hew Ross, born in 1842 at Greenwich, with a sister named Eliza who was three years his junior. Although Ross's account remarks that the workhouse he entered was 'on the west side of London', it is clearly the Greenwich Union workhouse whose long-serving Master was Mr J.R. Ellis (transformed into 'Willis' in the report). Ross and his sister entered the workhouse in around 1849 when, following the desertion of the family by his father and the death of his mother, he and Eliza had been living with their elderly grandmother:

> I remember we went before a lot of gentlemen (the Board of Guardians) and they asked me several questions. Where that occurred I do not remember, but I do remember shortly after being put into an omnibus with my sister, and leaving my grandmother crying and clinging to my uncle on Market Hill. I was then nearly eight years old. We were put down from the bus opposite the gate,

and this conductor took us in. We were shown into the female receiving ward, and after waiting some time had dinner.

After dinner an old woman came and took all my clothes and then showed me into the bathroom, telling me to get in and not be afraid. I should think I was not afraid; indeed, I had been too much used to water. I was in the bath in a moment with a jump, but the next moment my screams and yells could be heard far and wide. The fact was, the water was hot, to me it appeared scalding hot. Mr Willis the Master came and several more, but could not get me in again. They lifted me, smacked me, coaxed, and at last used sheer force. I never was so afraid in all my life; I thought they were going to kill me. Never before had I had such a thing as a hot bath; and never shall I forget it. They thought I was afraid of the water; it was not the water but the heat. I must not forget to mention that a string of not very refined language was largely mixed with my screams. I was a marked boy from that time.

When at last I got dressed in the uniform, Mr Willis himself marched me off to the school, and, with a full and facetious account of my bath, left me in the custody of Mr Darley the schoolmaster. It was Saturday afternoon, and the boys were 'kept in' for previous bad behaviour. They were all standing stock still round the school, and as quiet as could be. I looked at them and wondered at seeing so many and so still. Mr D. asked me my name. I wouldn't answer. He asked me two or three times, but no answer. At last he got off the stool at the desk, and took hold of my shoulder, and said, 'What is your name.' I was out of his reach in a moment, and shouted out as loud as I could, 'Find, out, carrots.' He had red hair. There was a titter all round the school, and one of the monitors caught me by the collar, and got a punch in the head for his pains, which did not seem to hurt him in the least. He was a big boy, and had me up to the desk in no time. Mr D. opened the desk and brought out a cane, and told me to look at it. I looked at the cane, but paid far more attention to the monitor who had hold of me. Mr D. again wanted my name, and I wanted the monitor to leave go his hold and then I would tell. The monitor was ordered to leave go, and I sulked out in answer to the repeated query, Billy. At last he got my name, and to his credit he never touched me then to hurt me. It turned out that I was the smallest boy in the school, and had to stand at the end, as we were all in our sizes. I remember marching down the long passage into the dining hall to tea, and wondered whatever had become of my sister. When we got into the dining hall, the thought struck me I might possibly see her; but no. I found out after, that she was on the infants list, and they did not attend the hall. All this time I had been very sulky, and when at last I had my bed pointed out, and when Mr Waters the shoemaker had undressed me and put me into bed I felt so relieved. The boys soon began to make a noise in the bedroom, but not so myself. I remember putting my head right under the bedclothes, and having such a quiet cry. Night after night I did the same, and used to long for the night to come so that I might cry, without being noticed. The next day, Sunday, we went to church, the dining hall. Everything seemed very strange indeed. I had never before heard prayers of any kind, and of course did not understand them. I had often heard songs sung in a public house, and wondered to hear every one singing here. It did seem strange altogether.

I remember also when we came out of church the monitor came and pulled me out in front for having been fast asleep in church. Several others were 'stood out' as well as myself. I had also been talking, and that, coupled with what I had done the day before, I suppose it was, determined Mr Waters the shoemaker to punish me. He had a small cane behind his back when he told me to put up my hand. I had not the least idea what he meant doing, and when he took my hand and himself put it out, I simply looked sullenly at my own outstretched hand. Presently, and without my being aware of it, down came the cane on my outstretched palm. The pain to me was intense. I yelled and flew at him, and before he was aware, had given him one or two good kicks. He then belaboured me pretty much the same style I had been used to, viz., all over; but not one touch seemed to hurt me so much as that stripe on the hand. After giving me a good caning, he wanted the other hand, but it was no use, he did not get it. It was sheer fright that made me obstinate.

The next day, Monday, opened my eyes very considerably. All passed off well till 9 o'clock, when we went in school. I was put in the lowest class with the other little boys, but soon got tired of it. I longed to be about the streets again, and wondered when it would all come to an end. It seemed as though I must get into trouble, for that day I got a stripe on each hand from Mr Darley. This system of cutting the hand with a cane was certainly a new thing to me, and it seemed also to hurt me more than any other method of punishment could. I had never, before going to the Union, had a beating without seeing father or uncle, or some of them, who were beating me very much out of temper; but here the operation, let him be who he would, and we were subject to three, the tailor, shoemaker, and schoolmaster, always took it so coolly. It made me most awfully afraid of them.

I may as well here make a short digression to show how the school was managed. The schoolmaster and pupil teacher, together with four monitors, who were dressed differently to the rest, had entire charge of us during school hours. Apart from school time we seldom saw the schoolmaster, except in the dining hall, but were under the control of either the tailor or shoemaker, or both, together with pupil teacher and monitors. The tailor and shoemaker had just the same power of caning as the schoolmaster. Between the three, there was a great deal of caning, and I shall have occasion to speak of it again presently.

I looked upon all three as brutes, and as far as the shoemaker is concerned, I have not yet altered my opinion. He did really seem to me to love to flog the boys. I once saw a boy with the two sides of his face black and blue. He showed it to the Master in the dining hall, and I believe Mr Waters, the shoemaker, got into trouble over that. I also saw him once in the shoemaker's shop offer a boy a penny to take four cuts on one hand without flinching. The boy put his open hand on the cutting board and took the four cuts, but Mr Waters would not give him the penny.

I suppose it must have been about a month after admission that I first saw my sister, although every Wednesday afternoon we were allowed to visit each other. I had no idea, nor did my little sister, why the boys went after supper into the dining hall; it was to see their relatives. The first Wednesday afternoon in the month was visiting day, and my grandmother was at the gate punctually at 1 o'clock, and so I was brought from the infirmary to see her. I had been ill, and was getting a bit better, and so was allowed to go, but it was not without the doctor's permission. He happened to be in the surgery, and the old nurse took me to him. How pleased I was to see her, also my sister for the first time. I begged hard of my old grandmother to take me away, but it was no use. I may as well here mention that all the time the old lady lived, which as near as I can guess, must have been about 13 months after my admission, she never but once missed seeing me on visiting day, although she had to walk all the way from Woolwich, 3 miles, and she was aged and walked with a stick. I was always the first they called, to the porter's lodge to see her. I never had a Christmas dinner at the Union, though I must have been there about seven years. My uncle James was doing pretty well, having got a tidy little business as fishmonger, and he always contrived to have me out at Christmas. My little sister never went out from the day she went in.

To resume my tale of Union life, I seemed somehow to fall in with the discipline after a bit, and when finally I knew right from wrong, I did not get beaten nearly so much. Mr Waters, I think, was the first of our Masters to leave. I remember most of the boys seemed half wild with joy when he left. He must have been very much disliked. Mr Darley, the schoolmaster, was the next to go. For my own part, I was rather sorry when he went. I should say now he was a kind-hearted man. He was succeeded by a Mr Mullen, who had not been in the school a couple of days before he made himself a hero with us boys, as he was the means of taking the power of flogging from the tailor and shoemaker. We loved him, they disliked him. However, I don't think he stayed long, but he used to work us very hard in school. I remember his leaving one Sunday, and I remember Roberts, the pupil teacher, crying. I was well-up in the third class when Mr Mullen left. He was succeeded by Mr Saltley, and I believe him to be about the best schoolmaster we had. By the time he left I had worked my way from the third to the first class, and thence to a suit of blue, the uniform of a monitor, and a class of my own, the fourth.

It was shortly after Mr Saltley came that the then master tailor took me away from the school and I was made a tailor; three days I worked in the shop and three days weekly were spent in school. By that time I had become thoroughly used to my lot, very seldom was in trouble, enjoyed the sports in the boys yard, did not seem to have that longing to leave that I used to have, and in fact, was as happy and as hungry as ever I was in my life.

Things with me went on well till Mr Allen came as tailor. He early took a great dislike to me. Why, I cannot say, but certain he did. Three days in the week I was under him, and except the first month or so, got regularly two thrashings a day. I think I mentioned before that through the instrumentality of Mr Mullen neither the tailor nor shoemaker were really allowed to beat us. Allen, however, did it, but though we did not dare tell the schoolmaster, yet we knew that he did not dare let Saltley know it. I say it now fearlessly, and I am well aware who will read these words, that Allen had me thrashed by the schoolmaster, Mr Saltley, on an average twice a day, that is twice a day on three days of the week. He seldom pretended in the shop that I was guilty of any wrong, but as regularly as he went to his luncheon I went with him to the school, and a few words whispered in Mr Saltley's ear did the business.

I should just like to say a few words more of the workhouse. In the first place, the diet of boys from 6 to 12 was the same. It was not enough. Every boy had the scraps of bread, 'odds and ends' in fact, put into a basin and filled with water and milk, not milk and water. If you would, sir, just take 4 oz of bread and cut it into eight parts, then put the water and milk on it, you would see what sort of a breakfast a boy turned 11 years of age had to last him from 6 o'clock in the morning, till 12. The dinner was in proportion; if we had meat for dinner, it was 3 oz, and the potatoes were never weighed; but I have been so very hungry, that when I have seen the small piece of meat, and perhaps three potatoes come for me, I have felt as though it was not near enough before I tasted it. If, as was not unfrequently the case, one or two, or perhaps all three of the potatoes turned out bad, why, there was the meat only. At supper there was the half slice of bread and butter (4 oz bread) and a half pint of water and milk. I am of short stature, and I always put down my stunted growth to the fact of my being under-fed at the Union. As a result of this under-feeding, I may say that nearly every boy who was fortunate enough to have a halfpenny or a penny would directly after breakfast hang about the stairs leading to the bedrooms to catch the old women who used to make the beds, and ask if they had an allowance of bread for sale. Many is the allowance (6 oz bread) I have seen boys buy of the old women, and have also bought many myself. Boys also got into the habit of buying and selling their own rations. Thus, if Bob Jones coveted Joe Smith's top, he would offer Joe half his supper for it. At the same time, perhaps, Bob had a mother in the house, who was certain to send by one of the bedroom women an allowance of bread for her boy Bob in the morning. If I remember rightly, nearly all our meat dinners consisted of salt beef. It was very salt, there was no water, and the wash-house was generally locked, except when we were washing. How I have

suffered with thirst. Not one drop of water to be got, except during washing
time. The only kind act I ever remember Mr Allen doing me was when he first
went to the workhouse. It was one Sunday afternoon. I was locked in school
by myself on account of bad eyes, and was almost mad with thirst. The day
was fearfully hot, and I lay on the gallery at the far end of the school all alone
moaning, and I suppose making too much noise for Mr Allen, whose room was
just the other end. How long I had been so, I cannot say, but while my face was
buried in my hands and knees Mr Allen touched me, and asked what I wanted.
I begged him to give me a drink, and he did. I fancy I see him now with a large
jug of water. To me it was delicious. He went straight to the playground and
opened the wash-house, and so every boy had a drink.

   I had a great deal to be thankful for at the workhouse. I entered it like a
little heathen. Before going there, I had roamed unchecked about Woolwich,
learning all kinds of wickedness and vice. Had that life continued, with no one
but my poor old grandmother to look after me, I should soon have been far
beyond her control, and I believe must eventually have been sent to prison, and
perhaps as a transport. By the bye, I knew what convicts were from my earliest
infancy, having seen them at Woolwich. As it was, I was now nearly 14 years of
age, knew how to read, write, and calculate pretty fairly, had learned that God's
name was sometimes mentioned without an oath, and also outside the walls
of a public house. I had read well lots of Scripture tales, and had also a small
library of any own. I had about eight or nine books, which I used to lend out
on Sundays to the other boys. I generally took a little pride in my work too.[27]

In 1871, Ross was working as a schoolmaster at the West Ham workhouse. As
the 1874 report notes, W.H.R. was 'above that position now, but is still worthily
filling a high post, whence he can influence the fate of many destitute children,
who recognise and bless his fatherly care of them.' The high post in question
was his appointment in 1872 as Master of the Stamford Union workhouse in
Lincolnshire. The following year he married Rachel Finley, whose father was
former Master at Lincoln workhouse.

John Rutherford
Indoor Paupers

Indoor Paupers was published in 1885 under the pseudonym 'One of Them' and
purports to give an insider's story of life in an unnamed London workhouse. The
book is unique in providing such a lengthy and detailed portrait of a workhouse
from an inmate's point of view. As well as its narrative of daily life, brought to life
by descriptions of the other inmates and their backgrounds, the author makes a

number of serious allegations about the misconduct amongst workhouse officers such as the embezzlement of foodstuffs. What is perhaps most striking about *Indoor Paupers*, though, is that the picture it paints is often very much at odds with the conventional image of workhouse inmates being wholly oppressed and submissive. Instead, they employ whatever means – or guile – they can in order to make institutional life more tolerable.

The writer's obvious literary talents raise some questions on how authentic his account actually is, a matter commented upon by some reviews of the book when it was first published. The *Law Times*, as well as seeking confirmation of its veracity from the publishers, Chatto & Windus, claimed to have 'obtained some corroborative evidence that the publishers have not themselves been deceived by some fraudulent person'.[28]

Like many publishers in modern times, Chatto & Windus has been through a number of mergers and takeovers. It now forms part of the Random House Group who, even today – because of the terms of the author's original contract – still decline to disclose the identity of 'One of Them'. However, delving into the Chatto & Windus company archives, now deposited at Reading University Library's Special Collections department, reveal him to be one John Rutherford who, on 14 July 1885, at the age of sixty-one, had entered the Poplar Union workhouse. It was from there, at the beginning of November 1885, that the author contacted the company, offering them the manuscript of *Indoor Paupers* – presumably composed over the course of the previous three months. The company offered the sum of £20 for the copyright of the work, which Rutherford accepted, and within a week his manuscript had been despatched to the printers. He departed from the workhouse on 18 November and in January 1886 his author's complimentary copies of the printed book were despatched to him at 16 Strafford Street, Westferry Road, Millwall. Little else is known about John Rutherford – assuming that to be his real name. He apparently never made a personal visit to the publisher's offices, with the payment being arranged through an intermediary. As well as *Indoor Paupers*, Rutherford had written a play entitled *A Day at Holyrood*. However, this was not a work which the company had any interest in publishing.

Like all new workhouse entrants, Rutherford's circumstances were assessed by one of the union's relieving officers.[29]

I found the process of becoming an indoor pauper easy enough. The relieving officer was kindly disposed, did not ask any superfluous question, and gave the order without demur. This took place just inside the gate. I was then ushered into the receiving ward, a detached building of two floors, in charge of a pauper. Here males, who present their order after the departure of the doctor, spend the rest of the day and the following night, nobody being passed over to the body of the house until examined by the medical man and pronounced free from skin-disease.

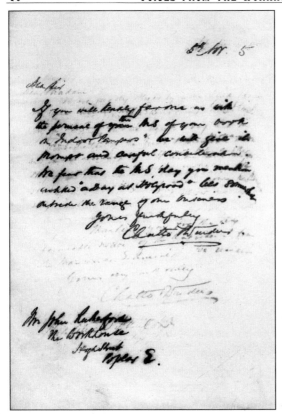

The reply from Chatto & Windus expressing interest in seeing the manuscript of *Indoor Paupers*, addressed to Rutherford at the Poplar workhouse. (Courtesy of Random House Group Ltd and University of Reading, Special Collections)

I was then taken to the bath-room and treated with, what was to me a luxury indeed, a dip in clean warm water. Then my own clothes were taken away, folded up and ticketed, while I was supplied with a workhouse suit. In the process the ward-man made a merit of supplying me with an extraordinarily good suit, and a still greater merit of letting me have a flannel singlet. This latter act he took care to tell me was a very great favour indeed, and therefore, well worth a bit of tobacco or a copper. And he got a penny – my last – a part of a small sum raised the evening before by the sale of a handkerchief. But the old fellow lied in every particular. The singlet, as it turned out, was a portion of the ordinary workhouse dress, while the clothes were so bad that the taskmaster ordered them to be changed for better ones a few days later. Thus my first experience of the place was to be victimised.

Immediately after my change of clothing the doctor made his appearance. I passed the scrutiny successfully, and was immediately transferred to the house, being sent incontinently to the stone-yard, a place where, according to rule, all males must spend their first week. There was no stone-breaking, however. Myself and about ten others were employed for the rest of the week in removing the hemp from a lot of telegraph-wires. There was no hurry over the job – very much the contrary – but plenty of chatter and larking when the taskmaster was out of sight.

The following Monday I was transferred to the oakum-shed, where I have remained ever since, and where the task imposed is anything but killing. The younger men are supposed to pick four pounds of oakum, and the older two pounds. A few of the latter do their work regularly – only a few, however; but no young man that ever I saw completed his four pounds.[30]

The male inmates of the workhouse had entered the institution for a variety of reasons:

The general run of indoor paupers richly deserve their fate, and a great many seem to like it better than any other. There are dozens of men under my view at this very moment who have been removed from the house and been given opportunities of making themselves comfortably independent out of doors – many of them several times over. Yet here they are again as hopeless and helpless as ever.

A few feet from me sleeps a man once well-to-do as a shopkeeper. He is barely forty, but already a pauper who is not likely to be anything else. He ruined himself by incorrigible vices. He was a betting man and a profligate in every sense. Moreover, nobody living could place the slightest trust in anything he ever said, or rely upon him in any way. His wife put up with him for years upon years. At last, the workhouse, with its miserable prison life, being full in view, this woman, several years her husband's junior – fine-looking too, full of vigorous life and womanly feelings, and exasperated by a long course of something worse than neglect – gave way to the solicitations of an old sweetheart who had remained single for her sake; and, taking the youngest and most helpless of her children, emigrated with this old lover.[31] The husband incontinently broke up house and became an indoor pauper. The fact that he had held a respectable position, and that his nearest relatives still filled respectable positions, disposed the Guardians to befriend this man. Once and again he obtained a permission, occasionally granted in hopeful cases, to go out into the world and make a home, leaving his children behind him. On each occasion he went direct to a situation, receiving a suitable outfit from the Guardians. On each occasion he made not the slightest attempt to make a home; and on each occasion the Guardians were compelled to have him arrested and sent to prison for a term.

A very different set of men, however, are the few husbands who are here through the death of cherished consorts. Such losses, as I have seen, break up men between forty-five and fifty-five very rapidly. They lose, or rather have lost long before, the qualities which keep households together. Those desolate old men are greatly to be pitied.[32]

We also learn about the backgrounds of some of the female inmates and the sometimes corrupting effect of living in a workhouse:

> First come the young women with illegitimate children, who, having been compelled to resort to the house in the first confinement, are sure to renew their acquaintance with it again and again on the like errand. Their experience of the house, indeed, encourages them. They are incomparably better cared for in their trouble than they would be elsewhere. And they fall at once into companionship that suits their situation exactly. There are no weeping mothers or sisters to reproach, and no indignant fathers or brothers to go somewhat beyond reproach. There are no former acquaintances to look at them askance, no prudes to preach to them officiously and mercilessly, and no sneering and jeering gossips to be dreaded. They are surrounded by women who have done the like or worse, and who, therefore, are the last persons in the world to throw verbal missiles at them.
>
> The mother of successive illegitimates is of another sort. She is usually self-supporting – a tailoress or factory hand, given to different flirtations every night she goes out to 'enjoy' herself, and whose 'mishaps' are not the result of attachment to any particular man or men, but of a spree with a casual acquaintance – one, it may be, picked up at haphazard in the street and seen for the first and last time on that particular occasion.
>
> In addition to such lost women as the foregoing, the workhouse opens its gates to others who have fallen somehow into the trick of alternating spells of indoor pauper life with spells of common prostitution. This sort of existence is seldom commenced before the individual has attained her thirtieth year, and is usually suggested by experience of the place and its ways during a severe fit of illness, when, having neither friends nor means, and no other shelter, the poor creature was compelled to resort to the infirmary of the Union.
>
> At first her spells in the streets are much longer than those in the house; but by degrees the former diminish, and the latter lengthen, until, by the time she reaches her fortieth year, she limits her street life to two or three days a month. When such a woman discharges herself, she makes not the smallest secret of her purpose. The thing, and the probabilities thereof, are discussed by herself and her ward and workshop acquaintances in all their details. Guardians and officers are aware of it, too, but they are powerless to prevent. Now and again, an inexperienced chairman will take such a hussy to task; but, as a rule, to get the worse in the encounter. She is dead sure, when challenged with quitting the house for an 'immoral purpose', not only to acknowledge the fact, but to exult in it; and, while justifying it, she invariably contrives to make a laughing-stock of her assailant.
>
> As to the very young girls, who are no longer children, they are shut out from all that intercourse with the other sex which is a necessity of their nature, and

which, under judicious direction, is the very best teacher of true modesty. Their strong but uncultured instincts turn eagerly to the conversation of the fallen women, and luxuriate in every sentence. Thus they become utterly depraved in sentiment before they are afforded an opportunity of entering the world. How can young wives subjected to such an ordeal retain a due regard for the marriage contract? How can young girls similarly dealt with ever entertain any such regard at all?

With all her stronger feelings seconding the precepts of the temptresses, the young indoor-pauper wife is not long in coming to the conclusion that they are quite in the right as to manners and morals, while she herself has been, so far, altogether in the wrong. In short, she adopts their principles in the bulk, and longs for an opportunity of reducing them to practice. Nor in many instances is the opportunity long withheld.

Now and again the professional procuress makes her appearance in the house as an indoor pauper, and mostly finds the minds of the women, married and single, who suit her best, ready moulded to her hand. She has no difficulty at all in enlisting them; and seldom finds any in procuring their release. She may posture as a friend of the family, and so tempt her out into the world, or procure somebody else to do the trick. And out again in the world the discontented wife is sure to disappear, with the 'family friend', at an early date, leaving husband and children to return to the workhouse at their leisure. It needs hardly be remarked that the work of the procuress is still easier with the very young girl.

But, even without the aid of the procuress, the fate of the young girl is determined in the very worst way. Sooner or later she is sure to be tempted into the streets by one of the harlots, and, a certain age attained, there is nothing to prevent.[33]

Although workhouses operated a strict segregation of the sexes, there were still means by which romance could be pursued:

Nearly all the work of the house is done by inmates – the women taking the laundry, the sewing, the mending, and other feminine occupations, and the men the whitewashing, painting, etc. Obviously a good deal of intercourse must take place between males and females while these matters are in progress.

Again, in nearly every instance, the officers are mere over-lookers and preservers of order. The real work of their posts is performed by pauper deputies, who are thus carried all over the house every day in the week. Necessarily these underlings must have the full use of their faculties in order to be efficient. In other words, they must not yet be 'old'. Moreover, they must be selected from the best material in the house; and human beings whose prime is not yet past, and who are pent in from year's end to year's end from the outer world, cannot meet, even for a few seconds, without plunging up to the eyes in flirtation.

Both sides, indeed, are eager for it. In consequence, more progress in an intrigue is made in five minutes, by a pair of indoor paupers when they happen to meet, than is made in as many weeks by persons more fortunately placed.

A couple of meetings will suffice to engage a pair. And once the engagement is formed, the parties to it must have frequent communication, and all sorts of tricks and contrivances are employed to secure it. Confidants on both sides are indispensable, and found without difficulty. All other paupers, indeed, make it a point of honour to further such an affair. Messages are exchanged; so are little notes, most of which are curiosities in their way. Many are penned on the margins of old newspapers, in the queerest possible hands, and in such spelling as is scarcely to be met with elsewhere. I have seen a pauper love-letter scratched with a nail on the bowl of an old iron spoon.

Flirtations among paupers on very rare occasions end as elsewhere, in marriage; and such marriages, when they do take place, are not so unhappy in result as might be supposed. They tempt the parties into making a vigorous and therefore successful effort at independence.

As a rule, however, a pauper flirtation is evanescent – a matter of six weeks or two months. Within that time it attains full intensity. Then – no better means presenting itself – the enamoured pair discharge themselves on the same morning, and go out to spend twelve to forty-eight hours together, according to the amount of money at their disposal. This is at once the consummation of the love-fit and its close. They resume their places in the house completely cured of it.[34]

One further category of inmates was known as the 'ins and outs':

Indoor paupers admit of many subdivisions. We have the old and the young, the hopeful and the hopeless, the married and the single, the permanent and the transitory, and, finally, a class by themselves – the Ins and Outs.

The class last named is a remarkably troublesome one. As a rule, its members are completely worthless to themselves and to everybody else. They leave the house at regular intervals, putting the officers to an infinity of trouble in the process; for precisely the same lengthy forms have to be gone through at every fresh exit and entry as at the first.

Some of these fellows go out to a job, keep at it as long as it lasts, lay in good stores of tobacco at the end, and then spend every farthing left of their earnings in a 'topping spree', lasting one to three days, according to the amount received. Then hey for the workhouse, or 'spike', once again! Here the blackguards recover from their debauch, and drown away the days until they are ripe for another job and another 'topping spree'.

Such fellows are exceedingly provoking. They are men varying in age from 21 or so to 45 – all abounding in life and vigour, and, without exception, perfectly

The men's ward block at Poplar workhouse, where John Rutherford was 'One of Them'.

capable of maintaining themselves by their own labour. They prefer this sort of life, however, and are not to be roused out of it, as things legal go. They are quite shameless, laugh at the heaviest toils of the house as being, what they really are to them, the merest child's play. The reasons adduced by these Ins and Outs for leading this sort of life are very convincing to themselves. The spike is infinitely cheaper and cleaner than the common lodging-house. It saves their own clothing, and, when the thing becomes absolutely necessary, provides them with more. It 'doctors' them when their malpractices result in foul diseases. And though the food is poor, it is regular, and greatly superior, besides, to what they can hope for when out of work and depending on themselves.

The Ins and Outs, without exception, are profligates in the extreme. Many of them are just the fellows to insinuate themselves into the good graces of thoughtless girls of the lower classes; and precisely the lads also to take base advantage of the trust. Most of them have illegitimate children, and not a few two or three, for whom the unfortunate mothers have to provide as best they can. It is obviously useless to sue the fathers. When such a fellow finds the agents of the law at his heels, he becomes an indoor pauper incontinently, and so justice is baffled.

There are twenty-five or thirty men of this kind in the house with me at the present moment, all exceedingly sociable and jolly in their own estimation; and in the estimation of everybody else. They are all full of fun and frolic, and as full of good stories of their own reckless doings.[35]

Workhouse life was largely one of monotonous routine, but the inmates could always find ways to provide themselves with entertainment:

> Saturday night, for various reasons, is a lively night in our workhouse dormitories. It is the close of the week here as well as elsewhere, and the morrow is a day of rest, with an additional hour in bed. Therefore the younger men, at least, are disposed to lie awake longer on that night and amuse themselves somehow or other.
>
> Up we go to the dormitories at a quarter to eight. Ten minutes or so are occupied in changing under-clothing and getting between the sheets. The Labour Master goes his round and sees that all is right. By a quarter-past eight at latest all doors are locked, and all lights, save that of the recently introduced night-lamps, extinguished, and the men are left to themselves for eleven long hours.
>
> There is a good deal of desultory chat between the occupants of adjoining beds, who are always more intimate than the rest – comrades, in fact. This, however, soon drops. Then comes a voice, belonging to one of the influential personages in the room, calling 'Order – order!'
>
> Order it is in an instant – a pin-drop silence, in fact. This obtained, the influential personage requests in his politest manner Mr Nameless to oblige the company with the story of one of his innumerable thrilling adventures.
>
> Mr Nameless is a white-haired man, rather under the middle height, spare of figure, but broad-shouldered and long in the arm, with an erect form and a firm elastic tread. His face is frank and open, and his dark eye remarkably brilliant.
>
> His story is a vivid account of a tiger-hunt in Upper India. The speaker never uses the first person, but it is clear that he was an eyewitness of what he describes, moreover an actor in the affair. The incident is admirably told in a series of word-pictures. Evidently the man is an artist in narrative. How well he recounts is evinced in the breathless interest and hasty exclamations of the audience, who manifest almost as much emotion as if they were there and then taking part in a tiger-hunt. The story occupies about half an hour, and is followed by a storm of applause.
>
> Silence once again secured, somebody is called upon for a song. There is seldom any reluctance in acceding. The song over, the singer uses his privilege in calling upon somebody else. Now and again a recitation or an anecdote is accepted instead, but there are no more set stories.
>
> 'Tune up, Mac!' calls out a fellow from the other end of the room.
>
> 'Yes, yes,' repeat a dozen voices. 'A song from Mac. Order for a song from Mac!'
>
> 'Well, I suppose I must,' replies Mac. 'A few more whiffs of the pipe, and I am ready.'
>
> A few minutes of conversation follow while Mac finishes his smoke. Then he pulls his pipe from his mouth and clears his throat – a signal that he is ready.

It is also a signal for silence, which is instantly obtained. Then he pours forth in a rich mellow voice, and in right good style, 'The Old Musqueteer'.

The song is received with enthusiasm. When the applause dies away, Mac exercises his right, and calls upon somebody else to aid in entertaining the company.

Somebody else, it is well known, *can* sing; but he either is, or pretends to be, out of voice, and recites with deep feeling 'Lord Ullin's Daughter' instead. It takes almost as well as a song. Then the reciter calls upon our singer of singers – the Sims Reeves[36] or Braham[37] of the house, Jack Blades.

'Hear, hear!' respond all the rest; 'Jack Blades, Jack Blades! One with a chorus, Jack, one with a chorus'; and several of Jack's favourites are suggested. Jack, however, gives none of these.

Even before the last voice is silent, Jack commences one as yet unheard in the dormitory from his lips. Beginning low, almost in a whisper, but such a whisper! – one heard distinctly in every corner of the room – Jack's splendid baritone is heard rising higher and higher – piling note upon note, as it were, gathering power as it peals, until it develops into a perfect torrent of richest music; then it sails down the gamut in a lilt without words. All this by way of prelude.

Everybody is now still as death. When the lilt ceases you may hear even the hearts around you beating. Not for more than five seconds, though. That short interval past, Jack bursts forth in a grand old sea song, with the right sort of chorus, commencing 'A long, long pull, and a strong, strong pull,' and does it ample justice. The splendid voice – for such it really is – absolutely fills the room with delicious sound.[38]

Although inmates performed no labour on Sundays, it was not a day they relished:

Sunday is not a pleasant day in this house of ours. But as it is, in all its weary dreariness, so it was intended to be, and nothing else. The principle of its managers, that is to say, its Guardians, has been from the first to make the place anything rather than an agreeable sojourn; and they have succeeded perfectly in realising their intent.

The Sabbath among us is a day of rest; emphatically so, or of stagnation rather. We have an hour longer in bed of a morning in the summer. We go to divine service once a day – that is, those of us who belong to the Established Church – and, immediately after supper, we have a troop of preachers let in upon us, who howl at us in the most uncompromising manner, without ever asking leave – very much against the will of many of us, indeed – from half-past six until bedtime.

The letter-writing of the place is not much: perhaps fifty letters a week may be received and replied to by its hundreds of inmates. Some of the replies are penned as soon after the receipt of the letter as circumstances will permit, but the greater number are deferred till Sundays. Then – always after church – about a dozen men wait their turn for the use of the solitary ink-pot and pen belonging to the apartment.

Letter-writing, however, occupies but a few inmates out of many; and these few for no more than half an hour or so apiece. They get through the rest of the time as the others get through the whole of it – anyhow, and mostly very drearily. The lazy fling themselves on the benches or on the floor in the corners, and doze through the day in a way utterly beyond the comprehension of people with active brains.

Others lounge about the yard in listless fashion; and a most uninteresting promenade that said yard is. It is a broad quadrangle, girt in by the main building and its offices on three sides. The fourth side is bounded by a lofty wall, beyond which rises a high-level railway. We can hear the snorting of the engine, and we can see the steam and smoke, as a train passes; and that is the sum and substance of our intercourse with the world, apart from letters and from the visits of friends once a month.

There are a few tattered novels about the room – only a few – which have been passing from hand to hand for months, continually losing leaves in the process, and which will continue so to pass until the last leaf has been consumed as a pipe light.

Newspapers, however, form the favourite intellectual fare. Three or four fortunate inmates receive a weekly journal regularly, and these are the men of standing of the place. They are deferred to, sought after, courted, and even paid in bits of bread or tobacco, for half-hour loans of the journals at their disposal.

Other men gather round the story-tellers, who are almost exclusively of the In-and-Out order, whose discourse is always of their own adventures, and who never by any chance have good to relate. On Sundays they dilate to attentive and sympathetic listeners concerning life on the road, and in the streets, prisons, casual wards, harlots, fences, thieving exploits, pugilistic encounters in the ring, ruffianly debauches, with their supplementary rows, dodging and squaring bobbies, and athletic competitions.

In spite, however, of all the methods of getting through the day just mentioned, the Workhouse Sunday, as we have it, is emphatically dull and dreary.

Some of the inmates, indeed – the married men – are allowed to pass an hour, immediately after divine service, with their wives and children; but in by far the majority of cases there is no pleasure in the interview. Such meetings take place under official supervision and in the sight of dozens. Tender feelings, therefore, must be suppressed, if such have survived the miserable period preceding the break-up of the home and the still more miserable – because in so many cases hopeless – imprisonment in the house that followed.

However, when the feelings are not tender, no great care is taken to suppress them at these interviews. Husbands and wives, who bear one another grudges, take advantage of them to 'speak their mind,' and spend them for the most part in mutual recrimination.

The only features about these Sunday meetings between members of the same family that excite sympathy are witnessed in the cases wherein husbands and fathers, who have lost cherished wives, meet children of tender years. The way in which the youngsters fix themselves on a father's knees, and nestle in his breast with arms round his neck and cheeks against his, the way in which they lie there to the end of the interview, the melancholy aspect of the man, the silence of the group – for hardly a word is dropped among them – and the reluctance with which father and children tear themselves asunder, when they are compelled at length to quit the scene – are things that go straight to the heart.[39]

If Rutherford is to believed, workhouses were riddled with corruption, with larceny (theft of property) and peculation (embezzlement) being commonplace:

Foremost among indoor pauper vices I take leave to place larceny. However, if all be true that we hear, the offence is far from being confined to them. There never yet was an establishment of any size or age in which abuses did not prevail, simply because no system of management can be devised free from flaws. As soon as servants are accustomed to a place and discover its weak points, some of them are sure to turn these defects to their own advantage. This remark applies more particularly to public establishments than to any other.

My own particular workhouse is an old one, and abounding in defects. Some of its sections are too large, and others just as much too small, while a number of necessary offices are altogether wanting. Further, there are no architectural arrangements for completely isolating the various departments, and for preventing subordinate officials and their pauper deputies from prowling all over the place whenever they feel so inclined.

Certain necessary offices being wanting, so also are the officers. There are, therefore, no arrangements for supervising and checking a good many proceedings. As a matter of course, certain abuses were developed in the place immediately after its opening, and have continued to flourish ever since. Certain people connected with the place, indeed, have become so accustomed to peculation that they have come at length to look upon its exercise as very much a matter of right.

Perhaps no form of workhouse larceny is so objectionable as that which deals with the food of the inmates. The supplies are strictly in proportion to the numbers to be fed, such and such a quantity of potatoes, flour, oatmeal, meat, etc., per head being issued daily. Thus, if a subordinate officer should appropriate a certain quantity of the raw stuff, the portion of each individual would be correspondingly reduced; and if his or her pauper assistants made raids on the cooked food, the individual shares must undergo still further diminution.

There are countless ways of smuggling articles out of a workhouse. Here much depends on the quality of the persons engaged in the transaction. Manifestly it is much easier for a highly placed official than for a subordinate; while any subordinate, however mean, has many more facilities at his disposal than a pauper.

A very common method is by coming to an understanding with the contractors or their men. Then – this according to the defects of the workhouse system and the character of the officer superintending the departments attached – the stores are either delivered short of quality, or the full amount is deposited in the house and a portion conveyed away – often at the moment by the vehicles that brought them.

When the food is plundered on system by officials, this is the method adopted: Different days are selected for the raids on the different sorts of food – one day for the meat, another for the flour, a third for the vegetables, a fourth for the meal, and so on.

Tuesday, let us suppose, is one of the porridge or gruel days. The paupers will receive precisely the same quantity morning and evening – say a pint and a half on each occasion. But the quality? The best answer to that question is a fair statement of what ought to happen, contrasted with what has happened. A pound of meal to a gallon of water is the regulation amount; but on the raiding-day the proportion is known to have been seventy pounds of meal to one hundred and twenty gallons of water, or fifty pounds of meal – nearly one-half – short.

The paupers complain; but of what use is that? The Master admits that there is some justice in the complaint. He calls for the cook, and receives a plausible excuse which he does not care to search too closely, orders that the thing shall not occur again, and then forgets all about it. Next day the gruel is all correct, and the next, and the next, until the raiding-day returns, when what has just been described is repeated.

It is the same with the meat, which is stolen on one of the days when there is soup for dinner; and the same with everything eatable.

Of course this sort of thing cannot take place without the notice and connivance of the paupers employed in the kitchen. Of course, also, the said paupers do not fail to take full advantage of what is going on. Seeing their superiors steal the raw food, they do just the same with the cooked food. They carry it off by wholesale, gorge themselves till they can gorge no more, and sell the rest openly to such paupers as can purchase, while the impecunious have to look on, half famished, regarding the whole thing in their own perverse way.

Theft is especially rife among the Ins and Outs; and they have more opportunities of displaying their dexterity than would readily be imagined. Indoor paupers gradually acquire various little things, as books, pocket-knives, writing materials, sets of chessmen, and so on. Much of this kind of property is carried constantly about the person – stuffed into the breast, or stowed away in pockets which the poor creatures construct in their clothes wherever it is possible to place them.

But pockets cannot be multiplied as wanted. Such property, therefore as cannot be crushed into them is stowed away in the beds, every one of which is more or less of a magazine.

When an In and Out is about to discharge himself, he ascertains quietly which bed contains the more valuable articles; and, let the owner watch as he will, the thief will contrive to get at his hoard and strip it of whatever has excited his cupidity.[40]

Charlie Chaplin
Newington Workhouse and Hanwell School

Perhaps the most famous of real-life workhouse inmates was Charles ('Charlie') Chaplin – best remembered for his comic 'little tramp' character in the silent-film era. Chaplin was born in south London in 1889, the son of two music hall performers, Charles and Hannah Chaplin. His parents separated before he was five years old. Hannah struggled to make a living and in May 1896, she, Charlie and his elder brother Sydney, entered the Newington workhouse:

Although we were aware of the shame of going to the workhouse, I didn't realise what was happening until we actually entered the workhouse gate. Then the forlorn bewilderment of it struck me; for there we were made to separate, Mother going in one direction to the women's ward and we in another to the children's.

How well I remember the poignant sadness of that first visiting day: the shock of seeing Mother enter the visiting-room garbed in workhouse clothes. How forlorn and embarrassed she looked! In one week she had aged and grown thin, but her face lit up when she saw us. Sydney and I began to weep which made Mother weep, and large tears began to run down her cheeks. Eventually she regained her composure and we sat together on a rough bench, our hands in her lap while she gently patted them. She smiled at our cropped heads and stroked them consolingly, telling us that we would soon all be together again. From her apron she produced a bag of coconut candy which she had bought at the workhouse store with her earnings from crocheting lace cuffs for one of the nurses. After we parted, Sydney kept dolefully repeating how she had aged.[41]

Three weeks later, the two boys were transferred to the Central London District School at Hanwell, about twelve miles out of London:

Charlie Chaplin – his childhood experiences of poverty no doubt provided material for his screen portrayal of a down-at-heel tramp.

It was an adventurous drive in a horse-drawn bakery van. On arriving we were delivered to the approbation ward and put under medical and mental observation before entering the school proper.

The first few days I was lost and miserable, for at the workhouse I always felt that Mother was near, which was comforting, but at Hanwell we seemed miles apart. Sydney and I graduated from the approbation ward to the school proper, where we were separated, Sydney going with the big boys and I with the infants. We slept in different ward blocks, so we seldom saw each other.

But, to our happy surprise, within two months Mother had arranged for our discharge, and we were dispatched again to London and the Lambeth workhouse. Mother was at the gate dressed in her own clothes, waiting for us. She had applied for a discharge only because she wanted to spend the day with her children, intending, after a few hours outside together, to return the same day; Mother being an inmate of the workhouse, this ruse was her only means to be with us.

Before we entered our private clothes had been taken from us and steamed; now they were returned unpressed. Mother, Sydney and I looked a crumpled sight as we ambled out though the workhouse gates.[42]

After a day spent enjoying themselves in Kennington Park, eating cherries, and visiting a coffee shop, the family presented themselves back at the workhouse 'just in time for tea'. They again had to go through the whole admissions procedure, with the boys being returned to Hanwell a few weeks later. The school at Hanwell

– one of several so-called 'barrack schools' in London – was enormous, providing accommodation and education for more than 1,000 workhouse children. Inevitably, discipline was strict:

Hanwell School was divided in two, a department for boys and one for girls. On Saturday afternoon the bath-house was reserved for infants, who were bathed by the older girls. This, of course, was before I was seven, and a squeamish modesty attended these occasions; having to submit to the ignominy of a young girl of fourteen manipulating a facecloth all over my person was my first conscious embarrassment.

At the age of seven I was transferred from the infants' to the older boys' department, where ages ranged from seven to fourteen. Now I was eligible to participate in all the grown-up functions, the drills and exercises and the regular walks we took outside the school twice a week. Although at Hanwell we were well looked after, it was a forlorn existence.

The boys' playground was approximately an acre, paved with slab-stones. Surrounding it were one-storey brick buildings, used for offices, storerooms, a doctor's dispensary, a dentist's office and a wardrobe for boys' clothing. In the darkest corner of the yard was an empty room, and recently confined there was a boy of fourteen, a desperate character according to the other boys. He had attempted to escape from the school by climbing out of a second-storey window and up on to the roof, defying the officials by throwing missiles and horse-chestnuts at them as they climbed after him.

The massive District School at Hanwell, also known as the 'Cuckoo School'. Part of the building is still in use as a local community centre.

Pauper children in the dining-hall at Hanwell under the watchful eye of the school staff.

For major offences of this nature, punishment took place every Friday in the large gymnasium, a gloomy hall about sixty feet by forty with a high roof, and, on the side, climbing ropes running up to girders. On Friday morning two to three hundred boys, ranging in age from seven to fourteen years, marched in and lined up in military fashion, forming three sides of a square. The far end was the fourth side, where, behind a long school desk the length of an Army mess-table, stood the miscreants waiting for trial and punishment. On the right and in front of the desk was an easel with wrist-straps dangling, and from the frame a birch hung ominously.

For minor offences, a boy was laid across the long desk, face downwards, feet strapped and held by a sergeant, then another sergeant pulled the boy's shirt out of his trousers and over his head, then pulled his trousers tight.

Captain Hindrum, a retired Navy man weighing about two hundred pounds, with one hand behind him, the other holding a cane as thick as a man's thumb and about four feet long, stood poised, measuring it across the boy's buttocks. Then slowly and dramatically he would lift it high and with a swish bring it down across the boy's bottom. The spectacle was terrifying, and invariably a boy would fall out of rank in a faint.

The minimum number of strokes was three and the maximum six. If a culprit received more than three, his cries were appalling. Sometimes he was ominously silent, or had fainted. The strokes were paralysing, so that the victim had to be carried to one side and laid on a gymnasium mattress, where he was left to writhe and wriggle for at least ten minutes before the pain subsided, leaving three pink welts as wide as a washerwoman's finger across his bottom.

The birch was different. After three strokes, the boy was supported by two sergeants and taken to the surgery for treatment.[43]

Chaplin later experienced the cane himself after confessing to an offence he had not committed. He also underwent the ignominy of being treated for ringworm – a highly contagious fungal infection of the scalp common in pauper schools – with his head shaved and stained brown with iodine.

Charles Burgess
Shoreditch Union Cottage Homes

Charles Daniel Burgess was born in 1911 in the back streets of London's Bethnal Green. He was the first of three further children of the marriage between Richard Burgess, a widower with four sons and one daughter, and Mary, a widow with one daughter, Jinny. In 1919, the family was devastated by Richard's death following an accident at work in the local gasworks. As a result, Charles and two of the other children ended up at the Shoreditch Union's 'cottage homes' at Hornchurch. Unlike those of Stanley and Chaplin, his memories of the homes were relatively happy:

There was no widows' pension on Social Security in those days, so Mum had to approach the Board of Guardians attached to the Local Council, otherwise known as Poor Law Relief, also nicknamed 'The Bun House'. Mum was given vouchers that had to be changed at the local butcher shop for meat. She was also issued with vouchers for bread, coal and dairy products. The rent was paid and she was also given money for clothes and vegetables etc. She was told that the three oldest children would have to go into a children's home, meaning Mary and Tom and me. Tom contracted ringworm – a skin complaint, and was allowed to stay at home. He had to have all his golden ringlets shaved off so that the ringworm could be treated. Before going, we spent the weekend in the local workhouse at Shoreditch.

The children's home was called The Hornchurch Cottage Homes for Children, and it was situated between Romford and Hornchurch in Essex. It was then all just farms and meadows. The home was in a country lane and was entered via large gates with a lodge house at the side for visitors. You entered a long drive and the first house was where the superintendent lived, further along were six cottages, each named after a famous woman. There were three each side, each housing approximately 35 girls.

After growing up in the Hornchurch cottage homes, Charles Burgess lived for many years in London, before leaving for a new life in Stevenage New Town in 1954. These two pictures show him aged sixteen and in later life.

Then on the left were the school (which doubled as the chapel on Sundays), the swimming baths (rarely used) the gymnasium, and the drill hall. Opposite the school stood the administration buildings. These consisted of the dairy, the bakery, a tailor shop and a boot-repair shop. There was also a shop for the maintenance of the cottages, and a place for the resident gardener. Fresh milk was delivered daily from one of the nearby farms, and one of my first jobs was to collect a two-gallon churn of milk each day for my cottage. Next there were six more cottages named after famous men (mine was to be 'Landseer'). Again, there were three each side and each was capable of housing 35 boys. Each cottage had a large entrance hall, a kitchen with a huge double oven fire grate and a dining room. There was a day room for reading, playing chess, draughts, and children's card games. There was a plot of land at the rear with a few apple and pear trees, redcurrant and blackcurrant bushes, and a small playground. On the first floor of each cottage, were three dormitories and the washroom. Each dormitory held twelve beds, and the washroom contained three bathrooms. There was also a bedroom with its own bathroom for our foster parents (who we had to call 'Mother' and 'Father'). Our foster parents also had their own sitting room on the ground floor. Each boy had a towel and soap, and a drawstring bag containing a brush and comb. All belongings were marked with a personal number – all his clothing, slippers, and nightshirt, even his best Sunday suit. My number was two. Our weekday clothes consisted of short trousers, a shirt (cotton for the summer and flannelette for winter), a jersey, black stockings and boots. We all shared boot-cleaning brushes and blacking. All boys up to sixteen years old wore shorts. Our Sunday-best suits were made from Yorkshire tweed and consisted of a single breasted jacket, and trousers. The jacket was buttoned to the neck and collarless. A separate stiff white cotton collar and a clip-on bow tie were worn outside, on top of the jacket neckline. The jacket had two breast pockets and two side pockets, all with buttoned flaps, and a buckled belt, which was sewn to the jacket at the back but left loose at the front. The trousers were... wait for it... breeches! They were cuffed just below the knee and fastened with two buttons on each cuff. Together with black stockings and boots, we must have looked a real treat. I still don't remember how we kept those stockings up, but I do remember that the first thing I learned was to darn the holes when they appeared... and darn them properly too!

Classes were held in a very large hall in the schoolhouse. The wooden desks and fixed benches were in two rows of about twenty desks with an aisle down the centre and an aisle on either side. Each desk had a hinged lid with a space beneath to keep belongings in. The backrest of the bench was hinged so that it could lean forward towards the desk. Unlike the two-seater desks that I was used to in London, these desks each seated six boys.

In the first two or three rows in each line of desks sat the youngest boys, the next two or three rows were taken by older boys and so on with the oldest boys at the back. There were only two teachers, both male, who gave lessons to each boy suitable for his age group. The boys attended school in the mornings, and the girls attended school in the afternoons. On Sundays, the girls and boys attended Service together, with the boys on one side and the girls on the other. That was the nearest we got together, the girls and boys looking at each other out of the corners of their eyes. After Service, the girls were led out first and after a short period, the boys followed. The same hall was used for Sunday Chapel. The backrests were pushed towards the desks so that we sat facing the back of the hall, and towards a shutter which, when rolled up, revealed the Altar and the bible stand.

When I took my first bath, there were about five other boys of about my age and we bathed two to a bath and were all washed by our foster mother. I was so embarrassed. Well, it's not like being washed by your own Mum is it? There were no lavatories in the cottages. They were outside, at the back, and were known as 'the dykes'. If you wanted to go during the night, there were chamber pots outside each dormitory, three to each dorm, and had to be emptied each morning by the eldest boys. There was also a laundry at the back of the cottage, and several boys were detailed each week to do all the washing and ironing (including ironing the stockings). The washing was done in a wooden tub and a 'dolly'. A dolly is like a ten-inch, three-legged wooden stool on the end of a long handle, which has a crosspiece grip at the top. The tub was filled with boiling water with some sort of washing powder added (probably soda), then the dirty clothes added. The dolly was put in the water, legs first, and holding the crosspiece grip, it was rotated to agitate the contents of the washtub until deemed clean. Thirty pairs of stockings at a time were washed this way.

The first thing I was taught was how to make my own bed, and make it properly according to the rules. Another job I had was cleaning the cutlery. Spoons and forks were cleaned with a cloth and white paste and then polished. Knives were cleaned in a knife-cleaning machine. I also had to polish the brass knob on the front door and the backplate of the bell-push, which was about six inches in diameter. But the longest and the worst job I had was peeling enough potatoes for 36 boys every single day.

Our breakfast every day was a plate of porridge cooked the Scottish way; with water not milk, salt not sugar. It wasn't compulsory to have it if you didn't want it. It was so thick, you could turn the plate upside down and the porridge would stay on the plate! We also had two slices of bread and margarine, which was known as 'two dorks', and a mug of cocoa. I didn't see a cup of tea for about three years. We had a hot midday meal every day. Sometimes it was stew, or 'sausage toad', or roast meat with boiled potatoes and cabbage. On Saturday we would have mashed potatoes, cabbage and corned beef. But on Sundays we always had a roast dinner; roast beef with roast potatoes and all the trimmings. We always had a pudding: sometimes rice or tapioca, or boiled suet pudding with golden syrup, or 'roly-poly pudding' with currants. On Saturday we had jam tart and on Sunday we always had 'jam roll'. For our tea on weekdays, we would have the same 'two dorks' and cocoa, but on Sundays we also had a piece of cake. Every two or three months the Homes Committee from London would visit. Then, in the middle of the week, we would get a roast dinner!

There was nothing Dickensian about the home. I never once saw corporal punishment. They had other ways of punishing naughty children. One way was to make you stand under the clock that hung on the wall out in the entrance hall. You stood there nearly all day facing the wall, but this was a rare punishment. There were no 10ft high walls or iron fences surrounding the buildings, in fact, only a 4 or 5ft hedge bound the playing fields where the football pitch and the cricket field were. In the five or six years I was there, I think no more than a couple of boys ran away. They were all brought back, and anyway, most of the boys had nowhere to run to. These runaways were the only ones punished with six strokes of the birch and 'sent to Coventry' to one of the cottages that were empty.

I can't say that I was unhappy there – I had a clean bed to sleep in (in it at 8 o'clock and up at 6 to the sound of a bugle played by one of the band boys). We had our own military band. I tried to get into the band to play the clarinet.

Some young inmates of the Shoreditch cottage homes in the early 1900s. As well as the children's houses, the homes had their own school, chapel, infirmary, workshops and swimming bath.

I was learning to run up and down the scale by music score for about two months, I then had to have a medical and was told I didn't have enough wind. I was a bit choked at this news. We had a good band, with the boys ranging from seven to sixteen years in age. We were not allowed to mix with the girls except at Sunday Chapel, and even then we were at a distance from them. The Superintendent conducted the service, and also played the organ, which was pumped by one of the older boys. Further down the drive from the cottages was a small infirmary, further on there were two cottages for tiny tots – boys and girls. Even they were kept separated. That's where my sister Mary was. I rarely saw her. She didn't go to chapel.

My Mother wasn't able to visit us very often. She probably couldn't afford it. I suppose when she did visit, that was the only time I was able to see and talk to my sister Mary.

Every six months, a dentist would call to examine our teeth. Each cottage was visited separately. Although there was a dentist's chair in the surgery, it wasn't used. We just stood in front of him, were told to open our mouth as wide as possible while he poked the fingers of his left hand around our mouth and teeth. He always held his right hand firmly behind his back. If he found a bad tooth, before you could close your eyes, his right hand was there with the pliers and your tooth was in the tray... no gas and no cocaine! He wore knee-high leather gaiters and it was rumoured that he only wore them because he was kicked so often!

Once a year, in the summer, we had Sports Day, and quite a lot of the boys had visitors. The Homes Committee also attended. Each cottage competed against all the others. There was running, high and long jump, obstacle races, and tug-of-war. There was a prize of a shield for the tug-of-war contest, and only two cottages competed for it – 'Landseer' (my cottage) and 'Nelson'. I was always in the 'tug' and we won the shield almost every year. The shield was engraved with the winning cottage's name and held for a year. After the field sports finished, everyone went into the swimming pool house, where swimming races and diving were held. After the competitions were finished, all the competitors dived into the pool. Then the visitors and staff would throw coins into the water and laugh at the antics of the boys trying to get to the bottom of the pool to retrieve them. After this jollity the visitors and staff adjourned to the Drill Hall where they were served tea and cakes. Some of the boys then put on a show with Indian clubs and dumbbell drill, and the evening finished with dancing to the boys' Military Band.

I had been in the home for about three years, when one Sunday after Service, the Superintendent told us that all the teachers had left, and until new teachers were employed, there would be no lessons. He added that if no teachers were found who were suitable, then it was possible that we would all be going to schools in the surrounding villages. That Sunday, my education ceased until I returned to London.

Bill Golding
Stockbridge Workhouse and Southampton Cottage Homes

In 1925, four-year-old William (Bill) Golding and his mother entered the Stockbridge Union workhouse in Hampshire. A little later, he was placed in the Southampton Union's Hollybrook cottage homes at Shirley Warren where he spent the next ten years:

My mother was born in 1900. She had me when she was about twenty, and her father had just remarried and his new wife was much younger than him and he didn't want any children hanging about. So she was kicked out and lived with her sister. Then four years later she had another child and for some reason or other she couldn't bring it up, so we landed in the workhouse, the two of us. I didn't know I had a brother until I was about twelve years old and we were introduced to one another.

I was born, actually, in Southampton – at an address which is not to be found anywhere. I found out later that it was a sort of an accommodation address for unmarried mothers.[44] It was the local infirmary. Any of those born out of wedlock were given that address. I went with my son down to Southampton some years ago to try to find where I was born – 2A Chilworth Road. And it didn't exist, you see.

My most vivid memory of the workhouse was the smell – the smell of carbolic soap and stale bread. There were old women who were forever on their knees scrubbing the floors. And the bare wooden floors and the mixture of carbolic soap and stale bread seemed to cement the floorboards together. There were long wooden tables and benches in the dining hall. They were subjected to the same treatment – carbolic soap and scrubbing. And these old women, no-one spoke – as if they were ordered not to. And the sound of scrubbing, and the smell of carbolic soap and stale bread, lingers on to this day.

I didn't see my mother much at all. She had to go out to work, you see, to pay towards my keep in the children's home – monthly I think she paid. And I didn't get any visits from her until I was about ten or eleven I suppose. That was discouraged – children having parents coming down to see them.

The first home was called Oaklands. You sat on long forms and in the afternoon you leant against each other and you went to sleep. And you woke up and had a walk round the estate and that was about it. You went to bed about six o'clock or whatever. I started at the local school at about the age of five – we were marched off to school at that age. In the first home, that was from age four

Like many homes for workhouse children, Hollybrook had a boys' wind band, with members often going on to careers as army or navy bandsmen. This picture of the band dates from the early 1900s.

Bill Golding, who, in his eighties, visited Southampton to track down the homes where he grew up. The surviving parts of Hollybrook have now largely been converted to residential use.

to eight. Then you went into another home, which was a cottage-type home and contained about ten children, which was a lot better. And you stayed there from age eight to twelve.

Then from twelve to sixteen you went in what they called the Big House where there was about seventy of us. We were regimented like along army lines. You know, bugle in the morning, bugle at night. You were marched off to school and marched home again. But it wasn't too bad, you know, roly-poly pudding, spotted dick. The only thing that didn't go down too well was semolina. If there was any fat, you had to eat that otherwise you got a clouting. Yes, everything had to be... you know, whether you liked it or not. It was life on its own. Very sheltered – you didn't have any contact with the outside world.

We never had any names, we were all numbers. In the first home I was number 2, in the cottage home I was number 8, in the Big House I was number 64. If the Master wanted you he'd shout your number... or your surname. And if there were two, older and younger, if your name was Coster, say, it was Big Coster and Little Coster, or your number. I remember this particular boy, his name was Campbell. No-one knew his first name, no-one knew his parents. But he died at the age of eleven – some mysterious... well people died off like flies, in that time. And I remember going to his funeral. There was only about two of us went. I remember going along the short distance from the infirmary to the graveyard. He was wheeled along on one of the basket-type biers on wheels. He was buried in a pauper's grave, in an unmarked grave, and that was it.

We went to Sunday school. We were marched off to Sunday school. We had an annual treat in the New Forest. One year we went to Stonehenge. We went to the local gasworks – a tour round the gasworks. And every year, in the second home, you had a trip to the store to see Father Christmas. We got no toys, right through. But when you saw Father Christmas, he gave you a bottle of hair oil, or something like that – something they wanted to get rid of.

I was lucky enough to get in the band and the choir. In the band, we used to have band outings. Our longest trip away was to the Isle of Wight when we played at some fete or other. I played the drum – the side-drum. We had big playing fields. Not that we had any instruction in any games or anything, but we used to kick a football about and we used to run around the place. It was all fenced in though, you didn't escape although some tried it and they were hauled back. They never said what happened to them.

In the second home, from eight to twelve, there was about ten of us there, and run by a 'mother'. But she was a Miss Lovealock, I remember. If you were naughty, you had a choice. You had a smacked bottom or stand in the corner with your hands on your head. At night, if you spoke in your dormitory, she could hear it. 'Those who are speaking come down,' she said. Well, for some reason, I'd be the only one caught at that – speaking after lights out.

When you left Hollybrook, that's the Big House, you... most of them went in the army – in the boys. It was either that, the army, or going to skivvying – housework, or to go on a pig farm round Oxford way, Wallingford. That's where they ended up. No training, it was just elementary schools. And you left elementary school at the age of fourteen – you were in the Big House then, and they paid you fourpence a week. For that fourpence a week you did all the darning, darned the socks, sewed on buttons, peeled potatoes, things like that. The plum job was to get to be servants to the staff. There was one job in the staff room and another job was in the Master's room where you served, you waited and you cleared the things away and washed up everything. You might get a tip now and then off the staff. Well I happened to get one of the plum jobs – not the highest one, the next one down, looking after the staff. The staff consisted of four or five women dressed up as nurses. It wasn't too bad that.

The punishment you got there was medicine, you had a choice of medicine – brown medicine, white medicine or castor oil. Three grades. The brown medicine wasn't too bad, the white medicine was horrible, and the castor oil was the worst punishment, as you can imagine.[45]

Bella Aronovitch
A London Workhouse Infirmary

In 1928, Bella Aronovitch, a teenager from a poor East End family, suffered acute appendicitis. Because of complications, she spent the next four years being shunted between various London hospitals. These included 'voluntary' (charitably funded) hospitals, a council-run hospital, and a workhouse infirmary, possibly the one at Archway run by the Holborn Union, whose appearance shocked her:

As I was wheeled through the door I was astounded by the size of the ward – it was simply enormous. It was not only long but exceptionally wide. There were four rows of beds very close together, with only just enough room between each row to move around. I was put into a bed along one of the inner rows, far away from the light of any of the windows. My spirits sank and I felt overwhelmed as I looked round this sea of beds and faces.

The nurse came over, looked at me and my belongings and told Mother to take my nightdress home. She said that the hospital supplied nightwear and did not allow patients to wear their own clothes. I took off my thin nightie, gave it to Mother, and I was given the hospital nightgown. This garment, made from coarse, grey flannelette, was so hard and stiff I did not have the strength to unfold it and Mother helped me to get into it. The weather was very hot, and on this summer's day I was enveloped in this monstrous garment, which dragged a full half yard over my legs, with wide, gathered sleeves almost twice as long as my arms – I felt I could scarcely breathe because of the weight. It is difficult to imagine such a scene in the twentieth century; it was more in keeping with 1829 than 1929.

The two previous hospitals I had been in were voluntary. I now found myself in a Poor Law hospital attached to the workhouse. This explained the rules with regard to clothing and why people appeared so odd when I first saw them – they were, in fact, dressed in the workhouse regulation clothes. I was in an institution which belonged more to the London of Charles Dickens than the beginning of the nineteen-thirties.

I have never, before or since, been in a hospital ward where so many people died. Almost every night someone died and occasionally there were as many as four deaths. All this was not as sinister as it sounds. Then, as now, the problem of the aged sick was a very difficult one. Not to have to die in the workhouse was the unspoken prayer and greatest wish of many aged, working-class people. The family of the aged did their best, often in the face of unemployment and great poverty. Having nursed an aged person for a long time, the difficulties towards the end became more than the ordinary family could cope with, so it was that many of these old folk were finally brought into hospital, literally dying. Sometimes they would last a few weeks, whilst others died overnight.[46]

Len Saunders
Croydon Union Workhouse and Children's Homes

In around 1929, at the age of four, Len Saunders arrived at the Croydon workhouse, apparently 'dumped' there by his parents of whom he knows nothing. His memories of the next decade are largely of hard work in the laundry, beatings, and abuse. He finally escaped what by then had become council children's homes by climbing over a wall and running away. He eventually became a miner in Yorkshire after lying about his age. Over sixty years on, many of his memories are still too painful to recount:

I take it that my parents dumped me there, I suppose. That's the only word I can use. And which I think was a terrible thing to do to anybody. There was no birthdays, no Christmas, there was just nothing. They used to give a bit of fruit out at Christmas. I remember I got an orange once left in my sock. At Christmas we never done so much work.

At five we were working. Used to do a lot of laundry work, sheets and that. If you was young like what I was, you used to stand behind the mangle. The older boys would turn the mangle and you would get the sheets, and we would hold them and fold them and give them back and they would turn the mangle down and go through again. Any bloodstains, if you could put them inside so nobody could see it, sort of thing. If you turned to catch them as they come through – make sure they didn't hit the ground or there would be trouble straightaway. Then as you get older you'd be turning the handle, screwing it down. The older boys used to boil them in these coppers – they [had] sticks and that to get them out. The water just run anywhere until you got them to the mangle. We used to get up about six and we'd be working until six then clean up. We used to light the fires, the boilers, with hot the water up to clean the sheets. You just had to do as you were told. If you didn't, well, you know... I know at first I didn't. I learnt very quickly you got to. Whether you were five or fourteen or twelve, you were there to do a job. It made no difference. You had to prepare the dinners and that, the potatoes. The windows need cleaning, the place need cleaning... it wasn't much of a place to start with.

They'd tell you to do something and you done that – obviously there was no 'ask' – you learned very quickly not to ask. There was a man who used to have a nail in a bit of wood. And he would... I've got an ulcer on the bottom of my left... he would just, you know, for nothing at all. And you were put in these prisons and that... it was always down in the dungeon sort of thing.[47]

We used to put cardboard in our shoes where the holes used to come through. Used to cut cardboard out to put in the shoes to keep it dry. All the boys used to do that. They used to have short trousers and a shirt – you used to have to keep that clean. You used to have to clean that before you had

The children's cottage homes at Croydon, now demolished, where Len Saunders spent a miserable childhood before finally running away.

your food. We'd all try to – you could have some hot water out the boiler if you wanted to. You done the best you could with what you got. If you got a bed you was lucky. Otherwise you slept on the floor. You used to get some porridge, well they called it porridge, watered down. And if anyone was missing you could tell they'd said the wrong thing. They'd be in the dungeon and they'd get no food at all, just a bit of bread and water in the morning and evening.

I did escape. I'd had enough, I had to get away. I got over the fence. And that's what I done, getting over – I caught my fingers as I was coming down somehow. I can't bend that one. I didn't get caught. I went to the hospital. I came out and made my own way. I thought I could get away from Croydon. I reckon I was about twelve or thirteen when I left there. Like I say, I don't know. After I left there I was around Reading, Croydon, until I went in the mines. I did make lots of friends after I come out of there which I didn't in the workhouse. And I met a lady and I kept friends with Mark who's just recently died. He was in the workhouse – I don't know which one. 'Cause I talk about them now but I haven't talked about them for a long time. And Mark would never tell me. Young boys who had just been discarded by their parents.

I thought it was all my fault. All the boys thought it was their fault. That's the way they saw it. It's the way I saw it. I can speak about it more now without breaking down. I still don't like small places. You can always tell a workhouse. We got one in Reading and when I come to Reading I knew straightaway it was a workhouse. I can tell a workhouse. I was never in there but I know it was. It's going to be pulled down shortly. Sooner the better. It didn't affect me so much but it did my wife. She hated going past there. In fact she hated it so much I got some other digs so she didn't have to stay down there. But you could always see the chimneys.[48]

TWO

WORKHOUSE STAFF AND ADMINISTRATORS

THE ADMINISTRATION OF a parish workhouse was through the parish committee, known as the vestry, with the parish overseers[49] responsible for any financial matters. Workhouses set up under Gilbert's Act[50] or under individual local Acts[51] were generally administered by a committee of directors or 'Guardians'.

These early workhouses generally had fairly few paid staff, typically just a resident Master or Matron, with a married couple sharing the duties often being a convenient arrangement. Having a Matron to deal with the female inmates also reduced the possibility of any impropriety arising. In larger establishments, additional staff might sometimes be taken on. At the Bristol Incorporation workhouse, opened in 1698, the first inmates were a hundred pauper girls, with four 'tutresses' employed to teach them spinning, and a schoolmistress to teach reading. An old man was appointed as door-keeper and general porter. Servants were initially employed to do the cooking and washing but this was soon taken over by the older girls. The use of workhouse inmates to perform the domestic chores of the workhouse not only provided them with labour but was also a significant economy in the running costs of the establishment.

The 1834 Poor Law Amendment Act led to the creation of a central supervisory body known as the Poor Law Commissioners, succeeded in turn by the Poor Law Board in 1847 and the Local Government Board in 1872. Local administration was through groupings of parishes known as Poor Law Unions, each of which was to operate a central workhouse. Each union was run by a Board of Guardians elected by the ratepayers in each of the member parishes. The board met weekly or fortnightly, usually at the workhouse. A subcommittee of the Guardians known as the Visiting Committee was responsible for regular inspection of the workhouse. Large unions might also have one or more Relief Committees to process relief applications.

The staff in union workhouses were divided into 'officers' and 'servants'. The officers comprised the Master and Matron, a porter, one or more medical officers and a chaplain. Where a workhouse operated its own school, a resident schoolmaster and / or schoolmistress were also appointed – not just to provide lessons, but to supervise the children outside the classroom. Other potential officer posts included one or more nurses and an industrial trainer. The employment of 'servants' was generally to supplement or supervise the labour of workhouse inmates, for example in kitchen or laundry work.

Union workhouse officers were generally expected to be 'without encumbrance', i.e. single or widowed and without dependent children. The main exceptions to this were the Master and Matron, where a married couple often filled the role. Even then, children were deprecated and the cost of their maintenance was deducted from their parents' salary. Inevitably, though, children did appear and their recollections of growing up inside a workhouse provide another interesting viewpoint on the institution.

Richard Hutton
Steward of the Quaker Workhouse at Clerkenwell

The Society of Friends, or Quakers, set up workhouses at Bristol in 1696 and at Clerkwenwell in London in 1702, the latter intended to house fifty-six 'decayed Friends and Orphans'. Richard Hutton, the workhouse 'steward' or governor from 1711 to 1737, kept a 'complaints book' – a wide-ranging journal chronicling not only events in the institution and Hutton's thoughts about them, but a miscellany of other information ranging from details of the workhouse rules and diet to recipes for brewing beer, treating eye complaints, and killing bed-bugs.

Despite being an efficient manager, Hutton had constantly to deal with complaints, often unfounded, both from inside the workhouse and from the Quaker community outside. On 31 March 1718, he recorded:

> This day I was informed that the children under your care have not a sufficient allowance of food to fill their bellies... I am sorry that such a report should be raised among your people for I did think you always took the best of care amongst your poor. Children are hungry and growing and require more food, but hungry bellies and cold water betwixt meals do not agree, and raising them at five a clock in ... the morning and making them work without their clothes is very hard for children to bear. If the allowance is too little there ought to be complaint made to the committee. I know none of the committee or else I would lay it before them. I have the care of a great many children myself and

my comfort is I discharge a good conscience to them. I desire you to look into those things for fear there should come a sickness among them.

The behaviour of some of the residents caused considerable concern, such as the activities of a boy named John Gorden in 1713:

Besides several faults too tedious to mention here, he lately pick[ed] one boy's pocket of six pence and another of three pence and ran away and spent it. And at another time he went to a neighbour's and told them he had not victuals enough and desired trust for buns &c. He had then stole a knife and fork from [a] boy and one of the house knives and sold them for three half pence, which, when I knew, I sent for again, since we found a knife in his pocket belonging to the house. At another time he got a candle over night and got up about twelve a clock at night and took a pane of glass out of the storeroom window and got in, from whence he took about four pounds of plum pudding, although he, as well as the rest of the big boys, had a full pound for dinner besides their suppers. And he ate so much in the storeroom he could not come thence without leaving behind him what is not fit here to mention. And about a week ago he privately stole the key of the street door. Towards night we suspected him and tasked him with it, but he confidently denied with such a countenance, as if he had really been innocent, so that we searched diligently for it a great while, but in vain which made us very uneasy. However, about 5 next morning we went up where he lay and asked him about it again, but he denied it. Then we made him come out of bed and found the key under him. He intended, as he confessed, to have taken the knives out of the drawers and to have sold them with the key. We have since kept him as close as we can but he has been up, dressed in the middle of the night for what intent we do not certainly know, for there is no believing him.

The most troublesome inmate was William Townsend, who entered the workhouse in 1716 along with his wife and a maid. Unlike the other residents, who were funded by their Quaker Monthly Meetings, Townsend was a man of some means and contributed towards his own board and lodging. He also expected special treatment and was constantly ready to complain:

William Townsend went into the stable and the young man that looks after the children and brews &c asked William why he found fault with the beer, it being very good. William told him, he loved to find fault when he saw faults for he had been cruelly used since he came here. The young man asked him wherein he had been so cruelly used, and if he had not his allowance? Aye, William said, but I pay more than the rest. The young man said, but if thou should have a different diet from the rest it would breed contention in the family. Then

William said, but if they had been prudent managers they might have given us different from the rest and none of them have known it.

⌐⊶⊷⊷⌐

John T. Becher
The Anti-Pauper System

The Royal Commission set up in 1832 to investigate the operation of the Poor Laws frequently praised the Thurgarton Incorporation workhouse at Upton, near Southwell in Nottinghamshire. The institution, opened in 1824 under the provisions of Gilbert's Act, had adopted the 'anti-pauper system' previously instigated by local clergyman John T. Becher at the nearby Southwell parish workhouse. Becher had demonstrated that a strict workhouse regime – separation of the sexes, strict diet, the requirement of labour from the able-bodied – together with stringent control of out-relief, could produce a substantial reduction in the cost of poor relief. The layout of the Incorporation's workhouse was designed to support the use of these principles:

> We commenced our Undertaking by purchasing, in the Parish of Upton, at the distance of three quarters of a mile from Southwell, Three Fields, containing 10 Acres, 2 Roods, and 28 Perches, of Grass Land, immediately adjoining the Turnpike Road. In one of these Fields, measuring Six Acres, we erected the Workhouse according to a plan of mine, which Mr William Nicholson, our Architect, has delineated upon a small scale, for public Inspection. It is denominated 'The Thurgarton Hundred Incorporated Workhouse'. This Workhouse was completed and first occupied in December, 1824.
>
> On the Ground Floor, the Centre contains the Committee Room, used occasionally as a Chapel; and the School Room, which, by opening a Pair of folding Doors, may be united at pleasure with the Committee Room. On each side of the Centre, a Wing is attached. In the right Wing are the Kitchen, Back Kitchen, and two Day Rooms, for Females and Children. One for Paupers of good Character and Conduct; the other for the Idle, Immoral, and Improvident. In the left Wing are the Governor's Room, the Secretary's Office, and two similar Day Rooms for Males. A Court Yard, well supplied with Waiter and a Privy, are appropriated to each Class.
>
> From every Day-room a staircase ascends to the Dormitories, which are on the Chamber and on the Attic Story. The Children sleep in the Centre: the Females in the Right Wing: the Males in the Left. The Back yard is divided into two Parts, in which are situated the Wash-house, the Laundry, the Wards for Persons afflicted with Contagious Disorders, the Reception Rooms, the Strong Rooms for Punishment, and other Appurtenances.

The workhouse at Upton, near Southwell, erected in 1824 by the Thurgarton Incorporation, later became the Southwell Union workhouse. The site was acquired by the National Trust in 1997 and is here shown during work to reinstate and preserve the building in 2001.

In the Front of the Workhouse is a Garden containing one Acre and a Half. On the Grass Land two Cows are kept. The whole System is conducted upon the Principles of salutary Restraint and strict Discipline. With this intention the Males, the Females, and the Children, are separated from each other: but the Association of Husband and Wife, if specially requested, would not be prohibited during the hours of rest, except under very peculiar circumstances. The primary Classes are subdivided and distributed into distinct Wards, according to the Character and Conduct of the Paupers. This ensures subordination, and enables us to discriminate between the innocent and the culpable Poor.

No Fermented Liquors are allowed, except by an order of the Surgeon, in writing.

The Provisions are all of the best Quality. The Governor enters in his Order Book the Weekly Supply of Articles which he deems necessary, as well as the Names of the Tradesmen of whom he proposes to purchase them. This List is examined and revised by the Secretary, who subscribes the initial Letters of his Name; after which it is submitted for Confirmation by the Visitor. The Governor then purchases the several Articles, either at the public Market, or at the Shops of certain Tradesmen, selected by the Secretary, with the concurrence of the Visitor, according to circumstances.

The aged, infirm, and guiltless Poor, are not strictly subjected to the ordinary Diet; but are allowed Tea, a small quantity of Butter, and other little indulgences of this description. The Sick and the Infirm are sustained in such manner as the Surgeon directs.

The Apparel of the Poor is purified, ticketed, and deposited in the care of the Governor on their Admission. They are then dressed in the Clothing of the Workhouse until their discharge, when they resume their own Clothes.

The only observation suggested by the Materials of the Apparel is, that all Paupers, except the very Aged and Infirm, wear Clogs with wooden Soles, instead of Shoes. These are more economical; they are of little use if carried away; and, if tendered for sale, excite suspicion. They do not injure even the tender feet of Children.

This Workhouse will contain commodiously 158 Paupers.

The moral and religious care of the Poor is confided to the superintendence of the Chaplain, who reads divine Service and a Sermon on every Sunday; visits the Sick; and attends the Workhouse from time to time, to inspect the instruction of the Children and the behaviour of the Paupers. Prayers are read by the Governor to the Males, and by the Matron to the Females, on every Morning, and on every Evening. The Publications circulated by the Society for promoting Christian Knowledge, are the only Books and Tracts provided for the Establishment.

Employment is principally found in the domestic occupations necessarily connected with the Establishment. The Males cultivate the Garden, and execute such laborious Work as may be required. The Females perform the Cooking, Washing, Milking, and House Work. They also spin, knit, and sew for the Establishment. The Children attend daily in the School-Room, where they are instructed, according to their Ages, by a Person selected from the inmates of the Workhouse. The Paupers are not allowed any Portion of their Earnings.

However it must be recollected, that our object is not to provide a permanent receptacle for able-bodied Adults, but a refuge for those who are rendered incapable of labour by mental imbecility, or by bodily infirmity; by the helplessness of Infancy, or by the decrepitude of Old Age. These are treated with all that tenderness to which they are entitled by their Misfortunes. But the Idle, the Improvident, the Profligate, and the Sturdy Poor, are subjected to a System of secluded restraint and salutary discipline, which, together with our simple yet sufficient Dietary, prove so repugnant to their dissolute habits, that they very soon apply for their discharge, and devise means of self-support, which nothing short of compulsion could urge them to explore.

Many Persons, on surveying the regularity and neatness which characterise our Workhouses, have been erroneously induced to imagine, that the Poor will be tempted to prefer such a Residence to their customary abodes. But we know from experience, that the cleanliness, temperance, decency, subordination, and seclusion, which administer essentially to the health and comfort of the friendless, impotent, and orderly Poor, are regarded with abhorrence by those who have depraved their feelings by habits of vagrancy, filthiness, and immorality. With this abandoned Class, Discipline and Punishment are convertible terms.

Hence it arises that we have not, either in the Southwell Workhouse, or in the Incorporated Workhouse, a single able-bodied Male Adult.[52]

Benjamin Woodcock
Master of the Barnet Union Workhouse

The surviving volume of Benjamin Woodcock's diary[53] runs from 1 September 1836 to 10 May 1838 and covers the period just after the formation of the Barnet Poor Law Union, when a new central workhouse was being erected to replace the old parish workhouses that were still in use. This is the very period during which Dickens' *Oliver Twist* was being written and first published in serial form, and with which the diary provides an interesting comparison.

Woodcock, a former draper, with no apparent previous experience of managing such an institution, had been appointed as workhouse Master in 1835. His diary was not a personal journal, however, but rather a notebook whose contents were open to scrutiny by his employers, the Barnet Board of Guardians. Despite this constraint, the writing discloses much about the author and daily life in the workhouses under his jurisdiction. Woodcock emerges as the antithesis of the stereotypically heartless and bullying workhouse Master, regularly (and convincingly) revealing his concern for the health and welfare of his charges. As the following extracts illustrate, life in the Barnet workhouse appears to have been a veritable soap opera:

19 September 1836 – About 6 Oclock this evening, we Buried Thomas Cheadle. Some of the inmates & three of his Relations followed. One of which, his Sister in Law, being desirous to know what money he left, States that About three Months back she gave him two Sovereigns, but I found but 5s in his box the following Morning. Old Tuckfield was very attentive at his Bedside from the time he was taken, till he died but he dennys knowing anything about the money.

20 October 1836 – Tomas Smith, the blind man, on his return this Afternoon, said the Resurrection Men[54] had Attempted the previous night to Steal his dead brother and askd me to let him go out the following day as he wished to watch the Churchyard all Night but I of Course refused.

7 March 1837 – Old Ned Hull, with whom I have had more trouble to Maintain Proper discipline than any other Man in the house, having Struck Another

A view of the Barnet Union workhouse, opened in 1837 with Benjamin Woodcock as its master. The building later became part of Barnet General Hospital, but was demolished in 2002.

inmate this afternoon, Contrary to the Rules & Orders, I was telling him the impropriety of such Conduct and that I should report him to the board when he made use of the Most Horrid & Abusive Language & said he cared for None of them. For which I pulld his nose, sent him to bed & Kept him the following Day without his Dinner. He Smelt very strong of Tobacco having been down the Garden Smoking, unknown to me. I hope the Board will be Pleased to award him some little punishment for such conduct, example being the only means to obtain Proper Order with such refractory paupers.

9 March 1837 – Between Saturday Night & Sunday Morning, some person broke through the Clamp & stole A quantity of potatoes in the Garden. They seem extremely fond of the Sort. This being the third time they have visited.

14 June 1837 – The Girl from Elstree who is in the family way, has not a Single thing for the Use of the Child. Had we better have some Linen made in the house?

25 June 1837 – Admitted in the Workhouse about 8 Oclock this morning an Irish Casualty Woman & her infant who was delivered a few hours before in a Ditch at East Barnet. I sent promptly for the Medical Officer who Promptly Attended. They are both in a fair way of doing well. She has nothing for the Child to wear.

26 June 1837 – Please let the Children have some books.

9 July 1837 – John Bell one of the inmates was bro[ugh]t home by two men about ½ past 4 Oclock on Sunday Afternoon in a State of intoxication. He went out after Dinner for the rest of the Paupers for the Purpose of going to Church instead of which he went to the Black horse Public house, where he remaind till he was unable to walk back by himself. He Swore when the Porter went to fetch him. We have not yet Punished him for it.

22 March 1838 – A Labouring Man named Stratton applyd at the Workhouse on tuesday for a house keeper but from what I could learn from his conversation Perhaps it would not be Prudent to send one.

<hr/>

Reverend Dennis L. Cousins
Extracts from the Diary of a Workhouse Chaplain

Published in 1847, the Revd Dennis Cousins' *Diary* is a series of 'sketches' relating to some of the inmates he encountered in his work as a workhouse chaplain. Perhaps more illuminating, though, is the work's introduction where Cousins makes clear his antipathy to the workhouse system, especially the way that families and elderly couples were separated.[55] Cousins also complains at some length about the meanness of Boards of Guardians in the salaries they offered chaplains – as little as £10 a year – in relation to the duties they were expected to perform. In short, chaplains were overworked and underpaid – to the great detriment, in his view, of the workhouse inmates they were expected to serve:

> It is not my purpose to dwell on the many social evils which arise out of certain glaring defects in the New Poor Law! My views as a clergyman – as one who has watched with some care the operation of this law in a spiritual light, are more than ever directed to the one grand defect which is so conspicuous in the whole system, the want of sufficient provision for what, in the ideas of every right-thinking person, is of far greater importance in *such* an establishment and amongst such characters, than mere temporal relief – *proper religious instruction and consolation to those who from a variety of contingent circumstances are brought to a workhouse.* I state it not as a mere unfounded assertion, but as what I believe to be a matter of statistical fact, that the balance between those who seek it as an asylum from misfortune, and those who are compelled to resort to it as a last refuge from their own vices, largely preponderates in favour of the former, and the sketches in the following pages will bear out this statement. Is then the union workhouse to be made a House of Correction?[56] – if so, why not at least

give it the same advantages which in a spiritual point of view are given to a house of the latter description? It would be difficult to find a gaol in any part of England which is not provided with a regular chaplain, whose remuneration is such that he is enabled to devote the due portion of his time to the religious instruction of those over whom he is placed.

But what is the case in the majority of our union workhouses? – in nine cases out of ten the chaplain appointed is already an over-worked curate, the small amount of stipend rendering it out of the question for any disengaged clergyman to accept the appointment. In many of our gaols, both in town and country, the chaplain receives a salary averaging from £160 to £200 a year; in few of our unions does a like official receive more than £50 per annum; those which exceed this amount are infinitely fewer than those which fall below it. I have now before me the official notification which I received on my appointment as chaplain to a union, and for which I was the only candidate:

'Rev. Sir,
I beg to inform you that you have this day been elected chaplain to the – union at a salary of £30 per annum. Your duties will be to read prayers and preach once on Sundays, to visit the sick, and catechise the children at – during the week, and to give the usual lecture on Friday evenings ...'

These duties, let me observe, were to be performed in a union which averaged 190 inmates (exclusive of the children) by one who had already the core of 2,000 souls in a parish with 30,000 inhabitants, and upon whom a proportionate part of the duties of so large a population naturally fell. I know that I am open to the inquiry, 'Why undertake such an addition to your labours, when you had already more than you could efficiently perform?' My reply is, simply because I knew that had I not undertaken the office (the duties of which I had for some time before my appointment gratuitously performed) those poor unfortunate ones in the workhouse would have been left, if not totally uncared for, at least dependent on the casual instruction of any who might have found 'a convenient season' to impart the bread of life to those who were hourly perishing for lack of it.

The result has proved the truth of this; for when on leaving the parish I resigned an appointment which I had held for nearly four years, the inmates of that union were left without any service being performed *except by the Master*, the utilitarian Guardians (after failing in the experiment of sending some of the paupers to church) having in vain repeatedly advertised for a chaplain to undertake the above-named duties at the *extravagant salary of £20 a year*!

None can know but those who have visited there, the sad scenes which call for commiseration; none can know so well as the minister of God who enters there on his errand of mercy, how rich the consolation which he can apply from the Spiritual treasury with which he is provided! For in that house he finds the buds which once gave promise of sweet flower insensible to the rays of hope which would beam upon it! There the cold hand of despair has seized with ruthless grasp upon its victim – there the world is excluded, life has lost its charm, and the angel of death is a welcome messenger, whose approach they long for as that which is to close their woes for ever! It is in the workhouse that the lessons of submission are to be learnt, but ofttimes they who should learn them have no teachers but their own rebellious hearts, and we speak advisedly when we say, that many have passed away to their great account in their solitary chamber of the union workhouse, without even the slightest consolations of a minister of God, who, although a frail and fallible creature as themselves, might at least, as every Christian knows, have been the means under God of soothing the pillow on which the dying head was laid.

Cousins has a particularly low opinion of workhouse schoolteachers who were often, he suggests, the subject of complaints and dismissal for drunkenness and 'other immoralities':

I have reason to believe great cruelties have been practised at times on the children, which probably do not always come to light, as a schoolmaster has no difficulty in awing an unhappy orphan, who probably has not a friend in the world, into silence, and suppressing all complaints. In one case a child was beaten so severely, that had not the punishment been stopped by the fortunate entry of the governor into the apartment, death would probably have ensued. In another the schoolmaster was in the habit of tying up with a handkerchief the jaws of those boys whom he thought deserving of punishment, to prevent their screams being heard, and then beating them in the most savage manner! The persons who were guilty of these cruelties had been village schoolmasters, where they could not have practised such conduct, as a child so treated would have immediately complained to its parents and would have been taken away from the school, which would quickly have shown the Master, from policy, if not from charity, the necessity of mildness in future. But where is a poor friendless orphan or foundling (for of these classes a great proportion of the workhouse children consist) to turn for assistance, when it knows no one in whom it can place confidence, or to whom it can utter complaints? Hence it seems incumbent on us, for humanity's sake, to be doubly cautious whom we select as schoolmasters for children thus situated, that is, 'whom we make rulers over these little worlds, lest we introduce a tyrannical despot, rather than a father! The following is extracted from a letter I received from the chaplain to a union workhouse. 'The evidence I produced against that man (the schoolmaster) was quite disgusting. I have now a schoolmaster and mistress of good principles. Their faithful discharge of duty has enabled me to exclude a man who, when schoolmaster, endeavoured at least to seduce several of the elder girls in the school.' This is a striking illustration of having chaplains, who are always regarded as the friends of the poor in the workhouses, who have no feelings of terror towards them. They come to the chaplain as to a minister of charity and mercy, as a friend of the wretch whom every friend forsakes.[57]

Richard Ellis
Profitable Employment of Paupers on Workhouse Land

Cultivation of the land was an activity that became popular with workhouse authorities. It not only provided a cheap supply of food for consumption by the workhouse, but was also a useful source of labour to keep the inmates occupied. As well as growing crops on the workhouse site itself, some unions even set up their own farms by hiring or purchasing additional land nearby.

Richard Ellis, the Master of the Abingdon Union workhouse from 1835 to 1861, was clearly a farming enthusiast, not only growing crops but also raising pigs, as indicated by his 1849 missive on the subject to the Poor Law Board:

> You understood me rightly that the produce of the ten acres of land adjacent to the Abingdon workhouse had enabled me, besides supplying vegetables for the use of the inmates, to credit the Guardians with £100.

Workhouse grounds under cultivation at Aylsham in Norfolk. The growing of crops not only provided fresh vegetables for the kitchen but was also a useful labour task for the male inmates.

The potatoe crop, although a failure in most places, has not been so to any great extent here. The soil being of a light description, and the system of planting in the autumn having been followed, conduced, in a great measure, to the preservation of this valuable crop. The quality of the potatoes was such that they were eagerly sought after, and realised an average price of 11s 3d per sack.

By keeping, upon an average, twelve large pigs, which we purchase in a very poor condition, (spayed sows being preferred,) we can use all our spare offal from the garden, and this description of pigs will eat it, and get half fat upon it. We obtain a large quantity of manure from them, and, with a small purchase of stable dung, are enabled to manure the ground sufficiently. The liquid obtained from the washhouses, privies, &c., is all conveyed into close cesspools in the garden, from which it is pumped, and conveyed between the rows of the crops, particularly mangold wurtzel, by which means this plant attains a weight of from 20 to 25lbs each, and sells at 20s per ton. In winter the liquid manure is pumped up and distributed over such parts of the ground as are dug in, and the ground is trenched and prepared for spring crops. A gravel pit is kept always open for the employment of those who are not otherwise employed; the gravel sold to surveyors and others produces more than sufficient to purchase manure and straw for the piggery. The seeds we grow ourselves, so that no extra charge is made upon that account in this return.

As well as vegetables, many workhouses raised pigs which were fed on workhouse kitchen waste. This 1896 view shows the piggery at the Mitcham workhouse farm, which also boasted its own gasworks.

In employing paupers in the garden, or on out-door work, one thing must be particularly attended to, that is, the character of the persons so employed. Unless upon particular occasions, I do not employ young able-bodied men, or even married men with families, if I can learn that they became inmates by their own misconduct. I make it a matter of favour to employ them there; and for those who do not work well while there, some sort of employment within the house is found. The old men and boys occasionally work in the garden, which makes them cheerful and keeps them in good health. The ground is worked by the spade and a light harrow, which is drawn by the boys.

You will perceive by the return herewith sent, that the common charges are credited with £52 for vegetables consumed by the officers and paupers, which number, including children, on the average, about 200 weekly.

Joseph Rogers M.D.
Reminiscences of a Workhouse Medical Officer

Joseph Rogers (1820–1889) became one of the most prominent crusaders for the improvement of medical care for the poor, especially those in workhouses. He also campaigned for better conditions of service for Poor Law medical officers.

As medical officer at the Strand Union's Cleveland Street workhouse from 1856 to 1868, Rogers battled at length for improvements in the building and its management in the face of opposition from within the Strand Board of Guardians and continual obstruction by the workhouse's tyrannical Master, George Catch. Rogers' pay at the Strand was only £50 per annum, out of which he had to pay for all the costs of any medicines that he prescribed. Following Rogers' campaigning, a parliamentary committee eventually agreed that expensive medicines such as quinine and cod-liver oil could be funded from the poor rates.

In 1865, Rogers assisted *The Lancet* in the journal's exposure of the appalling conditions that existed in many of London's workhouse infirmaries. The following year, he founded the Association for the Improvement of London Workhouse Infirmaries, many of whose aims were incorporated in the 1867 Metropolitan Poor Act.

In 1866, Rogers established the Association of Metropolitan Workhouse Medical Officers, later known as the Poor Law Medical Officers Association. The Association campaigned for better pay and conditions for doctors working in the Poor Law system.

Rogers' autobiography, published shortly after his death, describes conditions in the Strand workhouse and the internal politics of its management:

The Strand Workhouse in the year 1856 was a square four-storied building fronting the street, with two wings of similar elevation projecting eastwards from each corner. Across the irregularly paved yard in the rear was a two-storied lean-to building, with windows in the front only, used as a day and night ward for infirm women. There were sheds on each side for the reception of so-called male and female able-bodied people, whilst in the yard, on each side of the entrance gate, was a two-storied building, with an underground apartment lighted by a single window, and with a door for the reception of male and female casual paupers; the wards above being for those of both sexes admitted to the house.

The necessary laundry work of the establishment, which never in my time fell below five hundred inmates, was carried on in the cellar beneath the entrance hall and the general dining-room, whence it came to pass that the said hall, &c., was for four days in each week filled with steam and the odours from washing the paupers' linen. A chapel was contrived out of one of the male infirm wards on the ground floor on the Sunday, and utilised on that occasion for both sexes. On the left of the entrance hall was the Board-room; the corresponding apartment on the right, and the room above on the first floor, being the apartments of the Master and Matron. On the right side of the main building was a badly paved yard, which led down to the back entrance from Charlotte Street; on each side of this back entrance there was – first, a carpenter's shop and a dead-house, and secondly, opposite to it, a tinker's shop with a forge and unceiled roof. This latter communicated with a ward with two beds in it, used for fever and foul cases, only a lath and plaster partition about eight feet high separating it from the tinker's shop.

There were no paid nurses. Such nursing as we had, and continued to have for the first nine years I was there, was performed by more or less infirm paupers, with the occasional aid of some strong young woman who had been admitted temporarily and was on pass. Unfortunately it frequently happened that just as she was becoming useful she left, and there was nothing for it but to fall back upon the ordinary broken-down inmates, the selection of whom did not rest with me, but with the Master or the Matron, or both. Just outside the male wards of the House, at the upper end of the yard, there were two upright posts and a cross-bar. On this bar were suspended the carpets taken in to beat by the so-called able-bodied inmates, from whose labour the Guardians derived a clear income of £400 a year. In despite of the continued noise and dust caused by this beating, the Guardians persisted in carrying it on for ten of the twelve years that I was there. The noise was so great that it effectually deprived the sick of all chance of sleep, whilst the dust was so thick that to open the windows was entirely out of the question until the day's work was over. I attempted repeatedly to get this nuisance done away with, but so fierce was the antagonism of the majority of the Board that I had to abandon it.

The Master of the House, a certain George Catch, had been a common policeman in Clare Market, where he had made himself useful to the Chairman of the Board, who was the proprietor of an *à-la-mode* beef shop in that locality. Through this Chairman's influence he became the porter of the Workhouse, and the Master falling sick, he had performed his duty for him. The illness ending fatally, through the same influence Catch was promoted to the vacant office, though, at the time I first knew him, he was so ignorant that he could only write his name with difficulty. He was single on his appointment, but an alliance with the late Master's niece, who had acted as Matron for some time, was talked about on my taking office.

On the morning of my entering on my duties I went over the sick ward with the son of my predecessor. My curiosity was excited by sundry ill-shaped bottles, all of which contained the same description of so-called medicine. The salary did not admit of an extensive variety of medical necessaries, as it was only fifty pounds a year, out of which all drugs were to be found. It is true that this stipend was supplemented by an occasional fee from attendance on parturient women, in cases where difficulty or danger arose, or in any illness which took place prior to the ninth day after the confinement. That fee was limited to twenty shillings only. The decision as to the necessity for such attendance was vested in the midwife or Matron, and until that was given the medical officer was interdicted from entering the lying-in wards. This regulation was in direct contravention of the Poor Law Regulations, but then the Department were very unwilling at that time to interfere with the so-called discretion of the Guardians, however much their regulations were disregarded.

I have stated that the Chairman of the Board was the proprietor of an *à-la-mode* beef shop. During my first year of office this dignitary would often come to the House on Sunday morning dressed in the dirty, greasy jacket in which he had been serving *à-la-mode* beef the night before, and unshaven and unshorn, he would go into the chapel with the pauper inmates, and afterwards go to the Board-room, and have breakfast with the Master and Matron. Of course, between the three, there was an excellent understanding, and during this Chairman's reign all alterations for the better were resisted.

I have before stated that all my nurses were pauper inmates. The responsible duties they had to perform were remunerated by an amended dietary and a pint of beer. Occasionally for laying out the dead, and for other specially repulsive duties, they had a glass of gin. This was given by the Master or Matron, but I was expected to sanction the supply.

I have referred to the ward used for foul cases, which was in immediate proximity to the tinker's shop. It was altogether unsuitable for the reception of any human being, however degraded he might be; but it had to be used. I remember a poor wretch being admitted with frost-bitten feet, which speedily mortified, rendering the atmosphere of the ward and shop frightfully offensive.

At first I was at a loss to know whom to get to go through the offensive duty of waiting on him. At last a little fellow, called Wiseman, undertook the task, the bribe being two pints of beer and some gin daily, with steaks or chops for dinner. Presently the patient was seized with tetanus, and after the most fearful sufferings died. He was followed almost immediately afterwards by poor Wiseman, who had contracted from his patient one of the most malignant forms of blood poisoning that I ever saw.

These two successive deaths took place whilst the tinker was plying his business on the other side of the partition which separated this ward from his smithy. This place was an utter disgrace to the Board, but they never attempted to alter it whilst I was there.

The nursery ward was situated on the third floor, opposite to the lying-in ward. It was a wretched, damp and miserable room, nearly always overcrowded with young mothers and their infant children. That death relieved these young women of their illegitimate offspring was only what was to be expected, and that frequently the mothers followed in the same direction was only too true.

I used to dread to go into this ward, it was so depressing. Scores and scores of distinctly preventible deaths of both mothers and children took place during my continuance in office through their being located in this horrible den.

It frequently happened that some casual was admitted with her child, or children, to the room below the female receiving ward. On my visiting the House next day I would find that her child had got an attack of measles and could not go out; and in spite of my sending the mother and child to the children's infectious ward above, measles always broke out in the nursery some eleven days after, and I have had as many as twenty down with it at a time. I will not horrify my readers by stating the proportion of deaths to recoveries, but content myself with stating that the latter were very few.

What made these continuous outbreaks so vexatious was this, that I had laid down the most stringent regulations as regards isolation and disinfection; but unfortunately my orders could only be given to pauper women. I had no other persons to act with, and with that habitual carelessness which had led to their becoming paupers, they only in exceptional instances paid any attention to what I said.

Now and then a decent widow with an infant came in, and became an inmate of the nursery ward, there being no other place for her to go to. What her feelings must have been when forced into day and night companionship with some of the most abandoned of her own sex in this miserable Gehenna,[58] I will not attempt to portray, and yet the majority of the Board looked upon this den as a perfect paradise, and looked on me as an irreconcilable fellow for troubling them with my complaints respecting it. I had not been the medical officer for many months before I found that my pauper nurses were frequently under the influence of drink, and that, too, in the forenoon. On inquiring, I heard to my surprise that the Master was in the habit of giving out the stimulants at 7 a.m., and, as many of the inmates sold their allowance, the nurses had become partly or wholly intoxicated when I reached the House in the morning.

My first request to the Master was that some other time should be selected for the issue of stimulants. Such request was angrily refused, and it was not until I had appealed to the Board that I succeeded in effecting an alteration, but my success made the Master, henceforward, my determined foe. As I have stated, the medical officer's salary was intended to cover the provision of medicine. The Guardians, however, had supplied my predecessor with linseed-meal and mustard, but finding that I had a great many consumptive and bronchitic patients, I was induced to apply to the Guardians for some linseed, to enable me to give the patients some linseed tea. Now there was one nurse in the female sick ward, by name Charlotte Massingham, who had been in supreme authority there some years. She was nearly always muddled; to work with her was impossible; Charlotte invariably treated me with supreme indifference, not unmingled with undisguised contempt. I had introduced new-fangled notions, would have my medicines correctly given, and the patients well attended to. On hearing that my application for the linseed had met with success, I went up to the Workhouse. On going into the female sick ward I told Charlotte of my having gained the assent of the Board, when, suddenly springing up at least a foot, she came down slapping both sides, with her arms on to the ground, with the startling observation, 'My God! Linseed tea in a workhouse!' Charlotte's reign, however, was not of long continuance after this; she died, worn out by the effects of habitual intemperance. I heard, after she was dead, and the inmates were free to speak, that she systematically stole the wine and brandy from the sick.

It was obvious that one of the first points to secure was the removal of the laundry before referred to, situated in the cellar beneath the dining hall. The Guardians having assented to my suggestions, a contract was entered into with the builder to put up a laundry in the back yard. The structure was to cost some £400. On proceeding to dig out the foundation, the workmen came on a number of skeletons, the yard having been originally the poor burial ground of St Paul's, Covent Garden, for which parish the Workhouse, &c., had been built, and had been rented by the Guardians from that parish when the Strand Union was formed. So full was this yard of human remains, that the contractor was compelled to go down twenty feet all round, before a foundation for the laundry could be obtained. In making this huge trench, they disinterred the remains of the poor Italian boy, murdered by Bishop and Williams, whose murder was discovered by the late Mr Partridge of King's College Hospital, to whom Bishop and Williams had sold their victim for anatomical purposes.[59] Similar murders of the same kind in Edinburgh, led to the passing of the Anatomy Act, and to the suppression of the practice of body-snatching by the abandoned wretches who formerly supplied Schools of Anatomy with subjects. My next endeavour was an enlargement of the cellar at each wing so as to secure better accommodation for the reception of casual poor, and increased space for sick children and others. This was accomplished by nearly rebuilding the wings. Unfortunately these suggestions rendered me extremely unpopular with many of the Guardians, and delayed for some two years any increase of my wretched stipend, which would otherwise have been granted, if I could have remained a passive observer of that which I saw around me. But worse was in store.

My first serious quarrel with the Board happened thus. Many of the young women who came in to be confined, came under treatment afterwards, suffering from extreme exhaustion, and some were hopelessly consumptive. On making inquiry, I found that the practice in the lying-in ward was to keep the single women on a dietary of gruel for nine days, and then, at the end of a fortnight, to dismiss them to the nursery ward on House diet, with their children. Assuming, as I had a perfect right to do, that this dietary had emanated from an order of the Poor Law Board, I wrote to the Department telling what I had observed, and asking that Board's permission to introduce a more generous system. My communication was sent to the Guardians, and I was informed in a letter from the Board at Whitehall that it rested with me exclusively to order whatever form of dietary I chose, a power which I did not hesitate to use. The Board of Guardians condemned my conduct in writing to the Poor Law Board, in the strongest possible terms, and the use I had made of the power vested in me. The course taken by me was held to be in the highest degree reprehensible, as it traversed the deliberate action of the Guardians, who had established the starvation dietary for single parturient women, as a deterrent against the use of the Workhouse as a place in which to be confined. As the number of fresh admissions went on increasing, and I had not sufficient accommodation, I recommended that the side wings should be enlarged by carrying the building up a storey higher. This was done, and the pressure put on the accommodation was met for a time, but all these suggestions increased my unpopularity with certain of the Board, who condemned me for the expense I was putting them to. About this time the annoyance and obstruction I met with from the Master and Matron compelled me to apply to the Inspector for support. He came to the House to make inquiry, but so large a number of the Guardians attended to support the Master, that after a few questions had been put, he closed the inquiry. Some years after, he expressed to me his regret that at that time he could not see his way to aid me.

At the end of the first year some business took me to Scotland. The Board sanctioned my absence, and gave their approval of the gentleman who was to act as my substitute. On my return journey by the night train, on getting out at Peterborough at 6 a.m. to get some coffee, I was surprised to see the Master of the Workhouse and the clerk of the Board standing on the platform. On reaching King's Cross I remained in the carriage till all the passengers

Joseph Rogers, whose 1889 obituary in the *British Medical Journal* averred that 'if Howard was the Hercules of prison reform, as truly was Rogers the Hercules of workhouse reform'.

had alighted and had passed me. I was in doubt whether I had been deceived, but I had not been, for presently the pair passed the carriage, each carrying a small bag. About ten days after, a letter was sent from the Board, asking for an explanation of an alleged neglect of a sick person in the House. I forthwith called on my substitute and showed him the letter. He denied in the most positive terms the allegation of neglect. On visiting the House, no information could be gained from any one, but it occurred to me on leaving to ask the porter whether he could throw any light on the matter. After reading the clerk's letter he made the remark, 'Why, Catch was not in the House at the time he alleges the neglect took place, for he and the clerk went down to Peterborough from the Thursday to the Monday morning, to be entertained by the contractor who put up the laundry boiler.' In my defence, I stated this to the Board, when great was the indignation expressed by some of the Guardians; first, at his false charge of neglect, and secondly, that he and the clerk should have gone away without leave, and for their being entertained by the contractor.

The exposure of course intensified this Master's hostility, in which his friend the clerk cordially cooperated. The consequence to me was that I was continually sent for on most frivolous pretences. The messenger would come to my house and say, 'You are wanted at Cleveland Street;' if I asked for what, he was studiously ignorant. If I went, or if I sent my assistant, Catch would keep us waiting in the hall until it suited his humour to come out to me, when in a loud voice he would say, 'You are wanted in such and such a ward.' Hard as this was to bear with from this ignorant and incompetent official, I put up with it

A 1920s view of the Strand Union's Cleveland Street workhouse, where Joseph Rogers served
as medical officer. Originally erected in the 1770s for the parish of St Paul, Covent Garden, it is
a rare surviving example of a Georgian workhouse and was granted listed building status in 2011.

for a time, but at last I again called on the Poor Law Inspector, and asked him
his advice, when he informed me that the Master was bound to send a written
order, stating the name of the sick person, &c. On my having intimated to him
that I should not again notice his calls unless this requirement was complied
with, the annoyance was stopped – nearly all of these second visits having been
wholly unnecessary, and arranged with the view of wearing me out.

I have stated that, unless called on, either by the midwife, Matron, or Master,
to visit a woman recently confined, I was debarred from attendance on her,
and could not claim any fee. The Master and clerk arranged that no order
should be given until nine days had elapsed, when it was held that I was bound
to take charge of the woman as in an ordinary case of illness. This calling one
in on the morning of the tenth day was so frequently done that I saw that the
thing was arranged, especially as I learned on inquiry that the woman had been
ill for some days, and had asked that I should be sent for. I thereupon took on
myself to visit the ward daily, and to judge for myself as to the necessity for my
attendance. Some half-dozen of these cases occurred within three months. On
sending notice to the clerk that I had visited such and such a case, I received
the reply: 'I have made inquiries and find that you attended without getting the
necessary authority.' This I afterwards learned was done without any authority
from the Board. I therefore decided that I would give up going into this ward
for the future.

Some time after, and in pursuance of this man's policy of annoyance, a case
occurred just as I expected, which enabled me to get rid of him. On going

to the House one morning, the porter told me there was a woman ill in the lying-in ward. On going into my room the pauper attendant came and asked me to go to this ward. To the inquiry, 'Who sent you?' 'No one,' she replied. I then said, 'Go to the Matron, or if you cannot find her, to the Master, state that the woman is very ill, and bring me the authority to visit her.' She went away. Some half-hour after, I went by the ward door, and heard this poor wretch's cries for assistance, but I did not visit her. Again the attendant came to me and implored me to go up. I asked, 'Have you seen the Master or Matron?' 'Yes,' she said. 'What did they say to you?' 'Why, they only laughed.' I again declined to visit the ward. Shortly after I left the House. I had hardly passed the gate when the Master rushed into the hall and inquired whether I had left; on hearing I had done so, he said in a loud voice, 'I have caught that damned doctor at last,' and directed the porter to go for the nearest medical man. Some gentleman came and attended to her, and the bill, and a garbled statement of the facts, was sent by Catch to the Board. I was ordered to attend their next meeting and explain my conduct. I requested the attendance of the porter and of the pauper nurse at the Board's meeting. Catch gave his version of the story. When called on for my explanation, I narrated the course adopted by the Master, the Matron, and the clerk, and pointed out to the Guardians the evident intention of all three to prevent me being paid any fee; that in the case in question I had asked for an authority to visit the woman; that, although both of these officers knew of the poor woman's condition, they had maliciously allowed her to remain without proper attendance, and would not give any order, so that I should not be paid a fee. The defence was so complete, and so completely turned the tables on all three, that a severe censure was passed on the Master and Matron for their inhumanity, and a hint was given that they had better look out for some other appointment. This they did, and a vacancy for a Master and Matron having taken place at Newington Workhouse, Mr and Mrs Catch applied for the post, and, to the delight of all the inmates and officers of the Strand Workhouse, were selected. So intensely tyrannical and cruel had been the rule of this man, that the day he resigned the keys, and was leaving the House, the whole establishment – at least, all those who could leave their beds – rose in open rebellion, and with old kettles, shovels, penny trumpets, celebrated their departure from the premises. The incoming Master subsequently told me that he had never witnessed anything like it in his life, and that the row was so general and spontaneous, that he was powerless to check it.[60]

After later holding posts at the Newington and Lambeth workhouses, George Catch was eventually barred from ever again holding any workhouse post. He subsequently threw himself in front of a Great Western train and was cut to pieces.

William A. Bailward
Are Workhouses Made Unduly Attractive?

William Bailward (1852–1918) was a long-standing member of the Bethnal Green Board of Guardians and also its chairman for some years. He was also interested in promoting the role of charitable bodies in the relief of the poor and was a local secretary of the Charity Organisation Society which coordinated the efforts of different charities.

In 1899, Bailward addressed the South-Eastern District Poor Law Conference – an annual event where Guardians, union officers and other Poor Law officials met to hear and discuss papers on a range of topics relating to the Poor Law. The provocative title of his paper – 'Are Workhouses Made Unduly Attractive?' – reflected the concerns of many Boards of Guardians following various relaxations by the central authorities, such as elderly inmates not being required to wear workhouse uniforms:

> The question of Workhouse management has been very much to the fore of late years. We have had two circulars at least from the [Local Government] Board upon the subject. The first is general, and suggests various improvements in Workhouse and Infirmary such as classification, improvements in nursing, and various details, such as the abolition of distinctive clothing and other minor relaxations. The second deals chiefly with the treatment of the aged and infirm, for whom it prescribes classification as especially important, and reiterates the suggestions made in the former circular as to leave of absence and non-distinctive clothing. The circulars are only a reflection of what had been taking place in many parts of London prior to their issue. I think that we abolished distinctive clothing in my own parish at least a year before we received the circulars, and I expect that other Boards had done the same. Altogether no doubt the tendency of the last few years has been in the direction of greater indulgence for certain classes of the inmates of workhouses. With this, so long as it is rightly applied, none of us will quarrel.
>
> The Local Government Board in its second circular lays especial stress upon the importance of classification of the aged and infirm, and of separating those who have previously 'led moral and respectable lives from those who, from their habits of speech, or for other reasons, are likely to cause them discomfort.' It would be interesting to know how far this classification has been carried out. From the inquiries I have been able to make, I fancy in very few instances. We know, indeed, that a proper separation would involve the rebuilding of at least half the Workhouses in London. Most of them are already overcrowded, and want of space prevents any modification of existing arrangements. But even supposing there were room, the difficulties of classification are not surmounted. As I once heard it put, 'How are we to decide who shall be placed in the back row of the stalls, and who shall be in the front row of the pit?'

The Poor Law which divides those receiving relief into the able-bodied, the sick, the aged over sixty, and the young, rather naturally leads to the presumption that all those over sixty are to be treated alike. They are no longer 'able-bodied'. Relaxations of discipline and a more indulgent dietary scale is prescribed for them. If tobacco or snuff is given, it is given to them, and they are selected for any treats or outings which may be available. Their clothing is to be non-distinctive. In short, the sixtieth birthday is a milestone: all those who have passed it, whatever the cause of their entering the Workhouse, whatever their conduct whilst in it, can legally be treated by the Guardians with certain indulgences which are prohibited for those under that age. I think it will be found that the practice of most Boards of Guardians follows the presumption of the law, and that all those past sixty are in the main treated alike.

The importance of considering this question is obvious when we remember that the vast majority of the inmates of Workhouses, both in London and country, are above the age of sixty, and that the overcrowding of our Workhouses is chiefly due to the influx of this class of the poor. Are we to treat them all alike as a privileged class? Anyone who has had any lengthened experience of the matter, knows that inmates over sixty differ just as much, both morally and physically, as those under sixty.

Many people who have passed the age limit are physically much more capable than others many years their juniors. A typical case is that of an old man of seventy-four, who is, or was till quite recently, an inmate of a London Workhouse. He is as hale and hearty a man as anyone could wish to see. He has married a wife about forty years younger than himself, and has occupied his 'declining' years in begetting a family of five or six young children, the eldest of whom cannot even now be much more than ten years old. The Guardians have kept his children almost continuously for several years, and himself and his wife intermittently. He has always pleaded that he is unable to find work on account of his age, and he has been constantly given passes 'to look for work' for this reason. His wife also took her discharge from time to time, and only a few months ago returned to the Workhouse prepared to present the Guardians with another 'Poor Law child.' Subsequent inquiries have shown that upon at least one occasion when he was out on pass, and was representing to the Guardians that he was unable to get work, he was actually at work, and earning over a week. His employer spoke of him as a strong active man, and a good workman.

Another man, just over sixty – also strong and hearty – was let out repeatedly on pass to look for work. His want of success led to inquiries being made, and it was reported that he never prosecuted his researches further than 'The Well and Bucket'.

It would not be difficult to show that on the women's side as well as on the men's side the distinctions are equally wide. The woman who has led a drunken, disreputable life, and has passed the age of sixty, is unhappily no uncommon phenomenon in London Workhouses. I remember one such, who had also had two daughters in the Workhouse, both of whom had come in with illegitimate children.

Again, it must be well known to all of us here that a very large number of the old people – both men and women – return from their weekly leave of absence the worse for drink; also that many of them are by no means too refined in their language. It must necessarily be a considerable hardship to those who are decent and respectable to be mixed up with these rougher elements. Miss Twining[61] quotes a case in which a blind man in a London Workhouse was forced to go to bed at six in order to get away from the foul language used in the day-room. The notion that to be over sixty confers of itself a halo of respectability is a dangerous fallacy. A fair percentage at least of those who frequent our Workhouses need not be there at all if they behaved themselves even moderately well outside. We must all of us know cases, for instance, in which children would have kept their parents away from the Workhouse altogether but for their intolerable and continued misbehaviour.

The difficulties of classification are, as already pointed out, considerable. But we can, at all events, refrain from encouraging impenitent old age by gifts of tobacco, snuff, and sweets, by unlimited liberty to come and go, and by dressing it up in clothes which are sometimes better than those of the respectable tradesman outside. It is not at all necessary to go into people's past lives. The line of demarcation between those who behave themselves decently and respectably and those who do not is quite sufficiently defined, and no good Workhouse Master, if he has the support of his Board, will find much difficulty in doing justice, broadly speaking. But he must have the support of his Board, or he is powerless. If Guardians have no confidence in the Master of their Workhouse, the sooner they get rid of him the better.

The typical able-bodied 'in-and-out' is usually a happy-go-lucky, devil-may-care sort of fellow, whose chief characteristic is that he is totally devoid of any wish to maintain himself. He can often work and work well by fits and starts; but he has come to look upon the Workhouse or the casual ward as his home, and when he has once got that idea into his head, it is extremely difficult to get it out again.

I knew one such, a young fellow of about thirty, who has been in and out of the Workhouse since he was fourteen. He is short and thick-set, strong and well-made, not bad-looking, with dark curly hair. He has all his wits about him, and if there had been no Poor Law would undoubtedly have been earning his own living. Several times within my recollection he has disappeared for a short time, and it has been reported that he is at work. He has, however, invariably turned up again, stating upon almost every occasion that he has had 'an accident' which has obliged him to throw up his work. He is by turns threatened, cajoled, lectured, and prosecuted, but all in vain. He takes it all quite good-humouredly.

When I last had to do with him, he mildly remarked that 'he had not been in and out so *wonderful* many times.'

Another I remember was always in and out 'because of his leg'. It was quite true that he had a sore place on his leg, but the medical officer, who knew him of old, hinted that that sore place was as good as an old-age pension to him, and that it was not very likely that he would allow it to heal. He was otherwise an able-bodied, healthy man.

Another strong, active young man who 'could not get work', was passing his time in a flirtation with one of the ladies on the other side of the House. An intercepted letter, which ran as follows, was one day laid before the Guardians:

'Dear liz lizey I am going out on Monday. If you like you can come with me. I shall wait for you at the prince of wails – yrs truly, Bill.'

Flirtations of this kind are by no means uncommon in Workhouse life. Probably every Workhouse has its 'in-and-out' couple who have originally been 'married by the chaplain of the Workhouse'. Sometimes even the aged succumb. I know two old fellows who have taken to themselves wives from amongst the female inmates. In neither case, I regret to say, have the marriages turned out happily. 'She isn't at all the sort of woman I expected,' said one of them plaintively: 'She drinks a bit.'

There are some who think that the able-bodied day-room, both on the men's side and on the women's, has its charms for a certain class of inmate. They are said to be scenes of a certain rough conviviality, not always of too lofty a tone, which is dear to the heart of the able-bodied in-and-out. The supervision is, as a rule, not very stringent, and one has heard of such things as card-playing, chuck-penny, and other similar amusements being carried on there, *sub rosa*. One Board of Guardians at least has interfered with such amusements by appointing 'mental instructors', whose business it is to spend a certain time in the day-rooms, and to endeavour to influence their inhabitants in the right direction.

In illustration of the 'attractiveness' of the Workhouse for able-bodied women, I heard recently two stories, both quite authentic, from the same Workhouse. In both cases situations had been found for women by the Matron or otherwise. In the first case, the inmate in question consented to go to the situation, but represented that she must be back at the Workhouse in time for the 'Christmas entertainment'. In the other case, that of a girl with an illegitimate child, she went to the situation, but soon came back to the Workhouse, as she said that the work was not so hard there, and the hours were shorter. Moreover, in private service she had to get her own breakfast.

From all I can hear, the dietary scales of different London Workhouses vary considerably. I have one before me which is said to be 'the best in London' and which gives those over sixty butcher meat four times a week, bacon or pork the fifth, and meat puddings and meat broth on the other two days. Though this is said to be the best, I believe that there are several other Unions in which the scale is practically the same. I read in a paper the other day the following: 'Ample food supply at –' The Guardians had asked the Local Government Board to sanction an addition of half a pint of milk a day to the present dietary. The Local Government Board reply that they will do so, 'provided that some readjustment be made in the present dietary.' The Clerk pointed out that at present the inmates had a breakfast, lunch, a dinner, an early cup of tea and three ounces of cake, tea again with bread and butter and more cake, and then a supper. One of the Guardians, '*What* a day's feeding!'

Again, an inquest was held last year upon an inmate who had died suddenly in a London Workhouse. The doctor certified that the cause of death was syncope, produced by an overloaded stomach acting upon a diseased heart. The Coroner: 'One may say that he was killed by kindness. It may or may not be kindness to overload a man's stomach. Well, it shows that he did not go short of food.' The Doctor: 'Short! By no means. They have nothing to do but eat, drink, and sleep. And this is the third case from the same Workhouse where death has been due to an overloaded stomach.' A Juror: 'When I am out of work I shall want to go there!'[62]

Will Crooks
Evidence to a Local Government Board Inquiry

William ('Will') Crooks was born in 1852, the third of seven children from a poor family in Poplar. His father, George, a former ship's stoker, lost an arm in an accident in 1855, and the family relied on out-relief from the union to survive. When this was withdrawn in 1861, Will's father and the five of the children, including eight-year-old Will, were taken into the Poplar Union workhouse.

Three weeks later, the children were transferred to the South Metropolitan District School at Sutton. Crooks later recalled, 'every day spent in that school is burnt into my soul.'[63] He especially remembered the slow progress of time, especially Sunday afternoons when the children had to sit quietly in the day-room between dinner at noon and tea at six, with only the clock for entertainment.

His mother, Charlotte, managed to find enough money to reunite her family but the experience made a deep impression on him, as did the sight of a bread riot in the winter of 1866 when a lorry delivering bread to the workhouse was stopped and its cargo looted by the starving unemployed.

Crooks later became involved in local politics and in 1892 he successfully stood as a Progressive Party candidate in elections for newly inaugurated London County Council. He petitioned the Local Government Board to lower the property qualification for election to the Board of Guardians from £40 to £10.

As a result he was able to stand for election and subsequently became the first working-class member of the Poplar Board. On attempting to visit the Poplar workhouse, Crooks was barred by the Master, without whose permission a Guardian could be refused admittance. Following Crooks' protest about this regulation, Guardians gained the right to enter a workhouse at any reasonable hour. This small change resulted in an improvement in workhouse conditions across the country.

In 1906, Crooks gave evidence to a Local Government Board Inquiry and described what he saw when he first visited the Poplar workhouse:

We found the condition of things in the House almost revolting. The place was dirty. The stores were empty. The inmates had not sufficient clothes, and many were without boots to their feet. The food was so bad that the wash-tubs overflowed with what the poor people could not eat. It was almost heart-breaking to go round the place and hear the complaints and see the tears of the aged men and women.

'Poverty's no crime, but here it's treated like crime,' they used to say. Many of them defied the regulations on purpose to be charged before a magistrate, declaring that prison was better than the workhouse.

One day I went into the dining-room and found women sitting on the long forms, some sullen, some crying. In front of each was a basin of what was alleged to be broth. They called it greasy water, and that was exactly what it looked and tasted like. They said they had to go out and wash blankets on that. I appealed to the Master to give them something to eat, as they said they would sooner go to prison than commence work on that. Those women, like the men, were continually contriving to get sent to prison in order to escape the workhouse. After a few heated words between the Master and me he gave them some food, and none of them went to prison that day.

A few weeks later I was in the workhouse when these same women were creating a fearful uproar.

'Ah, there you are,' said the Master, meeting me. 'Go and look at your angels now! A nice lot they are to stick up for!'

I went to the dining-room. There was a dead silence the moment I entered.

'I am right down ashamed of you,' I said. 'When you were treated like animals, no wonder you behaved like animals. Now that Mr Lansbury and I have got you treated like human beings, we expect you to behave like human beings.'

They said not a word, and later in the day the ringleaders, without any prompting, came to me and expressed their regret. From that day to this no such scene among the workhouse women has ever been repeated.

The staple diet when I joined the Board was skilly. I have seen the old people, when this stuff was put before them, picking out black specks from the oatmeal. These were caused by rats, which had the undisturbed run of

Following his childhood experience of the Poplar workhouse, Will Crooks became involved in politics, eventually being elected as a Member of Parliament – a career that was summed up in the title of his biography *From Workhouse to Westminster.*

the oatmeal bin. No attempt was made to cleanse the oatmeal before it was prepared for the old people.

Whenever one went into the men's dining-room there were quarrels about the food. I have had to protect old and weak men against stronger men, who would steal what was eatable of their dinners. There was no discipline. The able-bodied men's dining-room on Sundays gave one as near an approach to hell as anything on this earth. It was everybody for himself and the devil take the hindmost. If a fellow could fight lie got as much as lie wanted. If he could not, lie got nothing. Fights, followed by prosecutions at the police courts, were common. The men boasted that prison had no worse terrors than that place. They were absolutely beyond control. They wandered about all over the place, creating all kinds of discord, and even threatening to murder the officers. Two Labour Masters nearly lost their lives in trying to control them.

The inmates were badly clothed as well as badly fed. Not one of them had a change of clothing. Their under-clothes were worn to rags. If they washed them they had to borrow from each other in the interval. The inmates' clothes were not only scanty, they were filthy. On one occasion the whole of the workhouse linen was returned by the laundry people because it was so over-run with vermin that they would not wash it.

One of the inmates – a woman–who was doing hard work at scrubbing every day, asked me whether she couldn't have a pair of boots.

'Surely,' I said, putting her off for the time, 'nobody here goes without boots?'

A second and a third time when I came across her scrubbing the floors she pleaded for boots. She raised her skirt from the wet stone floor, and showed two sloppy pieces of canvas on her feet, and that was all she had in the way of boots.[64]

Margaret Joan Wells-Gardner
Growing up in the Workhouse

Margaret Joan Wells-Gardner spent her childhood in the Lexden and Winstree Union workhouse in Essex, where her parents were appointed Master and Matron in 1906. Her memories of the institution were recorded in 1959:

Looking back, one of the clearest of my childhood recollections is of the bell. The bell punctuated the daily life of the closely-knit community which was 'home':The Workhouse.

There were about two hundred of us there. There were Master and Matron (my father and mother); a small staff called the Officers; and the Inmates. My sister and I were known as Miss Sybil and Miss Joan. We had been born in this Workhouse, and our father had been born there when his parents were Master and Matron. Three years elapsed between my grandparents' retirement and my own parents taking up duty, which they did in 1906.

The bell hung in its belfry on top of the octagonal tower which was the centre of the House. The bell-rope descended through the rooms below – part of the Master's apartments – to the ground floor. It included a length of chain, and made a fearful clatter. On weekdays the bell was rung to this timetable:

6.45 a.m.	Getting-up time
7.30 a.m.	Breakfast
8.00 a.m.	Begin work
9.00 a.m.	Master and Matron available for interview in their offices
11.45 a.m.	Cease work
12 noon	Dinner
1.00 p.m.	Resume work
5.00 p.m.	Cease work
5.30 p.m.	Tea
8.00 p.m.	Bed-time (8.30 in summer)

This showed that the Inmates normally worked less than an eight-hour day. They did not work on Saturday afternoons or on Sundays, unless in the kitchen or helping the infirm and so forth.

Many people living nearby relied upon the Workhouse bell as a time-keeper. Once, when for some reason it was rung later than usual, some of them came to complain!

The Inmates, other than the sick and aged, worked according to their ability – and of course without pay. Many of them seldom handled money, unless friends outside sent them small sums.

Many of the men worked in the garden, which provided nearly all the fruit and vegetables needed. The garden covered about four acres and a nearby field also belonged to the Workhouse. Other men looked after the pigs; some cleaned the rooms, some chopped wood or did other domestic or maintenance work. When I was very small, the water was pumped by hand from the well to the storage tank in the roof. I can just remember three or four men working together at the pump at intervals during the day. Then an electric pump was installed, and later an emergency supply was laid on from the public mains, which had not always been available.

The women worked in the kitchen or the laundry, in the sewing room, at cleaning or in helping to care for the infirm. Until about 1930 there was a nursery (later transferred to a neighbouring institution), and there the babies were looked after by their mothers. These mothers were nearly all single girls who had had their babies in the maternity ward. They were not allowed to leave the Workhouse unless or until they could take their children with them, which meant that some of them actually remained there for years.

Until about 1920, older children had lived in the Workhouse and gone out from there to the village school. Then a Home for them had been opened a mile or so away (and supervised by parents) and they did not come to the Workhouse unless they had parents there whom they visited. Much earlier on, the 'Workhouse children' had been taught on the premises by a schoolmaster and schoolmistress.

Each department of the House was supervised by an Officer. There were not many Officers when I was small, but the staff gradually increased as they came to have more time off duty and as the demands of the House grew. I can remember the days when my father had only two male officers – a porter, whose duties were many and various, and an engineer-handyman. About that time there were three nurses in the infirmary block. One was a midwife, and my mother shared the midwifery with her. There was also a cook, a laundress and one or two 'attendants'. All except the engineer-handyman were resident. Each had a fortnight's holiday a year – I think the head-nurse-midwife had three weeks – but otherwise they rarely had a whole day off duty. They were free after the mid-day meal once in the week and on alternate Sundays, and had one other evening 'off' during the week. Otherwise, although not actually working, they were on the premises in the evenings in case they were needed. Board and lodgings, uniform and laundry etc. were of course provided for them, and medical attention if necessary, and I think their salaries were about £50 in most cases. When my parents took up duty in 1906 their own salaries were £60 and £40 per annum, and they said their posts were considered handsomely paid at that time.

Father and Mother were very much tied to their work, or at least to the premises, and their responsibilities were great. Until 1930, when the County Council took it over the House was administered by the Board of Guardians who met fortnightly in the Boardroom, but the Master and Matron were responsible for the day to day management and for dealing with the many and varied situations, and indeed emergencies which arose. There were many aspects of their work: the care of the old, the sick, the infirm; of children; of mental defectives; of the vagrant men and women who came to the 'tramp wards' and who usually stayed two nights, working on the premises during the intervening day. The kitchen, the laundry, the boiler-house, the food and clothing and hardware stores, the garden, the office – all these had to be 'kept going', whilst the House itself had to be maintained in good repair.

Board Day was quite an event, especially before motorcars ousted horses from the scene. There were about 35 Guardians, for every parish provided for by the House had its own representative on the Board and the larger parishes had more than one.

Wealthy country gentlemen would arrive in carriages driven by their coachmen; farmers would drive up in high dogcarts; poor clergymen would come in modest traps. What must have been some of the last traces of the squire-and-parson hierarchy lingered on here, but the Guardians were genuinely concerned for the welfare of the House, and took personal interest in the Inmates coming from their own parishes.

Able-bodied men Inmates who were used to horses, and most of them were, were detailed to act as ostlers on Board Days. There was never any difficulty about this, the men welcoming the change of routine – and the tips they received. They would unharness the horses and overlook them in the stables until the early afternoon when, after the various committee meetings, the full Board meeting and a cold lunch (organised by Master and Matron), the Guardians would leave.

With the disappearance of the horses, Board Day lost some of its glamour; but the Guardians continued to come fortnightly, in their cars, until the House was taken over by the County Council and small house committees took their place.

This workhouse was built in 1837, of red brick with a slate roof. In shape it was rather like a wheel with four spokes. The hub was the tower I have mentioned earlier, topped by the belfry. It had three floors, the centre being one large room – the Master's drawing room – with windows facing north, south, east and west. This room was octagonal and between the windows were doors leading to each of the four wings which formed the 'spokes' of the 'wheel'. There were two bedrooms above, and the kitchens were on the ground floor below. The wings were the Inmates' and Officers' living quarters and also contained the stores and the offices. They consisted of three floors, but were not quite as high as the central tower. Single-storey buildings made up most of the circumference of the 'wheel'. Here were the laundry, the 'tramp wards' and various outbuildings, and quite an imposing Georgian entrance front facing the main road, with a large porch and entrance hall above which was the boardroom.

Behind the main House was the infirmary building. This comprised two blocks each of four wards etc. with a smaller block between them which was the nurses' home.

The chapel stood in the garden behind the infirmary. It was of red brick, well furnished and appointed, with a tiny chancel and a coloured east window. Babies born in the Workhouse were baptised here if their mothers wished it.

Between the four wings of the main building were open 'yards'. One was paved and was where the linen was hung out to dry after washing. The laundry led off this yard. The others were gravelled and decorated with flowerbeds, and had garden seats for the Inmates in their leisure hours. The main garden was outside all this. In front of the House was a wide lawn with entrance gates at each end and a broad curved drive between them. There were fine beech and other trees, and shrubberies. Further back were a flower garden, an orchard and a large vegetable garden.

In one corner was the Dogs' Cemetery. Here were the graves of the dogs, and one cat, which had belonged to the various Masters. Most of the graves had little headstones. They were kept tidy, and in springtime the little cemetery was full of daffodils.

By today's standards the inside of the House was austere. Some of the lower rooms had stone floors (all these were replaced by wooden floors in my parents' time) and many walls were of painted brick. Although none of the rooms was dark, the lower rooms had windows set high in the wall – these again were improved as time went on. The furniture was very plain and the mattresses, expect in the infirmary, were of straw. Nonetheless, there were certain comforts; and it must be remembered that most of the Inmates, though through no fault of their own, had come from homes which we should call poor today. There were coal fires in the day rooms and coco-matting and rag-rugs on the floors. There were pictures – perhaps not of high artistic merit – vases of flowers, and 'wireless'. A few newspapers were provided, and books and magazines were often given by people who lived nearby.

Washing facilities were rather crude: basins tucked away on landings, most of them with only cold running water. Hot baths were provided weekly. All these conditions were gradually improved.

The infirmary was comfortable and its standards were, I think, equal to those of most other small hospitals at the time. The wards overlooked the garden and were bright and cheerful, with open coal fires in winter. Each ward held about twelve beds, and there were armchairs for the patients who could get up. No surgery was done there. Patients who needed such treatment went to the local general hospital. Nor was the maternity ward in the infirmary itself, but in the women's wing in the main House. This was usual in Workhouses at the time. I never asked the reason, but it was probably to guard the maternity patients from any infection.

My mother and the head nurse were qualified midwives and, if a maternity patient was 'pending', they took care never to be out of the House at the same time. I have known my mother to forgo many outings on this account, and she accepted it cheerfully as part of her duty. The doctor was of course called if needed. In my childhood the doctor had no telephone, and the man who was the 'messenger' for several years, an Inmate named Harry Rogers, used sometimes to go out in the middle of the night to summon him. Harry would walk to the doctor's house, a distance of about two miles, and the doctor would drive him back in his car.

Sick persons had any special diet, stimulants or 'extras' they needed, without stint. Otherwise, in my early days, the Inmates' food was plain and uninteresting, although sufficient. There was a sort of rationing system which ensured that each person received a certain quantity of various foodstuffs. I think this system had been laid down by the Local Government Board, and was common to Workhouses everywhere.

For breakfast there was porridge, bread and butter or margarine, and tea. For dinner six days a week there was meat, soup or fish, vegetables and sometimes a pudding. Once a week, dinner was of bread and cheese. Mugs of tea were served after a meal of bread and butter or margarine, often with cheese or jam, and with cake to follow on Sundays. At this particular House, and no doubt at many other 'country Workhouses', there were plentiful supplies of vegetables and fruit from the garden, which were given to the Inmates. Some of them also received biscuits, cake, eggs, etc. from their friends outside. As time went on, the food became much more varied and eventually supper was also provided. The Officers had cooked breakfasts and two-course dinners every day.

It should be added here that the general health of the Inmates was good, and I cannot remember any epidemic illness occurring apart from colds and influenza.

Clothing was plain and serviceable. The men wore cloth jackets and caps, and corduroy trousers. Each man had a cloth 'Sunday suit' in addition. In my childhood the women wore blue print dresses, white aprons and frilled white caps. They had black woollen stockings and black laced boots, and their underwear was made of calico. In winter they wore shawls for extra warmth. Each woman had a 'best dress' for wear on Sundays and other special occasions. Stocks of other clothing were kept, and any Inmate going away for a holiday

At the gates of the former Lexden and Winstree Union workhouse, the painted instruction to modern drivers provides an ironic link with the predicament of its past inmates, many of whom were never able to leave the institution.

with friends, or leaving the Workhouse, was properly fitted up, using the clothes he had brought with him at the time of his admission if they were in good condition. The women's caps had been discarded by the time I grew up, as being too old fashioned. Old fashioned they no doubt were, but they were also decidedly becoming. The other clothing was modernised as time went on.

People were admitted to the House by the Relieving Officers for the areas from which they came. If they were ill or very old, they came directly into the infirmary. Otherwise they were placed in the Receiving Wards until it had been ensured that they were clean and free from any infection. Their own clothing and any valuables which they brought with them – there were seldom any of these – were kept safely for them, but they themselves kept any small personal articles they wished always to have with them, and, of course, their wedding rings. If they brought money with them, or were sent money by friends, it was kept for them and given to them in small sums whenever they asked for it. This was done entirely in their own interest, as there was a risk of theft by some of the other Inmates.

People were occasionally admitted who had considerable sums of money. Fixed weekly deductions were then made for their maintenance, and any money still in hand when they left was returned to them. If they died in the workhouse, the balance was handed to their relatives.

The Inmates could be visited by friends on Sundays and on one weekday afternoon, but visitors coming long distances could come at any reasonable time. When any sick person was on the danger list, his relatives were sent for. If he died, the relatives made their own arrangements for his burial or, if this was impossible, the Master arranged for his burial in the parish from which he had come to the Workhouse. Some of those who died had no friends, and the Workhouse was indeed their only home. However humble, their lives they were properly cared for and finally laid to rest with every respect.

The chaplain visited the sick Inmates and, on Sundays, after a rather prolonged ringing of the bell, Service was held in the Chapel. It was a simple service. The psalms were read, and the hymns and chants sung to familiar tunes – and sung heartily, as I remember. Some of the men had been choristers in their parish churches, and a few had really good voices. Holy Communion was also celebrated in the infirmary wards for those who could not go to the chapel, and eventually the chapel was also used for non-conformist services. Very few of the Inmates were Roman Catholics, but those who were, were visited by priests and nuns.

The chapel was specially decorated for Easter and Christmas, and for Harvest Thanksgiving. For this last there was always a special preacher, sometimes the Bishop. There were hot cross buns for breakfast on Good Friday and eggs on Easter Day.

Christmas was the highlight of the whole year, and preparations began weeks beforehand. Puddings were made, and decorations and presents were arranged for. Many local residents and firms sent gifts in money or in kind, and some of these gifts came from people who could not have had much to spend on their own festivities. With these and the money the Master was allowed to spend, every Inmate was sure of having at least one present.

By Christmas Eve, the day rooms and the infirmary wards were gay with paper-chains and holly. On Christmas Morning the staff rose very early, and after the bell was rung at 6.45 they would sing carols beneath the dormitory windows. After breakfast the gifts were distributed, and then it was time for the Service in chapel.

For dinner there was turkey and pork, potatoes, Brussels' sprouts, Christmas pudding and mince pies, beer and lemonade. There were crackers for everyone. The preparation and serving of Christmas dinner naturally caused much work, and several people living nearby came each year to give voluntary – and very welcome – help. Other people came as visitors, mostly the Guardians or, later on, the members of the House Committee.

On Christmas evening, all who could gathered in the dining hall for a party. The tables were moved back and the chairs set in a big circle. There were games and an impromptu concert when, year after year, some of the Inmates sang their favourite songs. There was much enjoyment, even if little musical talent. Lucy Webb, I remember, always sang 'The Old Rustic Bridge Beside The Mill', and Alice Kate Smith a fascinating song called 'When I Touched My Seaweed I Knew It Was Going To Be Fine'. Winnie Keating danced a hornpipe. Some of the men, too, sang or recited, and the staff provided a few rehearsed items. The Assistant Master regularly sang 'The Mountains of Mourne' in a bass as deep as the sea to which those mountains sweep down.

Refreshments were handed round, and were taken to those who could not join in the party. The evening ended with 'God Save The King' and with 'Three Cheers for Master and Matron' – but it was not the end of the Christmas festivities, the men and women having separate little parties in their day-rooms on Boxing Day and New Year's Day.

All through the year there were other occasional 'treats' – concerts given by people from 'outside', and one or more outings by coach to the seaside. There was an unofficial Ladies' Visiting Committee, whose members interested themselves in the Inmates and arranged little events for them including a 'tea' with games etc. in the summer. This took place in the garden if the weather was fine.

Here, then are my chief recollections of life in this particular Workhouse, which was, I think, typical of Workhouses everywhere. I visited a number of them, for my parents knew many other Masters and Matrons through what used to be called the Masters' and Matrons' Association. [65]

D.J. Evans
Workhouse Days Remembered

In January 1929, Mr D.J. Evans took up the post of porter at the Carmarthen Union workhouse at an annual salary of £52, plus £5 for hair cutting and shaving and emoluments which included living quarters, and free coal and light. His tenure continued into the 1930s when the running of the institution passed to the Carmarthenshire County Council's Public Assistance Committee:

In 1929 the staff at No. 1 Penlan, Carmarthen, or the Workhouse as it was still known, comprised the Master and Matron, the Porter, a female nurse, a cook and four or five maids. This might seem a small staff to be in charge of about a hundred inmates as well as a hundred or so wayfarers – tramps or vagrants, as they were called – who were admitted each week to the Casual Wards, which were housed in a separate block. But it should be remembered that duty hours were very long; furthermore, the Workhouse in those days was run by 'inmate labour', which meant that every able-bodied person had to contribute by performing various jobs, indoors and outdoors. Although far removed from that of Dickensian days, the regime was still strict and a far cry from conditions in today's Social Welfare Homes.

Cleanliness was the order of the day in respect of the person as well as the premises, bedding and clothing. In spite of primitive facilities the laundry work, done in a building behind the main block, was excellent. Sheets were pressed by using a huge box of stout timber, 7 feet long by 3 feet 6 inches wide and 2 feet deep, which was filled with stones. In the middle of the long side was a wheel with a handle and when this was turned it operated a cog system which moved the box to and fro upon rollers, which pressed the linen sheets. The stronger men were used for this job; often they were of child-like mind, but gentle and well behaved.

There was a good bakehouse in the small building south-west of the main building and backing onto Brewery Road; here all the required bread was produced by an inmate and his assistant. The bread-tins were very big, measuring 18 inches by 7¾ inches and 8 inches deep. The very large dining-room for the inmates had tables about 23 feet long and was in keeping with the general diet – plain and simple. For breakfast and evening meal, which were received without complaint by those poor souls, there was usually just one slice of bread, eight

The high walls surrounding the union workhouse at Carmarthen in South Wales. The porter's quarters were next to the arched entrance at the left of the picture.

ounces in weight and over an inch thick, very thinly spread with margarine, a basin of tea and sometimes a small piece of cheese. On Sundays there might be a piece of cake. Soup was the main feature of dinner. For many years the bread was sliced in a small room adjoining the main kitchen by an elderly and much be-whiskered inmate, who developed amazing accuracy in producing pieces of the right weight and thickness with a large knife having a wooden handle each end of the blade and measuring more than 2 feet overall.

A common sight in Carmarthen during the 'thirties was the four-wheeled wagon or truck, about 4 feet square and 3 feet deep, which was drawn by a T-handle. Loaded with bags of chopped firewood, this vehicle was hauled and pushed by three or four inmates. In charge of this enterprise was an unforgettable character with a limp, who wielded absolute authority over his mates and although he was of simple mind he never erred in rendering accounts to the Master's office at the end of the day's trading. The firewood was produced in the Woodshed. The sawing and chopping was done by tramps rather than the regular inmates. Inmates were used to help in the boiler-house, where steam was provided for various uses. Other cost-saving work done by inmates was gardening. For many years there were five large gardens, which produced enough for almost the whole year. Legislation after World War II was aimed at removing the image of the Workhouse and as a result the Carmarthen institution became known as No. 1 Penlan and no inmates, now called residents, were allowed to be employed. And so the gardens were disposed of and all the other services by inmates came to an end. The new attitude is understandable; on the other hand purposeful occupation, sympathetically supervised, often had a therapeutic effect.

There were bright occasions even in the old Workhouse. Around Christmas it was pleasant and there were colourful decorations hung about. With Christmas dinner extra fare was provided and there was even beer – the gift of a local brewery– for those who wanted it. Occasional visits were also arranged by local organisations to provide entertainment, sweets and tobacco. Every Saturday afternoon the inmates were allowed to go out into the town, but before leaving, all in their best, their names were recorded by the Master. They also wore their best clothes for religious service in the dining room on Sunday afternoons, when only a few were reluctant to attend. Church clergy and chapel ministers took it in turn to conduct the service and the Sankey and Moody[66] hymns were sung with joyful enthusiasm.

The main block, which housed the inmates, was known as the House. The 'knights of the road' were accommodated in another block known as the Casual Ward; otherwise it was called the Tramp Ward and to those who sought shelter there it was The Spike. Conditions in the Casual Wards were bad and cleanliness was not up to the standard which prevailed in the House, but there was a gradual improvement and diet got better. The wards were cramped and there were inadequate facilities for the maintenance of cleanliness. There were two day-rooms, each measuring 10 feet by 8 feet; there was also a small open fire, which heated a copper cylinder to provide all the hot water there was. Some tramps used the open fire to cook food they had begged. An enamel bath was fixed in one of the day-rooms. Adjoining the day-rooms was a long passage, in which there were benches for use when the place was full. The passage also gave access to ten cells, which were locked at night when occupied. A wooden fold-away board about the size of a narrow door served as a bed; this could be folded to the wall during the day. Upstairs there were small dormitories containing eight or ten beds, narrow iron frames with wire mesh to hold fibre mattresses. The help which the Porter relied on came from one of the casuals, either voluntarily or after persuasion, who was universally known as the Tramp Major. One such, although harmless, roared and cursed terribly in an effort to terrorise the others into submission, but they took little notice of him.

Conditions improved in time. Shower-baths were installed and a steam disinfector was connected to the boiler to treat clothing infested with fleas and lice. The clothing was put into a container, from which air was then drawn out before steam was injected. Anyone doing this kind of job usually daubed his own clothing with paraffin to ward off contamination. Each tramp had a bath on admission, after which he was given a night shirt of very coarse calico as well as a towel. All had to come naked for their shirts. They were also provided with slippers, but few used them on the stone-flagged floor, partly covered with coconut matting. Their clothes, which they were not allowed to take into the cells or wards, were stored away, but by some magical ingenuity some would still manage a surreptitious smoke although smoking was forbidden. The shirts were numbered to ensure that a tramp received the same garment each night of his stay. There was never any problem in accounting for night shirts when tramps were discharged, because each was required to hand in a garment with the appropriate number before he could depart. Towels were not so strictly controlled and occasionally one would be missing – usually the dishonest tramp kept his own and purloined another's to hand in. But steps were taken to stop this abuse. On discharge each tramp was given a 'bread and cheese' ticket. In those days there were casual wards in the Institutions at Llanelli, Llandeilo, Lampeter and Narberth and on each route there was an appointed shop where the ticket could be exchanged for bread and cheese. Sometimes old hands who were addicted smokers were able to persuade a sympathetic shopkeeper to supply tobacco instead.

For many years the Porter's off-duty time was one half-day every Wednesday and after the religious service on Sunday afternoon, but only once a fortnight. This was because only two men were employed – the Master and the Porter – and it was desirable that a man should be on duty to deal with unruly behaviour which sometimes, but usually unpredictably, arose. Mostly, trouble resulted from drunkenness, more often than not because of addiction to methylated spirits.

The tramps and casuals were required to work for the food and shelter they received. One of the tasks was stone-breaking and for this purpose there were six cells, each with a stout wooden door and a barred peep-hole. Each cell was about 5 feet long and 3 feet 6 inches wide and had a small skylight. These cells were lined against the boundary wall adjoining Penlan road and set in this wall at a lectern angle at the end of each cell was an iron grille 2 feet 6 inches high by 2 feet 3 inches long. The grille comprised holes 1⅝ inches in diameter, through which stone, broken with a hammer, was screened. Because of constant hammering, the centre of the grille had worn into a larger hole about 3 inches in diameter, so that a lot of the screened stone was larger than the prescribed size. The broken stone fell through the grille and was conveyed along a chute (one for each cell) onto the roadside, where it was collected by a council lorry for road-work.[67]

THREE

REPORTS AND INQUIRIES

FROM THE TIME that workhouses first came into use, those outside them have sought to monitor and appraise their operation. The reasons for doing this have varied, ranging from routine inspections by local officials to sociological investigations, the collection of evidence in relation to legislative reform, exposure by campaigning journalists, and official inquiry into alleged misconduct or scandal. Although the reports from such investigations often dwell on the negative aspects of workhouse operation, they can also reveal valuable detail that would not otherwise have been recorded.

Anonymous
An Account of Several Work-houses

The year 1725 saw the appearance of *An Account of Several Work-houses for Employing and Maintaining the Poor* – the first ever workhouse guidebook. Published by the Society for Promoting Christian Knowledge, an organisation which encouraged the establishment of workhouses and charity schools, the book detailed the setting up and management of more than forty local workhouses then in operation, as well as noting the existence of almost a hundred more. A typical entry was that for Barking ('alias Bury-king') in Essex:

> In the Year 1721, the Parish took a House upon a Lease for 30 Years, at £10 per Annum, and having fitted up with necessary Accommodations for receiving the poor Pensioners of the Parish, they opened it at Christmas the same Year. It will conveniently lodge about 48 People, two in a Bed; and there is a small Infirmary built on the Backside of the House, but the People are generally in so good Health, that there has been hitherto little Occasion to use it.
>
> The Number of Poor now in the House is:

4 old Men	}	from 50 to 80 Years of Age.
10 old Women		
3 Boys	}	from 4 to 7 Years of Age.
3 Girls		

Their Employment is picking Ockam [oakum], at which they earn altogether about £20 per Annum; the Materials for this Sort of Work being pieces of old cable, or Junk (as it is called), are bought of two Merchants, one at Rotherhith, near Three Mariners Stairs, and the other at Cuckold's Point, and cost 7s per hundred Weight; which is sold again in Ockam for 10s per Hundred. Or in spun Yarn at 2½d per pound. Or in Rope Yarn at 2d per pound, or 16s 8d per C.Wt. For all these are made out of old Cable.

The Women knit, and mend Stockings for the whole Family, make Beds, and keep the House clean, and sometimes pick Ockam.

The Steward and his Wife have the Government of the Family; he buys all the Necessaries for Food at the Market, and she takes Care for dressing it.

The Victuals is divided into Messes, 4 Persons to a Mess; this being a cheap Country for Flesh, they have 4 Flesh Days in the Week, according to the following Bill of Fare, viz:

	Breakfast	Dinner	Supper
Sunday	Sheeps Head Broth	Beef, Pudding, and Broth	What's left at Noon
Monday	Beef Broth	Oatmeal Hasty Pudding with a quarter of a Pound of Butter to a Mess	Bread Butter or Cheese
Tuesday	Hasty Pudding[68]	Three bak'd Ox Cheeks	What's left at Dinner
Wednesday	Ox Cheek Broth	Pease Porridge	Bread, Cheese and Butter
Thursday	Hot Pease Porridge	Beef & Broth	What's left at Dinner
Friday	Beef Broth	Milk Porridge	Bread and Cheese
Saturday	Milk Porridge	Sheep's Head for each Mess	What's left at Dinner

Bread and Beer are allowed without Limitation.

They have Roast Beef at the Three Great Festivals,[69] and Plumb-Pudding at Christmas.

The Poor's Rate here is reduced from 2s to 1s in the Pound, and the Poor better provided for.[70]

The title page of *An Account of
Several Work-houses,* here in its
enlarged second edition of 1732,
which described more than a
hundred establishments covering
an area from Glasgow to the Isle of
Wight.

AN
ACCOUNT
OF SEVERAL
WORK-HOUSES
FOR
Employing and Maintaining the POOR;
Setting forth

The Rules by which they are Governed,

Their great Ufefulnefs to the Publick,

And in Particular

To the PARISHES where they are Erected.

As alfo of feveral

CHARITY SCHOOLS
For Promoting WORK, *and* LABOUR.

The SECOND EDITION very much Enlarged.

L O N D O N:
Printed by Jos. DOWNING, in *Bartholomew-Clofe*
near *Weft-Smithfield*, M.DCC.XXXII.

Sir Frederic Eden
The State of the Poor

The State of the Poor, published in 1797 by Sir Frederic Morton Eden, was a
pioneering work of sociological investigation which documented the lives
of the labouring classes. Much of the three-volume work comprised local
reports containing considerable detail about the lives of the poor in more than
170 parishes across England and Wales, with the workhouse often featuring
prominently.

Eden's report on Newark, compiled in 1795, judged its workhouse to be one of
the best in England:

> The Poor are maintained partly at a work-house, and partly at their own homes.
> The number of paupers, at present, in the work-house is 54; of whom, 20 are
> under 15 years of age (including 3 bastards;) 10 of the children work at the

cotton mill lately erected here: the other paupers are employed in such work as suits them, in different parts of the town: grown people are allowed 2*d* in the shilling from their earnings; children have no perquisites, but are now and then paid a halfpenny: the whole earnings, at present, from the Poor in the house, amount to about £90 a year. 42 regular pensioners (including 12 bastards) receive £3 2*s* a week: several house-rents are likewise paid; and a large sum is expended by the parish, every week, in discretionary payments; but, of these, the amount could not be ascertained. The badge[71] appointed by the Act of King William, is worn by paupers in this parish: it was laid aside a few years ago, but the Poor having increased very much, it was resumed last year; and the consequence has been that several persons who had before made regular applications to the parish, have now declined asking for relief.

The work-house here is one of the very best in England: it is sufficiently capacious, and well aired: the men are lodged on one side, and the women on the other; 2, 3, 4 or 5 beds (some of chaff, but mostly of feathers) are in each room: the house is well supplied with vegetables from a good garden; and in all other respects, both within and without, it exhibits a degree of comfort and cleanliness that is seldom to be met with. A few apartments, rather neater than the rest, are appointed for the reception of such persons, as have been unfortunately precipitated from an early station in life, to the humiliating condition of subsisting on a parochial allowance; and their situation receives every attention that humanity can dictate.

The following is the Bill of Fare observed in the work-house:

	Breakfast	Dinner	Supper
Sunday	Milk-pottage	Bread-puddings, beef, bread, broth, and roots.	Beer and bread, with cheese, or butter.
Monday	Ditto.	Bread, and pease-pottage.	Ditto.
Tuesday	Ditto.	Bread-puddings, beef, bread, broth, and roots.	Ditto.
Wednesday	Ditto.	Frumenty of wheat, and milk.	Ditto.
Thursday	Ditto.	Same as Tuesday.	Ditto.
Friday	Ditto.	Suet-pudding.	Ditto.
Saturday	Ditto.	Dumplins, with sauce, composed of vinegar, sugar, and water.	Ditto.

At supper, 1 pint of beer, and 2 ounces of cheese, or butter, are allowed to each adult; and to children in proportion: at dinner, all have as much bread and meat as they can eat; but they are not suffered to take any away.[72]

In the same year, things were in a rather less happy state at Knighton in Radnorshire:

The Poor, till half a year ago, were farmed, by a contractor in Ludlow, for £148 a year, the parish paying all expences of funerals, contagious disorders, appeals, &c.) but they are now partly maintained in a work-house, and partly by out-pensions. 17 persons are in the work-house, and 12 poor families receive 17s a week. The overseers now find a great deal of trouble in managing their Poor; particularly in the work-house, which is under the direction of a governess, who is perfectly incompetent to enforce obedience to her orders: the Poor seldom obey, and often beat her; and, even among themselves, they have continual disputes: so that the parish regrets the alteration which has taken place in their system; particularly as they find the Rates will be considerably higher this year. The breakfast in the Workhouse is milk, or broth; dinner mostly meat and vegetables; and supper, bread and cheese or, milk.[73]

1832 Royal Commission on the Poor Laws
Bethnal Green Workhouse

In 1832, a Royal Commission was appointed to review 'the Administration and Practical Administration of the Poor Laws'. A team of Assistant Commissioners was appointed to collect information about the workings of the existing system, with visits being made to a large number of workhouse establishments. A typical report following such a visit was that submitted on the state of the Bethnal Green workhouse in London's East End:

London, 6 February 1832.

In conformity to your directions, we have the honour to report that we have inspected the workhouse at Bethnal Green yesterday, and conversed with the overseers of the parish respecting its condition.

We have, in the first place, to state, that the enormous pile of cinders, rubbish, &c. in the back yard of the building still remains in the same state as when the workhouse was inspected some weeks before, but that measures are in progress for its removal.

With respect to the internal of the workhouse, we have to inform the Board that it is at present unusually and alarmingly crowded, containing 1,044 inmates, male and female, the average population being about 100 less, a number still disproportionate to the extent of the house and the accommodation which it affords. The healthy paupers are lying three, four and five in one bed; from 60 to 80 in one narrow, low apartment, the windows all closed, the low rooms crossed with lines supporting their dirty clothes, interrupting the little remaining air, and the whole in a state of great filth, emitting a most intolerable odour. We can, however, state that two or three of the wards were cleaner and in a better state of ventilation.

We have also to report, that besides the ordinary diseases prevalent in this and similar asylums, there is a great and unusual number of cases of fever at present under treatment. In one ward, exclusively occupied by fever patients, about 30 feet long by 14 broad and about 12 high, containing nine beds, there were 14 adult females and seven children in various stages of disease, and lying one, two, three or four in one bed. When we entered the room, we found every aperture but the fireplace closed, and the smell and heat completely intolerable. In a second sick female ward we found four cases of fever amongst the other patients; the ventilation was rather better, the apartment cleaner and less densely crowded. In a third ward, occupied by boys and men in fever, we found 22 individuals occupying six beds, five in some beds. There were three grown boys, labouring under severe symptoms of fever, in one bed. The filth of bed linen, floors, &c. here was very great, the windows closely shut up, and the heat and stench excessive. The long ward immediately over this is allotted to healthy paupers. We found it crowded to excess, and the beds occupied by three, four and five individuals, In the furthest corner of the room we detected a man, named Headlam, who had been three days labouring under violent fever. He had, according to his own statement, and those of other inmates of the ward, received no medical assistance whatever. His bed was shared by three men; eight men were sitting round it when we entered, and two were dining with their plates on his bed. The state of crowding and filth in this ward was very great.

In the female lying-in ward we found 15 persons, women, infants and children, to whom were allotted to beds. One woman was in the last stage of smallpox, which disease she had been allowed to go through in this ward. A child was recovered from measles, and we were informed that some cases of typhus had taken place. The deaths during the month of January, (from the 1st to 31st inclusive) have been 50. Those in the same month for the preceding year (population of the house then 950), were only 23.

We have further to express our regret that, owing to the absence of the medical officer of the workhouse during our inspection, we are unable to report on the symptoms, rate of mortality, origin or mode of propagation of fever in the establishment, the parochial officers being unable to give us any precise information on these particulars; neither are they enabled to present any information as to the state of health of the parish, but they have made arrangements with the two medical attendants of the parish, who have promised to report them to the Central Board.

We the honour to be, Sir,

Your obedient servants,

(Signed) *John Anderson*, M.D. Surgeon R.N.

W.B. O'Shaughenessy, M.D.[74]

Charles Mott
The Bulcamp House of Industry, Suffolk

Following the passing of the Poor Law Amendment Act in 1834, a national system of poor relief was created under a new body, the Poor Law Commissioners. Assistant Poor Law Commissioners were appointed to begin the implementation of the new system across the country. Their visits to existing workhouses often produced interesting revelations as illustrated by Assistant Commissioner Charles Mott's report on the Bulcamp workhouse, an old establishment opened in 1766 to serve the Blything Hundred in Suffolk:

In the house of industry at Bulcamp, belonging to the Blything hundred, the most strange customs have obtained, and the paupers are indulged in a manner that render their situations far superior to that of the honest independent labourer.

A regularly licensed shop has for years been fitted up and allowed to be kept by a female pauper in the house of industry for the convenience of the other paupers. The exciseman attends periodically to 'take stock' the same as at any tradesman's shop or warehouse; and the last time I visited the house application was made to me, on behalf of this old pauper shopkeeper, as to the future prospects of her trade. The season had arrived at which it was customary to renew the licenses for the sale of her tobacco, tea, &c. I recommended, however, at the risk of lessening the revenue, that the old lady should relinquish business and retire, as her trade was not likely to be so good under the new arrangements.

The house is surrounded by a small farm belonging to the hundred. There are ten milch cows kept, and the paupers are supplied with the milk and best fresh butter; and I was informed that the Guardians had repeatedly declared that they could not get such butter at their own tables as the paupers were supplied with in the Bulcamp house of industry.

The want of classification and separation of the sexes is here exhibited in a frightful degree. Mr Willson, the governor, who is a respectable man, complained much of it, and related some disgusting effects of the system.

The following facts will serve to illustrate the encouragement held out to married couples who are disposed to become paupers: Many years since, two men of the names of Munn and Girling, with their wives and families, were admitted into this establishment. Several of their children were born and reared up in the workhouse until they attained the age of thirteen years, when they were apprenticed by the corporation. After serving their time, the sons married, and in their turn came with their wives to the workhouse. They were soon encircled by a rising family, who, having attained the proper age, were, as their parents had been before them, apprenticed by the directors and Guardians of the corporation. These children, at the expiration of their apprenticeship, likewise married, again became paupers, claimed their right of admission into their former asylum, the workhouse, were received, and are now living together, by the usage of the establishment.

Thus there are at this time, three generations of these paupers in the house of industry, and the same results are expected from the recently married couples as from their ancestors, namely, a perpetuation of the stock of pauper families.

I received much information upon the subject of early marriages from various officers of this incorporation. I was informed that early marriages are very frequent, and that parties have been known to go directly from church to the workhouse, where, having gained admission, they are placed just in the society which suits them, the male paupers and their wives being allowed to mix indiscriminately together in the day time, and at night a separate sleeping apartment allotted to each couple – a degree of luxury and comfort is enjoyed to which the honest and industrious labourer is a total stranger. This custom, however, is not confined to Suffolk, for on visiting one of the large incorporated hundred houses in Norfolk, I observed several of the doors of the rooms appropriated for married couples were nailed up; and on inquiring of the governor, I found that they had been occupied by able-bodied men and their wives and families, who had gone out harvesting, and that they had nailed the doors of their rooms up in order that no other persons should inhabit them during their absence.

To such an extent was this marriage system at one time carried in the hundred of Blything, that ten or twelve cases of pauper young men marrying young women, also paupers, and directly claiming their right to relief, occurred close upon the heels of each other. The visiting Guardian took upon himself the responsibility of publishing to the inmates, that if any more marriages occurred among the paupers, they would be prohibited from sleeping together. This had the desired effect of checking the practice as long as the prohibition was enforced.[75]

Samuel Green
Evidence to the Select Committee on Andover Union

In 1845, a major scandal surfaced at the Andover workhouse in Hampshire. Andover had a reputation as a strict workhouse, largely due its fearsome Master, Colin McDougal, a former sergeant-major and veteran of Waterloo. McDougal ran the workhouse like a penal colony, keeping expenditure and food rations to a minimum. He was revealed to be regularly drunk, to have had violent and bloody fights with his wife Mary Ann, the workhouse Matron, and to have seduced some of the female workhouse inmates.

Andover inmates were fed according to the Poor Law Commission's 'No.3 dietary' – one of the least generous of the six menu plans provided for workhouses to adopt. However, owing to an administrative error, the amounts of bread served to inmates at breakfast, and also some of the dinner rations, were even less than those officially stipulated.

The favoured labour for able-bodied men at Andover was the strenuous task of pounding old animal bones into fertiliser. In 1845, rumours began to spread in the neighbourhood that men in the workhouse bone-yard were so hungry that they resorted to eating the scraps of marrow and gristle left on the old bones they were supposed to be crushing. Fighting had even broken out when a particularly succulent bone came their way.

The Andover Union workhouse in Hampshire where, in 1845, the treatment of its inmates led to one of the worst scandals ever to hit the Poor Law system. The building, shown here in around 1905, has now been converted to residential use.

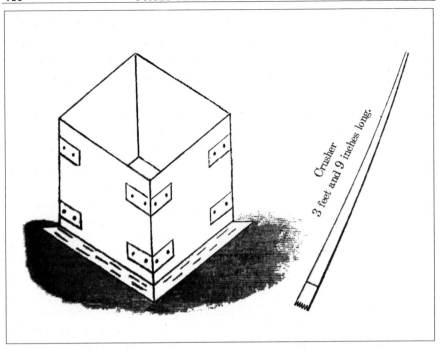

The bone-pounding equipment at Andover workhouse – a 28lb iron 'rammer' was used to pummel the bones in a tub. Apart from the appalling smell, it was back-breaking and hand-blistering work, yet boys as young as eight were set to it, working in pairs to lift the rammer.

Eventually, in March 1846, a Parliamentary Select Committee was set up to uncover the whole story. Amongst the many witnesses presenting evidence to the Committee was sixty-one-year-old inmate Samuel Green:

I reside in Andover; I have no wife, but I have five children; they are all grown up and off my hands. I came into the Union Workhouse about a week after last Christmas; I went out in May; I was employed in the workhouse at bone-breaking the best part of my time; the bones were got from different parts, some from one piece and some from another. There are people at Andover who collect bones. I have seen a great many marrow bones brought in; some of the marrow bones were beef, mutton, and some bacon. We looked out for the fresh bones; we used to tell the fresh bones by the look of them, and then we used to be like a parcel of dogs after them; some were not so particular about the bones being fresh as others; I like the fresh bones; I never touched one that was a little high; the marrow was as good as the meat, it was all covered over by bone, and no filth could get to it. I don't know as I ever eat a bacon marrow bone until I came into the workhouse; I found out in the workhouse that bacon marrow bones were good; I have eat meat off some of the bones; I have picked a sheep's head, a mutton bone, and a beef bone; that was when they were fresh and good; sometimes I have had one that was stale, and stunk, and I eat it even then; I eat it when it was stale and stinking because I was hungered, I suppose. You see we only had bread and gruel for breakfast, and as there was no bread allowed on meat days for dinner, we saved our bread from breakfast, and then, having had only gruel for breakfast, we were hungry before dinnertime. To satisfy our hunger a little, because a pint and a half of gruel is not much for a man's breakfast, we eat the stale and stinking meat. If we could get a fresh bone we did not take the stale and stinking meat. The allowance of potatoes at dinner on meat days is half a pound, but we used to get nearly a pound, seven or eight middling sized potatoes. The food we got in the workhouse was very good; I could not wish better, all I wanted was a little more. The bread was always as good as that (*pointing to a loaf on the table*), and no man has occasion to find fault with it. The cheese was very good cheese; it has been very good for the last year or two. I have been in the workhouse once every year since the house has been opened, excepting the first year; I was in gaol then; I am generally in one place or the other once a year.

I did not eat my bread any one morning in the week. I did not eat it, but not because I had too much. I used to sell it to buy a bit of 'bacco. I used to sell it in the workhouse. Most all the people who take 'bacco, sell their bread. 'Bacco is a very wholesome thing, especially in such a place as the workhouse. The fresh and stale bones used to be shot down all together. The Master once found that I had saved five allowances of bread, and he took them away from me, but afterwards gave them me again. He told me he should not allow us to save bread in that way. The saving of bread used to cause a good deal of quarrelling, because some of them would steal it. I used to save a bit of bread for Sunday, because on Sundays, when you are standing about the yard doing nothing, you want more to eat than when you are working; the time seems so long when you are standing about.

I have seen a man named Reeves eat horse flesh off the bones which had been brought from Squire Smith's; I have seen him do it often. I could tell it was horse flesh by the bone. I told him it was horse flesh, but he did not care; it went down as sweet as a nut. I have heard the medical officer inquire of Reeves if he had eaten horse flesh, and he always denied it to the medical officer; but I know he did eat it, because I have seen him. Reeves was a very dirty fellow; he could not keep his clothes clean for a week; his clothes in a week would be as dirty as a chimney-sweep's. The men would not answer when Mr Westlake, the medical officer, asked them if Reeves had eaten horse flesh. I once quarrelled with Reeves about eating it, and he asked me, what odds it was to me his eating of it. I said it was no odds to me, but I could not think how he could be so nasty as to eat such stuff.

I recollect Mr Westlake, Mr Hugh Mundy, and Mr Loscombe, coming into the day-room, and having the men round them, to inquire whether it was true such stuff had been eaten. The men said they had not seen him eat horse flesh; but I told Reeves I had seen him eat it. Upon that Mr Mundy shook his head, and turned himself round, and the gentlemen went away after that. The horse bones from Squire Smith's are boiled. I never saw any one but Reeves and Eaton eat horse flesh. I once saw Eaton take up a horse's leg, and take the hair off it, and eat the flesh. The leg was not cooked. No one saw him eat it but me. Eaton is weak in his intellect, and l don't think he has got any taste, or smell either. I have often seen the governor give Eaton extra food when he has not given it to other inmates.

The mark x of Samuel Green.[76]

The Select Committee's report was critical of virtually everyone involved in the affair, including the Poor Law Commissioners, who were abolished the following year and replaced by a new body, the Poor Law Board, which was more directly accountable to Parliament.

❧

The Lancet
Reports on Metropolitan Workhouse Infirmaries

In 1865, the medical journal The Lancet lent its weight to the growing campaign for improvements in the conditions of London workhouses and their infirmaries by publishing a series of reports based on visits to different establishments. The revelations about the shocking conditions that existed in many institutions were instrumental in the passing of the 1867 Metropolitan Poor Act which resulted in substantial changes in the capital's medical provision for the poor, most notably in the creation of the Metropolitan Asylums Board. The Lancet report on the Clerkenwell workhouse exposed it as having some of the worst conditions of any workhouse infirmary in London:

> If the infirmary of St Martin-in-the-Fields be very bad, there can be no question that the infirmary of Clerkenwell is worse; in fact, we here touch the lowest point in the scale of metropolitan workhouse hospitals.
>
> The parish of Clerkenwell elects its Guardians and manages its workhouse under special local Act of Parliament,[77] and it has certainly abused to the uttermost the opportunities for evading necessary reforms which are created by this position of affairs. The workhouse, in which there exists no trace of a proper separate infirmary, is a tall, gloomy brick building, consisting of two long parallel blocks separated from each other by a flagged court-yard not more than fifteen or twenty feet wide. The front and principal block does enjoy one fair outlook towards a wide street; but in other respects the whole house is

closely environed with buildings only less gloomy and unwholesome looking than itself. The hinder block, especially, wears an aspect of squalid poverty and meanness; and it is very old, dating from 1729. Both blocks are four stories in height. Entering either part of the house, we are at once struck with the frowsiness of the atmosphere which meets us; and we find the cramped winding staircases, interrupted by all manner of inconvenient landings and doors, which in these old buildings render the stairs a special nuisance, instead of an effective source of ventilation for the building, as they should be. Detailed examination of the sick ward implies detailed inspection of the whole house; for the sick, infirm, insane, and 'able-bodied' wards are jumbled side by side, and the whole place presents the dismal appearance of a prison hospital – not such as one meets with in civil life, but the sort of makeshift which might perhaps be seen in a garrison town in war-time, except that in the latter situation one would not be annoyed by the shrieks and laughter of noisy lunatics – one of the special features of the Clerkenwell establishment.

The Master is an excellent officer, accustomed all his life to the management of sick people, and with the valuable experience of a model prison (in which he formerly officiated) on matters of sanitary precaution; and his efforts are well seconded by his wife, the Matron. These officers work well with the surgeon, Dr J. Brown; and the most zealous endeavours are made by them to remedy defects which are really irremediable. They have one paid nurse under them, who is an experienced and valuable woman; and with her assistance, as much supervision as possible is given to the incapable paupers who do the real bulk of the nursing. As far as the strictly medical service goes, the sharp supervision of the superior officers seems to prevent the possibility of any such scandalous inattention to the wants of the sick as was noticed at Shoreditch; but the discovery which we made, that the disgusting practice of washing in the 'chambers' was carried on in several of the infirm wards, sufficiently showed the character of the pauper attendants, and prepared us for the very qualified encomium of the Master, who informed us that they were, on the whole, a sober, well-conducted set so long as they were never allowed outside the workhouse doors for a moment.

But it is the character of the wards, and their degree of fitness for hospital purposes, that we must chiefly pay attention to. It is necessary first to mention the elements of which the population is made up: in a total number of 560, which represents a crowded state of the house, there would be about 250 sick, and 280 infirm (including about 80 insane). This amount of population exceeds the Poor-law Board's estimate by 60, and the consequence is a reduction of the cubic space per bed, on the average of all the sick wards, to 429 feet, which of itself implies a dangerous state of things. But this imperfect allowance of entire space is aggravated greatly by the low pitch of the wards, the very insufficient number of windows (which are only on one side, except in a few wards), and the absence of any free currents of air circulating through the house.

A view of the Clerkenwell workhouse on Farringdon Road, erected in 1727 and enlarged in 1790 to house up to 500 inmates. The building was finally demolished in 1883.

Subsidiary ventilation has been attempted with much perseverance by the surgeon and the Master, and a great mitigation is, doubtless, effected of what would be otherwise an intolerable and very fatal nuisance; but still the atmosphere of the wards is very impure, and if the vigilance of the nurses, as is certain to be the case, at times relaxes, so as to allow the closing of ventilating orifices, a very dangerous foulness of air must ensue. And besides the deficiency of the wards generally in ventilation, there are some which are almost unique, we should fancy, for their badness in this respect. The four tramp wards (two male and two female) afford the following allowances respectively of cubic space – 120ft, 240ft, 198ft, and 184ft – to each sleeper: and two of these apartments may dispute the palm successfully, for gloom and stifling closeness, even with the St Martin's tramp wards. In one there is actually no window at all, but only a bit of perforated zinc over the door, and a solitary ventilator of very doubtful utility. In these nasty places the 'casuals' lie upon straw beds, spread upon a sort of wooden gridiron framework, and they must needs huddle so close as to be almost in contact with each other. (N.B. At Clerkenwell the tramps are not washed before being allowed to lie down.) The Master is well aware how improper a lodgment these wards afford; but, with the existing workhouse, it is impossible for him to find better accommodation for so many vagrants as he is obliged to admit.

Not to linger too long over the sanitary abominations of this house, we may mention one which seems to us most scandalous and disgraceful, but which the Guardians, one can hardly help thinking, must have been led to establish by a sort of sentimental feeling. They placed the parish dead-house in a snug corner of the yard before-mentioned, and with a ventilation capable of wafting reminiscences of departed parishioners to the inmates of the wards whose windows overlook the mournful edifice.

Perhaps the most painful consequence of the inefficient lodgment which the house affords to its motley population is the impossibility of classification, even where this is most urgently needed. The arrangements for the insane afford a shocking example of this. Such a spectacle as is presented by the two wards in which the more serious male and female insane cases are treated is not often to be seen in these days of enlightened alienist management. The women's ward, in particular, offers an instance of thoughtless cruelty which nothing can excuse the Guardians for permitting. Twenty-one patients live entirely in this ward, which affords them an allowance of only 459 cubic feet each; and the mixture of heterogeneous cases which ought never to be mingled is really frightful. There is no seclusion ward for acute maniacs, and accordingly we saw a poor wretch who for five days had been confined to her bed by means of a strait-waistcoat, during the whole of which time she had been raving and talking nonsense, having only had two hours' sleep: and there was the prospect of her remaining several days longer in the same condition. There were several epileptics in the ward, and one of them had a fit while we were present, and there were imbeciles and demented watching all this with curious, half-frightened looks, which said very plainly how injurious the whole scene must be to them. We are willing to suppose that the Guardians of Clerkenwell are unconscious of the great cruelty of allowing this wardful of women, who never ought to be associated, to sit gazing helplessly at each other, with no amusement but needlework, which they probably hate; or of leaving a melancholic patient whom we saw in the male ward (and whose condition was assuredly improvable) to mope, with his head in his hands, the livelong day. For our own part, we have never seen a sight which more thoroughly shocked us by its suggestions of the unlimited power of stupidity to harass and torment the weak and sensitive. But assuredly the stupidity and the ignorance are in this case a fresh crime, for no one who undertakes to manage the insane has any right to plead ignorance of the conditions necessary to their welfare.

The defects of the Clerkenwell Workhouse are so manifest, the house is so clearly unfitted for the purpose to which it is applied, that it might be supposed that nothing but intentional cruelty could lead the Guardians to the policy of retaining it. They have had many opportunities in past years of selling their property for a sum which would readily have purchased a site in their own parish, and paid the expenses of a proper new building. But they have constantly refused to take advantage of this, and have continued their present residence till it is now almost certain that when they are forced to a removal they will have to take their workhouse out of the parish.

We sum up our observations, therefore, in the same tone as that in which we concluded our report on St Martin's. There is no remedy for the evils of Clerkenwell Workhouse but immediate removal, and the sooner the Guardians put their house in order with a view to that course the better.[78]

Richard B. Cane
Poor Law Board Inspection Reports

Union workhouses were periodically visited by inspectors from the central authority – from 1847 until 1871 in England and Wales, this was the Poor Law Board. Responsibility for a large swathe of northern England which included Lancashire, Derbyshire, and a large part of the West Riding of Yorkshire lay in the hands of Mr R.B. Cane. Cane's area was one which had seen considerable resistance to the introduction of the New Poor Law in 1834 and, in many unions, a refusal to provide new workhouse accommodation. Instead, old and often very inadequate premises continued in use until being finally replaced in the 1860s and '70s. As well as the buildings, Cane found much to comment upon in the management of many workhouses, particularly in their infirmaries. His 1866 report on Preston's Deepdale Road workhouse was particularly critical (the italics are his):

This workhouse is old, ill arranged and unsuitable in every respect for the purposes for which it is used, namely, the reception of all classes of poor.

The classification is nominal merely, almost all the inmates meet together in the yard in the centre of the building. Ventilation, in the proper sense of the term, can hardly be said to exist in any of the wards.

The wards are for the most part dark, low, close, gloomy, and unhealthy; they are dangerously crowded with inmates, especially in the infirm and sick wards.

Many of the infirm people, men as well as women, *are sleeping together two in a bed*. The sick have not all of them a separate bed to lie upon.

In the '*venereal ward*' the patients affected with *syphilis* are sleeping together two in a bed.

Two women, owing to a want of room, have lately been placed together in the same bed in the *lying-in ward*, both having just been confined.

Four patients, *two men* and *two boys*, were lately sleeping together in the same bed in the 'itch ward'.

Six men occupied two beds in this ward to-day, *three* in each bed. The man lying in the middle of the bed had his feet to the top of the bed, and his head came out at the bottom of it. The feet of the other two men were placed so as to be close to the head of the man who was lying between them.

In the midst of this ward, and in full view of the others, boys and men, an adult patient was standing upright without a fragment of clothes upon him, whilst a pauper attendant painted him over with a brush dipped in an application for his disease. The 'itch ward' is at all times the most disagreeable to enter of any. The peculiar remedy prescribed, the nature of the treatment observed, and the use in such ward of the refuse bedding and linen of the house, necessarily render it the most offensive of all. But the close and stifling atmosphere of this ward in the Preston workhouse, its crowded state, the sight of these men lying 'head and heels' together, with the utter want of decency described, rendered a visit to it one of the most distressing and repulsive that I ever made to any workhouse.

There is no waterproof sheeting nor air cushions for the sick.

There are no water closets, or any other convenience at night, except some buckets placed in the wards for the use of the ordinary inmates.

The wards were (the Matron said) swarming with bugs.

The male inmates are not furnished with clothes by the Guardians; they wear their own garments as long as they will last; some of them were without stockings, and some had no shoes.

There is but one receiving ward; it contains no bed, and is common alike to men, women, and children.

All that can be said in favour of this workhouse is that it is kept as clean as circumstances will permit. The sick and infirm are looked after and attended to by a male and female nurse, who do as well as they can.

The Guardians find the drugs that are required, and medical attendance is reasonably well supplied, although the names of the patients as well as the requisite directions are not always attached to the medicines.

The beds, which are of sum and chaff, without mattresses, are in a cleanly state. The only effectual remedy for these evils is an entire new workhouse, with full and proper accommodation of all kinds.[79]

At Blackburn, similar miserable conditions were compounded by drunkenness and disorder amongst some of the staff, the workhouse Master included:

A nurse, under whose sole care the inmates are placed, has lately been appointed. She is assisted by pauper inmates, who act under her direction. There are about 80 sick cases in the infirmary, a much larger number than one nurse can personally attend to; she is, therefore, obliged to trust the giving of medicines to the pauper nurses in some cases, in others she depends upon the patients helping themselves. How this can be done with accuracy and regularity I cannot understand, for the medical officer leaves only verbal directions regarding the medicines, &c., for each patient. No written labels or directions are attached to

Despite the premises being only two years old at the time, the inspection of Blackburn's workhouse in 1866 found much to criticise in the construction of the building, as well as its management.

the bottles. Not a bottle or pill box (I examined them all) was marked even with the name of the person for whom it was intended.

Most of the beds in these wards are too close together; some of them touch each other.

There is no 'night nursing' unless the nurse is called up, and no other attendance is given at night beyond such as the pauper nurses may be willing to afford. Ventilation is exceedingly imperfect throughout the whole infirmary. There is no effectual classification of cases. Cases which in themselves are highly disagreeable are not separated from others; for example, in one ward is a poor woman suffering from cancer; she is reduced to a most distressing condition. Her disorder is so offensive that I could not remain near her; yet several other patients occupy this ward with her. The discomfort they experience must be extreme. All this is permitted to continue, although there are large and excellent wards in the workhouse which are unused. There is no proper supply of water in the waterclosets, and these closets are so constructed that the foul air arising in them is drawn into the wards.

There are large wards near the entrance lodge which contain cases of 'venereal disease' and 'bad legs'. The porter and his wife are supposed to look after these cases, but they appear for the most part to be left to themselves.

In the male ward were eight or ten men walking about almost naked. I was told 'they were getting their dinners'. The condition of the inmates of this ward was most distressing and painful to witness.

The accommodation for the sick is much too limited, and the nursing quite insufficient. The sick wards are being made somewhat larger, however, than they are at present.

The lunatic wards, and especially the men's day room, is too small and too confined.

Better kind of beds are requisite for certain cases. In the women's lunatic ward I found one of the beds mildewed and decayed owing to neglect.

Some of the able-bodied men sleep together two in each bed – a most objectionable custom.

There are great dissensions amongst the officers of this workhouse, and the management is therefore lax and disorganised. Almost all the male officers have brought charges against each other, chiefly of absence from duty, and drunkenness.

The Master especially is charged with intoxication; an entry to that effect was made in the porter's book on the 19th instant. Although the Master knew I was in the workhouse he did not appear. I sent repeatedly for him, and the reply was in each instance, that he could not be found. Under such circumstances I cannot but suspect that he was not sober enough to come before me. Of course this matter will be investigated, unless the immediate resignation of the Master should render that course unnecessary as regards himself.

Note. –The Master was removed from his office shortly after this report was made.[80]

Cane gained a rather better impression at Manchester. The old city centre workhouse at New Bridge Street was 'generally in fair order', although the food provoked some complaints:

This workhouse assumes largely the character of an infirmary and hospital, with a fever hospital, venereal wards, foul wards, and wards for cases of special infirmity, arising from paralysis, &c., attached to it. There is a resident medical officer. As many as 674 patients are on his list at this time. The drugs, which are of the very best quality, are found by the Guardians. Some idea of the extent of the dispensary may be formed when it is stated that 1,000 bottles of medicine, and other things in proportion, are made up and supplied to the inmates weekly. I saw and conferred with the medical officer, who assured me that he had everything that he required for the use of the sick, and that be only had to make application to the Guardians for anything he wanted, when it was immediately supplied.

Nearly all the beds, even for the sick, are of straw, though of course other beds are provided for particular cases. In visiting the sick wards, I specially and in the absence of the officer who withdrew at my request, inquired of each patient in a condition to understand and reply to my questions, whether he or she had any complaint to make either in regard to their food, their bed, their clothes, or their attendance, and whether generally they were contented and satisfied with what was done for then. The answers to my inquiries were satisfactory in these respects. I found that the sick were duly supplied with the diet, wine, beer, spirits, &c., ordered for them by the medical officer. Not only were they generally contented and satisfied, but I run happy to add that many of them expressed gratitude for the care and attention bestowed upon them.

There is, however, much dissatisfaction in regard to a portion of the diet. The pudding is considered hard and indigestible, and it is said to be absolutely rejected and wasted by a large number of the inmates. The rice as a meal is distasteful to many, whilst the pea-soup disagrees with some of the aged poor. The old women especially complain that their tea is not good of the kind, and that it is too weak. I tasted it myself and consider that it may well be improved in strength and flavour.

I found the workhouse generally in fair order throughout, but some of the beds are too near together. Ventilation is especially defective in the Magdalen wards, and I am inclined to think that one of the old women's wards is too full. Many counterpanes in the sick ward require washing, and there is not a sufficient supply of towels, &c., in those wards.

Prayers have not lately been said in the evening, and the chaplain's report book does not contain a report of the moral and religious state of the inmates of the workhouse.[81]

The imposing façade of the Manchester Union workhouse at Crumpsall, opened in 1857. Renamed Springfield Hospital, the establishment later provided treatment for the mentally ill. The building is now used as office accommodation.

For Manchester's recently built out-of-town workhouse at Crumpsall, however, Cane had the utmost praise:

> On the whole, this is the most complete as well as one of the best managed workhouses that I have ever inspected. It is in thoroughly excellent order throughout, and generally in such a state as to reflect the highest credit on all concerned in its management and care.[82]

British Medical Journal
Reports on Workhouse Infirmaries

Between 1894 and 1896, a self-appointed 'commission' from the *British Medical Journal* (BMJ) visited a number of workhouses and their infirmaries, first in England and Wales, and later in Ireland. Like *The Lancet* investigations thirty years earlier, the BMJ reports exposed the poor standards of care, comfort, and sanitation that still existed in many of the establishments they visited. The sometimes scandalous revelations led to improvements in workhouse medical care, especially with trained nurses being appointed to replace untrained staff or pauper nurses. The BMJ's report on Haverfordwest in South Wales was typical:

> It has rarely been our lot to visit a workhouse infirmary more unsuited for its purpose, or more ill-provided with all that is necessary for the comfort of the sick. The Master readily acceded to the request of Dr Williams, the medical officer, to show us the infirmary; but we must confess to a feeling of surprise that the Matron, whom we only saw for a brief moment, did not respond to the Master's suggestion that she should accompany us through the female department. This union embraces a large extent of country, and takes paupers from sixty-six parishes; the town is the centre of a wide district.
>
> The workhouse is well situated on a hill, and has extensive grounds around it; it is an old house, and in every part is quite behind the times. It is built round four courts, which form the airing courts of the various departments. There is accommodation for thirty-two sick, and there is besides a fever ward placed at the top of the house, at the present time empty. The wards are of variable size, and are distributed on the ground and first floors; the largest is for eleven beds, and the smaller wards hold two or three beds; the arrangement on the male and female side is the same. The wards are dreary places, the walls dirty, washed over with dingy yellow colouring, windows on one side, only one fireplace at one end, looking bare of furniture for the sick.
>
> The iron bedsteads are low and on them are three planks held by a crosspiece, not always laid close, and on this a chaff mattress about three inches thick.

We saw the helpless bedridden old people lying on these beds, and they must have found them a sorry rest for their weary bones. There are about four spring beds distributed in the wards, but they have only the chaff mattress over the springs. There is no means of ventilation but by the windows, and, as the fireplace in some of the wards is small it is hardly probable that the atmosphere is changed in the night.

The system of warming is peculiar to this part of the country. 'Culm', which is clay and anthracitic slack kneaded into balls, is used in the grates; when quite alight it is red hot and must throw out a good heat, but it is slow in kindling and can hardly be of service for obtaining a fire quickly.

The classes of patients are of the usual description found in the workhouses. On one of the spring beds there was an old woman with hemiplegia, helpless all but one hand and unable to turn herself; in the male ward was a fine man with erysipelas in his leg. On inquiring as to the treatment the 'nurse' told us that he washed it for himself twice a day with Condy's fluid, but that otherwise no dressing was used. We could not but think what a pity it was that more vigorous measures were not tried, since by a speedy curing of the leg the rates would be relieved of that man's keep. He was too long for his bed.

There were eight patients in bed in all; in this part of the infirmary, including senile debility, rheumatism, paralysis, chest complaints, and old age, and several very infirm men and women up in the wards. We were shown a small ward with four beds in it, all occupied; it opened immediately from one of the yards, it was without a fireplace, and was lighted by one small window. This is the tramps' sick ward. We could not ascertain that any one person was responsible for attendance in this ward, and, if assistance was wanted in the night, the most able-bodied of the tramps would have to go some little distance before lie could obtain it, as there is no communication bell.

The sanitary appliances are quite rudimentary; there is no water laid on to the upper floors; the only conveniences for the wards are commodes, of which there are a few in each ward; one is placed outside on each landing, intended for use at night, that for the men being enclosed within a screen, that for the women being open. It can hardly be expected that these poor infirm folk will go outside the wards on a cold night, nor is it well that they should. The commodes in the wards are emptied after 6 in the morning. On going round the wards we saw some ordinary utensils about, some of which were unemptied. The closets are all outside; they are simply cesspools, and some were very unpleasant. The water supply is ample, and is obtained from wells in the courts. The pumps in each court discharge over troughs down which the refuse water is emptied.

There is only one fixed bath, and that is in the tramps' room; it is a small one, sunk in the floor, with a tap to supply hot water, but the cold has to be carried in from the yard. We saw no baths which could be used for the sick, and, as every drop of water must be carried up or down, it is probable that bathing is not largely practised in this infirmary; indeed, the patients and their linen did not look particularly clean at the time of our visit.

The 'nurse' is untrained; she is solely responsible for the care of the sick and of midwifery cases; there is no night nurse nor regular pauper help at night. On inquiring how the helpless patients were attended to during the night, we were informed that they had to obtain such assistance as they could from the more able-bodied paupers who slept in the ward. As we found that bedsores were recognised as one of the usual ailments in the infirmary, it can be imagined how much help these paupers are able to render to each other. We pictured to ourselves the sad condition of these helpless old people, passing the long hours of the dark nights on their comfortless beds, uncared for, uncleansed, unfed. We say 'dark night' because we have ascertained that all lights were removed from the wards after the patients are in bed, nor did we see any appliances for lighting the staircases or passages. The labour ward is for two beds; it has no separate offices, and all refuse must be carried downstairs.

There is no system of classification; we saw the imbeciles and 'harmless lunatics' among the patients in the wards; one half-witted boy was busy serving the dinners. There were no lock cases in the infirmary, and we were informed that there were no isolation wards for offensive cases. The 'harmless lunatics' appeared to be straying about where they pleased.

On our way round the house we passed through the 'nursery', a large ill-furnished room, the floor laid down with paving stones; there was a large table, two benches, two wooden cradles, a few chairs, the latter round a fireplace which was most insufficient to warm the room in the winter. In this room the infants stay with their mothers until they are 2 years old. There was a baby in each cradle, one looking very ill; its mother thought it was 'sickening for something'. There was no rug, or even a bit of sacking on which the infants might crawl; a more dreary place to be called a nursery can hardly be imagined. Though not properly coming within the scope of this inquiry, we mention this room as indicating the lack of a kindly and sympathetic spirit on the part of those responsible for the management of the house.

The dinners were being served at the time of our visit. It was 'broth day'; the broth, made of mutton and vegetables, both looked and smelt good, but it was served in wooden bowls which were black with age and grease. We tasted the bread and butter, both of which were good. We saw no bed cards in the wards, but the Master informed us that the medical officer has a free hand in ordering extras, and that milk and beef tea are taken into the wards for the sick at night. As the last meal is given at 6 o'clock, and the first at 8 in the morning, it is necessary that the old people should have something to take in the night.

The day room on the men's side is used for sleeping purposes; there were four beds in it; it is also the tailor's shop where the male clothing is looked over and mended. It is a very small room, with one window, and at the time of

An aerial view of the Haverfordwest workhouse in Pembrokeshire, whose infirmary was heavily criticised by the *British Medical Journal* in 1894.

our visit the floor was piled with clothing, and the air of the room was quite unwholesome. On the women's side the day room is not used for a sleeping room; it had one large settle in it, but no comfortable chairs or anything to make it homely. On passing through one of the courts we were shown the disinfecting apparatus. It is a small galvanised iron box, like a good-sized tank, the lid broken at the edges, and having underneath it a tray for the fire; this was standing in a shed close to the closets.

It seems hopeless to make any recommendation in the case of this infirmary. The building is unsuitable for its purpose, and the system on which it is worked is faulty in every particular. [83]

The English workhouse system was introduced into Ireland in 1838 and from the outset Irish workhouses were of an inferior standard to those in England. Construction of the buildings was to be 'of the cheapest description compatible with durability... all mere decoration being studiously excluded.'[84]

By the 1890s, the poor conditions in many workhouses in Ireland reflected the relative neglect that the institutions had suffered. After visiting the Cootehill Union workhouse in County Cavan, the BMJ Commissioners found that, despite the efforts of the medical officer, the building was 'in all ways unsuitable for the work required of it':

We received a cordial welcome from Dr Moorhead, the medical officer of the workhouse, who very kindly took us round, giving us every help in his power. The house, a grey stone building, stands close to the railway station, but about a mile from the town, on rising ground, facing south and north. It is what is styled a 'second class house', a term describing its capacity (about 800 inmates), but not referring to its efficiency.

Passing through the lodge and the body of the house we came to the infirmary. As we looked at the exterior we were struck by the small slit apertures in the wall which serve as windows; they are a relic of the time when the therapeutic value of light and air was not understood. On the ground floor is the surgery, a small room full of drugs, and intended for the use of the medical officer; to the back is a disused ward holding 8 beds, now used for operations, or for the isolation of any case; opposite is a stone paved room intended for a men's day-room when the infirmary is full; the corresponding room on the female side is used as the infirmary kitchen; its equipment is a wide open grate, over which was suspended a large cauldron, containing water, we believe, a large iron boiler containing the only water at hand for use, a dresser, some tin plates, mugs, a saucepan, and a frying pan. There is a close range in the nurse's kitchen upstairs.

It is almost impossible to convey to the reader the picture of squalor and wretchedness that greeted our eyes as we mounted the stairs to the first floor where the sick are; long narrow rooms, beds on each side, 6 on a side in the first ward, and about 4 on a side in the continuation ward; the beds close together, on one side (the north) square windows in heavy iron frames, and opposite to them the slit-like apertures already commented on, rough colour-washed walls, roof open to the slates, an old-fashioned grate at one end, more chimney than fire, a bench and a few wooden armchairs; a bucket, chair, and a small table at one end completed the furniture. The bedsteads, close together, were many of them of the hospital pattern, but we saw the 'harrow' bed in use besides. On the spring beds Dr Moorhead uses a pad of old blanketing, this being, in his opinion, more sanitary than the hair mattress, as it can be washed, but on the 'harrow' beds there was a tick filled with straw, and all the pillows are of straw. On the old bedsteads the tick and pillow are placed against the wall, which is sometimes damp. As the square windows are neither weather-tight nor air-proof, the lower section has been boarded up, as some of the beds are across them; the whole of the ventilation is by means of the windows, the upper section swings on a pivot regulated by a toothed bar, but the frames are so heavy that it is a trial of strength to open them; such other openings as were in the roof or cornice were evidently out of gear. There are four such wards, two on each side, and it must be observed that those at each end are over the lunatics' quarters.

The patients presented all the variety of ailment that is found in a general hospital, though the larger number are chronic cases; the wards were comparatively empty, as it was the summer; there were 22 patients in the wards, and 35 in all on the medical relief book. Several of these were in bed; a man with rheumatic arthritis, a severe case of pneumonia, a case of intestinal obstruction, ulceration of the leg, senile debility, and some good cases of recovery from operation; all surgical cases are dealt with here, as it is practically the hospital for the district. There is no lying-in ward, the women being confined in the general wards.

The nurse, a trained midwife, has acquired her general training under the medical officer; her wards were clean and showed that much can be done for the sick by a zealous nurse, even under such unpromising circumstances. She has the assistance of an inmate in each ward, and on the male side there is a paid wardsman, who works under the nurse, and who has been of much service in inducing habits of order and cleanliness (Dr Moorhead's report). There is no night nurse. Dr Moorhead selects the wardswomen from the older women, rejecting, if possible, those who are in the house with infants, the latter being likely to neglect the patients for the sake of their child. The nurse is responsible to the medical officer for the infirmary, and she also is held responsible for the custody of the lunatics. There are bells from the wards to the nurse's room.

The lunatics were almost a sadder sight than the sick in the wards; they are in the two ends of the infirmary on the ground floor. Their quarters consist of the old cells disused by the medical officer, but not removed by the Guardians, and the corridor and dayroom attached. In the corridor were 3 beds head to foot against the wall, and the other beds were in the day-room, no furniture but a bench and a table, rough whitewashed walls, a small window, and an old grate protected by bars. The recreation ground, a stone-walled grass-grown yard, having a deal board as a seat; the woman standing up, herself feeble-minded, is the caretaker, the previous one having been discharged by the doctor for beating the poor creatures. These unhappy wretches are confined to this section, where neither treatment nor alleviation is possible. On the male side the section is the same, but many of the men were employed about the place.

The airing courts attached to the infirmary are small grass-grown courts at the back of the building. In this house Dr Moorhead has endeavoured to redeem the waste of desolation by laying them out somewhat like a garden, and placing a few seats for the old people, an act of kindness that has been much appreciated, the old people finding some relief to the monotony of their existence by the cultivation of the garden. The law of classification is so rigid that these poor people are practically imprisoned in the part of the house to which they are assigned. The rank grass that we saw in the lunatics' yard is anything but wholesome for the inmates.

We now turned our steps to the body of the house, where are the quarters for the aged men and women. These consist of long wards, low-pitched and unceiled, rough, whitewashed walls, windows at either end, and three at the side, a stove, harrow beds down each side, a few benches without backs, and a table at one end. The rooms were dirty, the patients were unkempt and unwashed, and as the only materials that we saw for the toilet were a tin basin

A men's ward at the Cootehill workhouse in County Cavan, showing the narrow, wooden-slatted 'harrow' beds. As can be seen in the background, bedding was rolled up during the day and the beds used as seating.

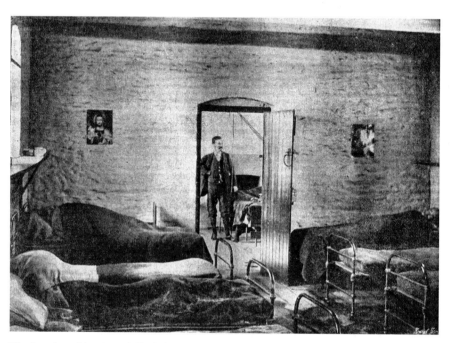

The interior of the Cootehill workhouse infirmary where *British Medical Journal* investigators found 'squalor and wretchedness'.

and a dirty round towel this was not to be wondered at. This ward is approached through a concrete-floored apartment called the dayroom, equally dirty and uninviting; most of the men were here, seated on a cross-bench in front of the comfortless grate; a long deal table, almost as black as the floor, was the only other furniture. On the female side most of the women were in the dormitory, many of them at needlework; their appearance was not quite so bad as that of the men, though the conditions in which they lived were the same. Both the men and women are in charge of an inmate, these caretakers themselves being old and infirm. In fine weather this class can sit under the sheds in the yard, but in the winter they are confined to their quarters. Before passing to the nursery we will describe the sanitary arrangements in these and the sick wards. It must be understood that there are no indoor conveniences, and that the privies are at some distance from the wards, and therefore unavailable in bad weather or at night; to meet this difficulty the old people are provided with open pails or buckets; in the sick wards these buckets are enclosed in a wooden chair. It must also be observed that the infirm wards are locked on the outside from 7 p.m. until 6.30 a.m. The greater part of that time the ward is in darkness, and the only assistance available is such as the inmates can render to each other. The pails remain unemptied until the morning in both the sick and the infirm wards. We pictured to ourselves these wards locked up, the windows closed to husband the feeble warmth of the stove; the inmates on their narrow beds, from which they may slip to the floor in their weakness and there remain until the morning; the filthy-smelling buckets, some doubtless upset in the dark; no water to be had, no help available except in case of dire need; we turned away sick at heart that such things should be. In the sick wards the nurse is at hand, but there is no night nurse, and the excreta of the sick poison the air in those crowded wards. In the lunatic wards the same unsavoury method prevails, and the well-known dirty habits of the feeble-minded add to the foulness of the surroundings. The privies in this house are on the waggon system; a movable trough receives the soil, and when full is drawn out of a door at the back and wheeled on to the land. We noticed that the trough was neither cleansed or purified before being returned to the privy.

There are no baths either in the infirmary, the fever hospital, or the infirm wards, nor is any water laid on to these departments, except to the laundry. The water for the infirmary is obtained from a tank in the body of the house, and that for the body of the house from a large well, from which it is pumped up by the inmates into the tank. The movable bath, having to be filled and emptied by hand, is now practically disused from lack of labour. The kitchen and the laundry remain as they were constructed when the house was built; in the former, three large boilers each, with its separate fire – one for the stirabout, one for potatoes, and one for holding cold water; in the laundry two old wash-tubs, a copper, and a box filled with stones on rollers serves as a mangle. Both these offices were very dirty – a dirty pauper was head cook, and two women were splashing dirty clothes about in dirty water in the laundry. The sole cooking utensils that we saw were two saucepans and a frying pan. It is no wonder that Dr Moorhead pathetically remarks in his report that it is no use his ordering meat, for he has no one to cook it. Under these circumstances we were not surprised to find that the dietary was as elementary as the appliances, consisting principally of porridge, milk and bread for the able-bodied and old people, and for the sick such food as could be cooked in the small ill-found kitchen in the infirmary.[85]

1905 Royal Commission
Visits to Poor Law Institutions

By the start of the twentieth century, pressures were mounting for a major reform of the poor relief system. In December 1905, a Royal Commission on the Poor Laws and the Relief of Distress was appointed to review the operation of the existing poor relief legislation and to propose any changes it considered necessary. The Commission assembled a considerable amount of evidence, also visiting a large number of urban and rural workhouses across England, Wales, Scotland and Ireland. The published reports of these visits were anonymised so that individual institutions could not be identified.

The first example (England and Wales – Provincial Urban No.20) includes an illustration on how conditions had improved for the elderly, particularly those judged to be of good character:

We visited the Workhouse, a somewhat artistic looking, old-fashioned building which has been extended from time to time, and which accommodated at the time of our visit 740 inmates. The interior of the house was beautifully clean, and there was an air of comfort about the wards that was particularly pleasing. Dinner, consisting of boiled beef, potatoes and suet pudding, was being served, and we could not help remarking on the smut appearance which the white tablecloths gave to the large dining-hall. These tablecloths, we were informed, are changed twice a week.

The sick are provided for in an infirmary, within the workhouse grounds, consisting of two pavilions – one for males and the other for females and children – and containing 260 beds. There is also a separate block containing two wards for fifty senile and chronic cases that are not ill enough for infirmary treatment. We visited one of the wards in this block, and were not particularly impressed with it. It had a heavy atmosphere – there being no proper ventilation. The sanitary arrangements were also faulty.

The nursing of the sick is done by one head nurse in charge of each pavilion, assisted by one senior probationer on each floor and one or two junior probationers. The infirmary is recognised as a training school for nurses but not for midwives. There is a visiting Medical Officer who attends when required and visits twice a day as a rule. He dispenses the necessary drugs. His salary is £200, and he also receives about £30 per annum in respect of midwifery and lunacy fees. On questioning him the Medical Officer quite frankly admitted that he was not able to give to the patients as much attention as they ought to have. This he laid at the door of the Guardians, who, he said, would neither remunerate him sufficiently nor provide him with an assistant. Cases requiring operation (about fifteen a year) are sent to the ★ ★ Infirmary to which the Guardians subscribe £50. On the other hand the ★ ★ Infirmary regularly transfers cases to the workhouse infirmary. Of such cases there were three at the time of our visit. One was a workman with a broken leg, who had been taken to the ★ ★ Infirmary, where it was set and bound up in plaster of Paris. After about a fortnight's residence in that institution he was sent to the workhouse infirmary until able to walk – in other words, when cured. The man would have been about twice as long in the workhouse as in the ★ ★ Infirmary. The other two cases were boys – one minus a leg and the other suffering from hip joint disease.

The female pavilion, directly over the nursery for the children, contains the sleeping accommodation of the nurses. This seemed to us to be objectionable, as the noise of the children must prevent the night nurses, who require to sleep during the day, from obtaining a proper rest. The children's nursery is a bright airy room in charge of two female attendants. The infants under their care looked healthy, but the other children, from perhaps about eighteen months to perhaps two-and-a-half years of age, had a sickly appearance. These latter children were having their dinner, which consisted of large platefuls of potatoes and minced beef – a somewhat improper diet for children of that age, and one which may partly account for their pasty looks. The attendants did not know the ages of the children; the children are not weighed from time to time, and a record kept.

There is no separate accommodation for imbeciles and epileptics, these inmates being scattered over the various wards among the other inmates.

In addition to the general air of cleanliness that pervades the workhouse the outstanding feature is the classification of the aged inmates according to character, each class having separate accommodation and being entirely separated from the others. The accommodation for the *first* or *highest class* provides for twenty-eight men and twenty-four women. Both the men and women have two dormitories and two sitting-rooms – the latter having linoleum or a canvas covering on the floor and being furnished with arm chairs, rocking chairs, tables and couches. Meals are served in the sitting-room that appears to be in daily use (the other being reserved for Sundays or for receiving friends). As regards food, the inmates get a loaf and a pot of jam for the 'cupboard' whenever they require them. They are also allowed a cheap and wholesome currant cake to their tea. The inmates may, with consent of the Master, go out any day after 'the performance of their small duties'. Friends likewise are admitted on any evening.

The qualifications necessary to obtain these privileges are good character, twenty years' residence within the Union area, freedom from connection with any crime and not having previously received relief within the period named.

The accommodation for the *second* or *middle class*, providing for thirty-six males and thirty-six females, is not quite so luxurious as that provided for the first-class inmates, nor have they the same privileges. They have their meals in their sitting-rooms, but no jam. Their leave of absence is only one half-day per week.

The qualifications for admission to the second class are ten years' residence and a slightly less unblemished character than that necessary for the first class. The rooms of the first and second classes are pleasantly situated, fronting the north and south quadrangles, which are laid out with ornamental flower beds, etc. Here the inmates can take exercise or sit when the weather is fine.

Misbehaviour on the part of an inmate in the first or second class is punished by reduction of class, and this is found to be a very effective method of enforcing discipline.

Third Class: No special accommodation is granted for this class, which is provided for in the general day-rooms of the workhouse. Meals are partaken of in the general dining-hall and leave is allowed one half-day per fortnight.

It should be pointed out that the classification of the inmates is made by a special Classification Committee, consisting of fifteen members, on the report of the workhouse Master and relieving officer. The Committee have power to place any case in the highest class, although not strictly complying with the whole of the conditions.

The work test consists chiefly of stick splitting, on which the Guardians realise a profit of 30 per cent. There is also a circular saw for cutting up the wood, which requires six men to drive and at which only the strongest of the men can be employed. The Labour Master informed us that he generally had a difficulty in finding sufficient men for the saw, and that most of the wood was cut by means of hand saws.

The casuals are generally employed at stone-breaking, the task being 8 cwt of stones passed through a 1½-inch grate: To the severity of the task the Labour Master attributed the fact that the number of vagrants during the last ten years had diminished from 6,000 to 800 per annum.[86]

At the same institution, the Commission observed a meeting of the Board of Guardians and its two Relief Committees – subcommittees dealing with out-relief applications:

The Board divided into two Committees for relief purposes, and apparently the Guardians wander from one Committee to the other at pleasure, which on the whole seems to be an unsatisfactory way of dealing with cases. Members administer relief to their own constituents.

There is a scale of relief and a scheme for Classifying applicants according to character, etc., but these, we were assured by the assistant clerk, are constantly departed from.

The relief generally granted is as follows:–

3s to 5s to an old person living alone and having no income.

1s 6d per child to a widow with children – nothing to the widow.

The Guardians used to give bread, but it was found to be so much abused that relief in kind is now limited to flour.

Committee No. 1.

A large number of Guardians was present, and they seemed to us noisy in their proceedings and rough in their handling of the applicants. One woman, e.g., who appeared on behalf of another, was told that she wanted a bath; and the circumstances and characters of all were freely discussed in their presence: Relief was given to deserted wives, and to women whose husbands were in gaol. The scale (not always adhered to) was good for the old people, quite inadequate for widows, and children. Much stress was laid upon the responsibilities of sons, who were summoned before the Committee, and who seemed to respond very well to what was expected of them.

Committee No. 2.

The meeting of this Committee appears to have been concluded in a more orderly fashion than the other. The Chairman dealt with the cases in a business-like way and frequently imparted good counsel to an applicant who seemed likely to benefit by it. One applicant; a marine fireman aged thirty-one, suffering from 'catarrh', with a wife, thirty, and children, twelve, eight, and three, was granted 1s 6d for two weeks on loan and was strongly advised to join a Friendly Society. As at the other Committee, out-relief was given to a woman whose husband was in prison.

There was one case (a widow) where the Committee discontinued her relief because she had married again. The relieving officer in whose district she resides was complimented on having had twelve widows married during a half-year.

One of the Provincial Rural workhouses visited by the Commission ('Rural No.65') can be identified as that at Leominster in Herefordshire. The workhouse there was dirty and infested by vermin, while the Board of Guardians appeared complacent and sometimes less than scrupulous in their administration of poor relief:

The workhouse at Leominster in Herefordshire; this picture shows the old priory building which formed part of the premises.

At the workhouse we found a Master who had only just come a week ago, his previous experience in Poor Law administration having been gained at ★ ★ and ★ ★ . The Matron is the widow of the late Master. The house is old-fashioned and was formerly a priory, which was adapted to its present use some 70 years ago. It is certified for 166, but now has only 62 inmates. Some of the old men were doing Brabazon Society work. At the same time there were more chronic infirms in their beds in the hospital than one usually finds; the worn-out agricultural labourer chiefly, whose wages in this union appear to be no more than 13s or 14s a week with perquisites, coming to 3s or 4s more.

Attached to this workhouse was an excellent kitchen garden, growing good vegetables and affording work for the inmates. We were told that a large portion of the produce, even of the potatoes, is sent to market, and we saw some of it ready to be sent there.

We attended a meeting of the Board at which 11 members were present, one being a lady. There had been another lady, but was beaten at the last election by a publican who was said to have brought 26 electors drunk to the poll. The out-relief was practically administered by the Chairman and the relieving officer; if the Guardian of the parish in which the applicant resided happened to be present he took some interest in the case; otherwise the Board were not concerned with the relief. One of the relieving officers was an ex-Guardian, a farmer who had failed, and therefore had been appointed to the office.

The Clerk was present, but left all the business to an assistant clerk, by whom he was corrected more than once and recommended somewhat shortly to leave the matter in his (the assistant's) hands. The publican interest, we were told, was largely represented on the Board, the assistant clerk being in intimate and close alliance with them. (One of the Commissioners fancied that the Clerk seemed ashamed of his position.) The Board as a whole seemed slack and uninterested and unintelligent.

For the most part the cases were merely renewed. Applicants appeared before the Board, and the Chairman addressed them with an invariable formula: 'Do you want the money to go on? Very well then.' One or two cases were of interest when interpreted by the lady Guardian, next to whom one of the Commissioners sat, otherwise the details were too meagre to be understood.

1. A man with one leg and 5 children applied for relief to be continued while he was unwell. In this case some of the Guardians had subscribed to get him a donkey and cart, and it was hoped he would do well hawking. 5s granted, for 4 weeks.

2. A widow, who works in the workhouse and takes away an indefinite amount of food, had 5s renewed.

3. A widow with 3 children receives 3s, being 1s 6d apiece for 2 of them, and is supposed to keep herself and the other. In this case the relief has been as much as 10s or 12s a week, but the elder children are now earning.

4. In this case we did not hear full particulars, but the woman was said to be dirty and the man given to drink; one of the Guardians mentioned having seen him at the public house that morning. Relief was granted at the instance of the Guardian of the parish, who was also the publican whose house the man frequented.

The death of a pauper being reported, the lady Guardian took occasion to appeal to the Board to take steps to provide a mortuary. She had visited the house of the pauper and found that the body had been attacked by rats. The Guardians were impressed and seemed likely to move in the matter, but one of them (the landlord of the house in question) intervened and said the harm done had been trifling, and the question dropped.

We afterwards went round the [work]house, which is old and unsatisfactory, the accommodation not being appropriate to the different classes. The boys' dormitory is on the ground floor and over the river; we noticed a large rat-hole, and were told by the Matron that rats came up at night. The bedclothes were not clean, and there were no pillowcases. The girls slept in double beds; their bath was dirty, and cockroaches had possession of the basins. The Matron explained that there were always cockroaches in workhouses. Although floors were well scrubbed and externals looked fairly clean, one of the Commissioners found cupboards very dirty, and the bedding in the babies' cots concealed stores of dirty food. This, again, was explained to be always the case in workhouses, both by the Matron and by the lady Guardian; neither of whom appreciated investigations.

Another, who visited the sick wards, thought the nursing insufficient; e.g., one mentally deficient patient keeps crying out, day and night, at frequent intervals, disturbing the other patients. He seemed to be in great discomfort, if not pain; but is not removed on the ground of economy.

The accommodation for casuals is unsatisfactory. There is no bath in the women's ward, and they are locked in at night without any means of communication with outside. The Matron maintained that there was a bell to the porter's lodge, and when it was pointed out that the wire was broken off close to the roof and could not be rung even by mounting on a chair, she said the plumber should see to it.

The Master, newly appointed, shares practically the quarters of the Matron (widow of the late Master). He seemed apathetic, with no proper standard for administration and no real interest in his work. One of the Commissioners perceived that by 11.30 a.m. he had already been having some beer, although the Board was sitting.

We were sorry to note that the Guardians spoke to us with the utmost complacency of their workhouse and its arrangements. Indeed, one of them formally complained at the Board that two of our colleagues, who had previously visited, had written no eulogistic remarks in the visitors' book.[87]

Although Scotland's poor relief system was independent of that operating in England, Wales and Ireland, the Royal Commission also examined its operation. A long-standing tenet of Scotland's provision for paupers was that it did not extend to the able-bodied. However, as in England and Wales, the offer of the poorhouse, as Scotland's establishments were usually known, could sometimes be used to test the genuineness of an applicant's claim of destitution. Poorhouse provision in Scotland was not compulsory but an option open to large parishes or 'combinations' of parishes – broadly equivalent to English unions. Here is the Commission's report on an unnamed 'rural or semi-rural' poorhouse, perhaps the Sutherland Combination poorhouse at Bonar Bridge, where those in charge were found to be 'not of the right stamp':

I visited the Combination Poorhouse in ★ ★ (erected 18--). The Combination consists of thirteen parishes, and accommodation is provided for 120 inmates, When I visited there were – men, 27; women, 19; boys, 2; girls, 4; of these, nine men and six women were in the sick wards, most of whom were aged and chronic eases. Straw mattresses are provided for all inmates – sick and ordinary.

There are no wards licensed for the reception of lunatics.

The staff consists of a governor (a pensioned sergeant-major without any previous experience), his wife, a Matron (who is responsible for the care of the

The Sutherland Combination poorhouse, opened in around 1865 at Bonar Bridge, was typical of Scotland's rural poorhouses. Later becoming Migdale Hospital, it finally closed its doors in 2011.

sick, but has had no training), a ward maid, cook, housemaid, porter and wife in charge of the receiving wards. The governor does not wish that a trained nurse should be appointed; he fears jealousy on the part of the Matron. There are three able-bodied men in the house, two of whom are about thirty years of age; the governor has no power to discharge them, and the inspector of poor of the parish to which they belong refuses to take action. The third is about sixty years of age, and has been in and out the workhouse for years. There are three unmarried mothers in the house, one of whom has had seven illegitimate children, but several of them have died. Twelve unmarried mothers were confined in the house last year. I was told that this county shows the highest percentage of illegitimate births in Scotland.

Some classification is attempted, based on record of character previous to admission, but modified by subsequent conduct.

The men are employed in a large garden, working under the superintendence of the porter. In bad weather they are occupied in stick splitting, and last year earned some £40 as profit on their industry. The surplus produce of the garden is sold in ★ ★.

The Committee of Management meet at the Clerk's office; they visit by rota, but irregularly; there are no ladies on the Committee; and no effort is made by any organisation or individuals to help unmarried mothers.

The institution left a not very favourable impression. The house was not tidy, nor did the inmates seem properly cared for; indeed, the tone of the institution was not satisfactory. I felt that the Committee made a great blunder when, six years ago, they appointed the governor and Matron to the posts which they now fill. I have nothing whatever to say against either of these officers, except that they are not of the right stamp. The governor of the house might be taken as an illustration of the need which exists for the establishment of a Government service on lines parallel to those which obtain under the Board of Education in reference to the qualification and appointment of elementary school teachers.[88]

Scotland's poor relief system also allowed smaller parishes to house their poor in a more informal style of accommodation, usually known as parish homes or almshouses:

The ★ ★ Parish Home.
This was the most delightful institution that I have seen. It was a large, comfortable, pleasantly furnished 'private house', with about thirty inmates. Some had their own bedrooms; others were in pairs; and others again in small dormitories. There were pleasant dining rooms and sitting rooms for common use. The one or two well-behaved defectives had separate rooms, under the immediate charge of salaried servants. All but these one or two defectives were either old men or old women, or prematurely infirm persons of good character, and they had full liberty to come and go as they chose. Some of them were of quite superior position, and had handed over their little remnants of property – in one case an income of fifteen shillings a week – to the Parish Council in return for maintenance and care. The Master and Matron were able and kind. One old German woman, who was delighted to talk to me in her mother tongue, explained to me that the Matron was a real saint. A large vegetable garden was cultivated by the more able-bodied of the men. The net cost of maintenance to the Parish Council was reported to me as being only trifling – something like a shilling per head per week – but the accounts were complicated by the property handed over by the inmates, the value or the work done, and free gifts of fish, etc., from the benevolent.[89]

Herbert Preston-Thomas
The Work and Play of a Government Inspector

Herbert Preston-Thomas (1841–1909) spent his whole working life in Government service, finally moving in 1894 from the Public Health Department to become an Inspector for the Local Government Board which by that date was responsible for the poor relief system. Apart from his work, Preston-Thomas was also a keen cricketer and mountaineer, being a member of both the M.C.C. and

Alpine Club. His autobiography, published in the year of his death, is laced with the good humour and sympathetic commonsense with which he executed his official duties:

> By way of preliminary, I was allowed to accompany some of my colleagues in their inspections of workhouses; and I remember well, on my first visit to an infirmary, being oppressed with an overwhelming sense of its sadness. It struck me as very different from the wards of a general hospital. There, the patients go to be cured; here, they come only to die. In Crabbe's words, they have 'Their graves before them and their griefs behind.'
>
> The pathos of the occasion and perhaps the thought of the responsibility which I was undertaking were for the moment so strong that I felt a lump in my throat. I was not sorry to go off to a lesson in the practical duties of workhouse inspection, which surprised me by its thoroughness. Beds were searched for (non-existent) intruders; children's eyes and teeth were carefully examined, and this or that case was referred to doctor or dentist; boys were stripped to ascertain their cleanliness; sanitary arrangements were closely overhauled; the food was minutely scrutinised, and so on. When we came to the books of the workhouse Master, I found them so numerous and dealing with such a multiplicity of details by a sort of system of quadruple entry, that I could only hope I should some day learn why they were all necessary. This, by the way, I have never succeeded in doing; and, but for the fact that officialism is a fetish to which I dare not be disloyal, I should contend that at least two-thirds of the number are absolutely superfluous, and give a great deal of trouble without any useful result.
>
> Another Sussex workhouse which I visited was the model of an institution in a small but rich Union. So far as the old folk were concerned it was a rather luxurious almshouse; and infinite pains seemed to be taken to make everybody comfortable, and especially to give the children a good start in life. I was not surprised when my friend the Inspector told me of a man who argued that if he had a family of five children, and his entire capital was five hundred pounds, he would do better for them if he spent it on horse-racing and died a pauper than if he bequeathed it among them. A hundred pounds apiece would give each child only three or four pounds a year, whereas, if they were handed over to the Guardians as penniless orphans, they would be brought up under the best conditions of housing and feeding, they would receive an excellent education, and would have a much better start in the world than would otherwise be their lot.
>
> A few days afterwards I saw a workhouse inspected by another of my colleagues, and was again impressed with the minuteness of the examination into all sorts of small details. For the first time I learnt the danger of allowing a baby to use a feeding-bottle with a long tube, which bacilli might make their home, and was taught the proper material and cut of a pauper's shroud. I also

visited the workhouse of a Metropolitan parish, but it was so enormous, and the different classes of inmates were split up among so many sections, that I was not able to glean much practical information in the short time which I could devote to it.

My district, one of the fourteen into which the country is divided, contained a population of rather more than a million and a quarter. Norfolk figured as the most pauperised county of England, and farming, the staple industry, was in a poor way.

In most Unions where pauperism was large I found that out-relief was dispensed with the utmost freedom; and at Guardians' meetings I constantly met with cases where the applicants, if it had been refused, would certainly have managed to maintain themselves or would have been maintained by their relatives. Everybody seemed to have a keen sense of the disgrace of entering the workhouse, but none at all of receiving outdoor relief, though in both cases alike the charge has to be borne by the ratepayers. The former was regarded as an open shame, the latter as a pecuniary arrangement not publicly known; and some Boards of Guardians favoured this view by not allowing the names of paupers to be published.

Probably much of the antipathy to workhouses is a survival from the times when the inmates dragged out a wretched and toilsome existence. At any rate, 'workhouse' is now a misnomer, as may be gathered from the fact that in many of them labour has to be hired, even for washing and scrubbing. The aged and infirm enjoy a large amount of liberty, they are only set to such light tasks as are sufficient to occupy them pleasantly, and in all material conditions of feeding, housing, and clothing they are much better off than the aged poor outside. When one sees knots of the old men gossiping by the fire or basking in the sun, when one finds the bedridden old women carefully nursed and appropriately fed, it is difficult to help contrasting their condition with that of some of the village poor, who live in miserable dwellings, and are half starved on the pittance which they obtain from their scanty earnings or from private charity. I have often heard an aged inmate say that he had always declared he would die rather than enter 'the house', but that if he had known that it was so comfortable he would have come there long ago.

I naturally found immense differences in the degrees of comfort in workhouses. In a few there were the bare whitewashed walls, the cheerless brick floors, the primitive sanitary arrangements, which used to be common a quarter of a century ago, but are now an exception. In a good many, where the administration had been liberal as well as intelligent, the inmates were excellently housed as well as fed. Most of the buildings were very old, but the difficulties thus caused had often been skilfully overcome. Still, the accommodation for the sick was usually far inferior to that afforded in the wards of general hospitals, and I made a point of impressing on Boards of Guardians that sickness, like love, levels all, and that the rates ought to provide as well for the pauper patients as voluntary contributions provide for the labouring classes in County Hospitals.

The nursing was the weakest point. Not infrequently a single paid nurse was in charge of thirty or forty patients, and this meant that almost everything for the sick had to be done by pauper inmates. They had nothing to gain if they did the duty assigned to them well, nothing to lose if they did it badly; the fact that, being able-bodied women, they were workhouse inmates proved, *prima facie*, that they were not of high character; so most of them were not disposed to take much trouble in attending to helpless old folk requiring assistance in various respects by night and by day. But things were steadily mending. Guardians were beginning to recognise the fact that nursing is a skilled business, and that it is worthwhile to pay for its being done properly.

I was always glad to receive information of some defect that ought to be looked into on my next inspection; although now and then it happened that I had to throw cold water on the suggestion of a well-meaning visitor. Here is some correspondence with one who found fault with the straw mattresses in general use:

'Will you kindly tell me (1) whether you do not consider that flock beds are more suitable than straw mattresses for use in workhouse infirmaries, and (2) whether it is not desirable to rouse and amuse the bedridden inmates, who now seem to spend their whole time in silently gazing at the ceiling?' My reply was as follows: 'I may answer your questions almost in Longfellow's words. You know his lines:

There is no flock, however watched and tended,
    But one dead lamb is there;
There is no household, howsoe'er defended,
    But has one vacant chair.

My version would be,

There is no "flock", however patched and mended,
  But some fleas will get there;
There's no old pauper, howsoe'er attended,
    But has a vacant stare.'

In plain prose, a flock bed harbours insects, to say nothing of the fact that the material has a knack of disposing itself in little lumps which scarify the backs of the patients; while straw mattresses, if properly filled, are very comfortable, and moreover, can be renewed at no cost whenever necessary. I believe that the opinion of both officials and inmates is unanimous in their favour. As to 'rousing' the aged paupers, I think that many of them prefer to be left in peace. I value visitors to workhouses enormously – especially such lady visitors as possess tact as well as kindliness – but I fear that now and then their attentions are thrown away on some of the very aged and infirm, who really only want to be at rest. By all means go and see the bedridden folk, but pray, let your 'rousing', like Bottom's 'roaring', be as gentle as that of any sucking dove. This advice, though not couched in very official language, was well received, for it elicited the answer – 'Thanks for your letter, which seems to me to contain more sound sense than I can find in most poetry.'

With a little more experience I should certainly have added a reference to the extraordinary success of the Brabazon Society in devising occupation for workhouse inmates. They have really done wonders in teaching old people, whose gnarled and gouty and rheumatic fingers often seemed absolutely incapable of any delicate work, to produce all sorts of quite artistic effects in wool, leather, or basketwork. The old, who used to have nothing to do but quarrel with each other, now thoroughly enjoy their lessons from the ladies of the Society. A pleasant rivalry is stirred up among them, and the sales of their productions from time to time yield a fund for such excursions and other treats as could not be paid for out of the rates.

The management of a workhouse depends mainly on the Master. He has to be a despot, and usually he is subject to very little control in the intervals between the weekly, or more commonly the fortnightly, meetings of the Guardians. Most of the Guardians, especially in rural Unions where the distances are great, rarely visited the workhouse. It frequently happened that the Visiting Committee met only on Board days; solemnly marched through the different wards under the guidance of the Master; inspected the provisions; examined the condition of the beds, or at any rate of the clean sheets which had possibly been placed on them an hour or two earlier; and had scarcely any communication with the inmates. This was the condition of affairs when I began my work as Inspector; and Mr Fowler's[90] Order of 1893, expressly giving authority to every individual Guardian to visit any part of the workhouse at any time, had an excellent effect in bringing abuses and grievances to light.

Even in the most trivial matters connected with workhouse visiting, tact and commonsense are required. Consultation with the officers in the first instance is always desirable, and I have known of a case in which a visitor, ignoring this rule, distributed flowers among occupants of the Infirmary, with the result that one patient, an imbecile, proceeded to eat them – stems, leaves, berries and all – and was nearly killed by this unusual food. Another most worthy and well-intentioned person habitually went to read to the patients just at their meal-time, when the old and sick particularly dislike being disturbed. Too often I found that visitors had suggested grounds of complaint to inmates who before were very well contented, but afterwards acquired a habit of grumbling.

As a rule they are inclined to make the best of things; and I came across one instance in which two bedridden men had for many months gone dinnerless twice a-week because the food happened to be such as they were unable to digest. When I told the Master that this fact, which I discovered in the course of a chat with one of the men, ought to have been observed long before, he could only say that they had made no complaint; and this was perfectly true. Of course I called the Medical Officer's attention to the matter, and they were at once put on special diet.

In other ways I found that the increase of workhouse visiting, especially by ladies, was valuable. The nurses, particularly in small, rural workhouses, often have a sadly monotonous life. They have few of what are called interesting cases, and lose their skill because they are rarely concerned with operations of importance, while their chief occupation is that of feeding and keeping clean a number of old people who are slowly dying. Much of their work is, in point of disagreeableness, akin to scavenging, and their lives are very solitary. Sometimes they do not get on very well with the Matron, for the duties of the two offices overlap in a fashion which ought long ago to have been set right; and now and then it happens that a nurse has scarcely any educated person to talk to. Lady visitors have done a great deal to supply this want, and many a nurse has been cheered and encouraged by their friendly sympathy.[91]

Since 1847, workhouses had been obliged to allow elderly married couples to share a room. Such accommodation was rarely provided, however, with Boards of Guardians usually arguing that elderly couples were happy to be segregated on the male and female sides of the workhouse. Preston-Thomas offers some evidence for this attitude:

I was present when the Chairman of the Board of Guardians, on being told by an old woman that she would not live any longer with her husband, asked 'Why? Does he beat you?' She answered, 'Beat me? Lord bless his heart, no. He treats me more like a friend than a husband. But I've tended him as long as I could, and I can't do it any longer.'[92]

FOUR

SOCIAL EXPLORERS

THE TERM 'SOCIAL explorers' refers to investigators such as journalists, novelists and social reformers who disguised themselves as down-and-outs in order to gain entry to institutions such as charity shelters, dosshouses and workhouse 'casual' wards. The casual ward, often referred to by its habitués as the 'spike', provided a night's accommodation to tramps, vagrants, and other 'houseless poor', in return for a stint of labour. Unlike the workhouse itself, where admission involved an official interview, entry to the casual ward simply required answering a few brief questions from the porter: 'Name?', 'Age?', 'Occupation?', 'Where from?', 'Where to?'

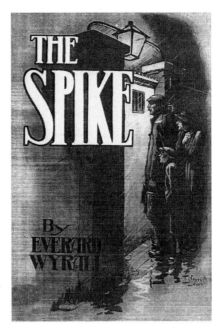

The cover of *The Spike* by Everard Wyrall, one of the less accomplished social explorers – early on in his travels, he aroused suspicion by his educated accent.

By use of disguise, social explorers aimed to gain the confidence of those they mixed with and so became privy to matters which might remain concealed from other forms of social investigation such as surveys or interviews.

Ground-breaking explorations by James Greenwood and J.H. Stallard in the 1860s were followed by a steady trickle of others treading the same path, such as F.G. Wallace-Goodbody[93] and C.W. Craven[94] in the 1880s, and Robert Sherard[95] and American Josiah Flynt[96] in the 1890s. The first decade of the twentieth century saw a positive deluge of explorers, amongst the most notable of which were Jack London, Everard Wyrall, 'Denis Crane' (Walter Thomas Cranfield),[97] the Revd George Z. Edwards,[98] Olive Malvery,[99] and Mary Higgs. The tradition continued in the late 1920s with Frank Gray and George Orwell, the latter recounting his real-life experiences through the medium of fiction in *The Spike* and *Down and Out in Paris and London*.

The approach pioneered by the early social explorers is continued in modern times in a variety of forms, ranging from academic anthropological research to undercover investigative journalism and television entertainment programmes such as *The Secret Millionaire* and *Undercover Boss*.

James Greenwood
A Night in a Workhouse

One of the earliest and best-known undercover reports is 'A Night in a Workhouse', by James Greenwood, published in January 1866 in the *Pall Mall Gazette*. Greenwood spent a night in the casual ward of the Lambeth workhouse and his titillating account described not only the repugnant conditions he experienced, but also the often rowdy behaviour of the other occupants of the establishment. The story, published over three successive issues of the paper, caused a sensation and was subsequently reprinted in pamphlet form.

Greenwood had not been keen to take on the assignment but was persuaded to do so by his brother Frederick, the editor and co-founder of the *Gazette*. Greenwood was promised an initial fee of £30-£40, with the promise of more if his articles significantly boosted the paper's circulation. Despite the impression given in his reports, Greenwood was not alone on his expedition, but accompanied by a stockbroker friend named Bittlestone who contributed his own observations to the story. The intrepid explorers were dropped off near the workhouse and picked up again the next morning by Frederick's carriage:[100]

> The day had been windy and chill – the night was cold; and therefore I fully
> expected to begin my experiences amongst a dozen of ragged wretches squatting
> about the steps and waiting for admission. But my only companion at the door
> was a decently dressed woman, who, as I afterwards learned, they declined to

admit until she had recovered from a fit of intoxication from which she had the misfortune to be still suffering. I lifted the big knocker, and knocked; the door was promptly opened, and I entered. Just within, a comfortable-looking clerk sat at a comfortable desk, ledger before him. Indeed, the spacious hall in every way was as comfortable as cleanliness and great mats and plenty of gaslight could make it.

'What do you want?' asked the man who opened the door.

'I want a lodging.'

'Go and stand before the desk,' said the porter; and I obeyed.

'You are late,' said the clerk.

'Am I, Sir?'

'Yes. If you come in you'll have a bath, and you'll have to sleep in the shed.'

'Very well, Sir.'

'What's your name?'

'Joshua Mason, Sir.'

'What are you?'

'An engraver.' (This taredaddle I invented to account for the look of my hands.)

'Where did you sleep last night?'

'Hammersmith,' I answered – as I hope to be forgiven!

'How many times have you been here?'

'Never before, Sir.'

'Where do you mean to go when you are turned out in the morning?'

'Back to Hammersmith, Sir.'

These humble answers being entered in a book, the clerk called to the porter, saying, 'Take him through. You may as well take his bread with you.'

Near the clerk stood a basket containing some pieces of bread of equal size. Taking one of these, and unhitching a bunch of keys from the wall, the porter led me through some passages all so scrupulously clean that my most serious misgivings were laid to rest. Then we passed into a dismal yard. Crossing this, my guide led me to a door, calling out, 'Hillo! Daddy, I've brought you another.' Whereupon Daddy opened to us, and let a little of his gaslight to stream into the dark where we stood.

'Come in,' said Daddy, very hospitably. 'There's enough of you to-night, anyhow! What made you so late?'

'I didn't like to come in earlier.'

'Ah! that's a pity now, because you've missed your skilley (gruel). It's the first night of skilley, don't you know, under the new Act?'

'Just like my luck!' I muttered dolefully.

The porter went his way, and I followed Daddy into another apartment where were ranged three great baths, each one containing a liquid so disgustingly like weak mutton broth that my worst apprehensions crowded back.

'Come on, there's a dry place to stand on up at this end,' said Daddy, kindly. 'Take off your clothes, tie 'em up in your hank'sher, and I'll lock 'em up till the morning.' Accordingly, I took off my coat and waistcoat, and was about to tie them together when Daddy cried, 'That ain't enough, I mean *everything.*' 'Not my shirt, Sir, I suppose?' 'Yes, shirt and all; but there, I'll lend you a shirt,' said Daddy. 'Whatever you take in of your own will be nailed, you know. You might take in your boots, though – they'd be handy if you happened to want to leave the shed for anything; but don't blame me if you lose 'em.'

With a fortitude for which I hope some day to be rewarded, I made up my bundle (boots and all), and the moment Daddy's face was turned away shut my eyes and plunged desperately into the mutton broth. I wish from the bottom of my heart my courage had been less hasty; for hearing the splash, Daddy looked round and said, 'Lor, now! There was no occasion for that; you look a clean and decent sort of man. It's them filthy beggars' (only he used a word more specific than 'filthy') 'that want washing. Don't use that towel – here's a clean one! That's the sort! And now here's your shirt (handing me a blue striped one from a heap), and here's your ticket. Number thirty-four you are, and a ticket to match is tied to your bundle. Mind you don't lose it. They'll nail it from you if they get a chance. Put it under your head. This is your rug – take it with you.'

'Where am I to sleep, please, Sir?'

'I'll show you.'

And so he did. With no other rag but the checked shirt to cover me, and with my rug over my shoulder, he accompanied me to the door at which I had entered, and, opening it, kept me standing with naked feet on the stone threshold, full in the draught of the frosty air, while he pointed out the way I should go. It was not a long way, but I would have given much not to have trodden it. It was open as the highway – with flagstones below and the stars overhead; and, as I said before, and cannot help saying again, a frosty wind was blowing.

'Straight across,' said Daddy, 'to where you see the light shining through. Go in there and turn to the left, and you'll find the beds in a heap. Take one of 'em and make yourself comfortable.' And straight across I went, my naked feet seeming to cling to the stones as though they were burning hot instead of icy cold (they had just stepped out of a bath, you should remember), till I reached the space through which the light was shining, and I entered in.

No language with which I am acquainted is capable of conveying an adequate conception of the spectacle I then encountered. Imagine a space of about thirty feet by thirty enclosed on three sides by a dingy whitewashed wall, and roofed with naked tiles which were furred with the damp and filth that reeked within. As for the fourth side of the shed, it was boarded in for (say) a third of its breadth; the remaining space being hung with flimsy canvas, in which was a gap two feet wide at top, widening to at least four feet at bottom.

This far too airy shed was paved with stone, the flags so thickly encrusted with filth that I mistook it first for a floor of natural earth. Extending from one end of my bedroom to the other, in three rows, were certain iron 'cranks' (of which I subsequently learnt the use), with their many arms raised in various attitudes, as the stiffened arms of men are on a battlefield. My bed-fellows lay among the cranks, distributed over the flagstones in a double row, on narrow bags scantily stuffed with hay. At one glance my appalled vision took in thirty of them – thirty men and boys stretched upon shallow pallets with but only six inches of comfortable hay between them and the stony floor. Those beds were placed close together, every occupant being provided with a rug like that which I was fain to hug across my shoulders. In not a few cases two gentlemen had clubbed beds and rugs and slept together. In one case (to be further mentioned presently) four gentlemen had so clubbed together. Many of my fellow casuals were awake – others asleep or pretending to sleep; and shocking as were the waking ones to look upon, they were quite pleasant when compared with the sleepers. For this reason: the practised and well-seasoned casual seems to have a peculiar way of putting himself to bed. He rolls himself in his rug, tucking himself in, head and feet, so that he is completely enveloped; and, lying quite still on his pallet, he looks precisely like a corpse covered because of its hideousness. Some were stretched out at full length; some lay nose and knees together; some with an arm or a leg showing crooked through the coverlet. It was like the result of a railway accident; these ghastly figures were awaiting the coroner.

From the moral point of view, however, the wakeful ones were more dreadful still. Towzled, dirty, villainous, they squatted up in their beds, and smoked foul pipes, and sang snatches of horrible songs, and bandied jokes so obscene as to be absolutely appalling. Eight or ten were so enjoying themselves – the majority with the check shirt on and the frowsy rug pulled about their legs; but two or three wore no shirts at all, squatting naked to the waist, their bodies fully exposed in the light of the single flaring jet of gas fixed high upon the wall.

My entrance excited very little attention. There was a horse-pail three parts full of water standing by a post in the middle of the shed, with a little tin pot beside it. Addressing me as 'old pal', one of the naked ruffians begged me to 'hand him a swig', as he was 'werry nigh garspin.' Such an appeal of course no 'old pal' could withstand, and I gave him a pot full of water. He showed himself grateful for the attention. 'I should lay over there if I was you,' he said, pointing to the left side of the shed; 'it's more out of the wind than this 'ere side is.' I took the good-natured advice and (by this time shivering with the cold) stepped over the stones to where the beds or straw bags were heaped, and dragged one of them to the spot suggested by my naked comrade. But I had no more idea of how to arrange it than of making an apple-pudding; and a certain little discovery added much to my embarrassment. In the middle of the bed I had selected was a stain of blood bigger than a man's hand! I did not know what to do now.

Following the sensation caused by James Greenwood's serialised account of his adventures in the Lambeth casual ward, the text was reprinted as a pamphlet whose attention-grabbing cover is shown here.

STARTLING PARTICULARS!

A NIGHT

IN A

WORKHOUSE.

From the PALL MALL GAZETTE.

HOW THE POOR ARE TREATED IN LAMBETH!

THE CASUAL PAUPER!

"OLD DADDY," THE NURSE!

THE BATH!

The Conversation of the Casuals!

THE STRIPED SHIRT!

THE SWEARING CLUB!!

"Skilley" and "Toke" by Act of Parliament!

The Adventures of a Young Thief!

&c. &c. &c.

F. BOWERING, 211, BLACKFRIARS ROAD,
MANSELL & SON, King Street, Borough, and all Newsagents.

PRICE ONE PENNY.

James Greenwood, whose undercover visit to the Lambeth casual ward gained him the soubriquet of the 'amateur casual'.

To lie on such a horrid thing seemed impossible; yet to carry back the bed and exchange it for another might betray a degree of fastidiousness repugnant to the feelings of my fellow lodgers and possibly excite suspicions that I was not what I seemed. Just in the nick of time in came that good man Daddy.

'What! Not pitched yet?' he exclaimed. 'Here, I'll show you. Hallo! Somebody's been a bleedin! Never mind; let's turn him over. There you are you see! Now lay down, and cover your rug over you.'

There was no help for it. It was too late to go back. Down I lay, and spread the rug over me. I should have mentioned that I brought in with me a cotton handkerchief, and this I tied round my head by way of a nightcap; but not daring to pull the rug as high as my face. Before I could in any way settle my mind to reflection, in came Daddy once more to do me a further kindness, and point out a stupid blunder I had committed.

'Why, you *are* a rummy chap!' said Daddy. 'You forgot your bread! Lay hold. And look here, I've brought you another rug; it's perishing cold to-night.' So saying, he spread the rug over my legs and went away.

It was about half-past nine when, having made myself as comfortable as circumstances permitted, I closed my eyes in the desperate hope that I might fall asleep, and so escape from the horrors with which I was surrounded. 'At seven to-morrow morning the bell will ring,' Daddy had informed me, 'and then you will give up your ticket and get back your bundle.' Between that time and the present full nine long hours had to wear away.

But I was speedily convinced that, at least for the present, sleep was impossible. The young fellow (one of the three who lay in one bed, with their feet to my head) whom my bread had refreshed, presently swore with frightful imprecations that he was now going to have a smoke; and immediately put his threat into execution. Thereupon his bedfellows sat up and lit their pipes too. But oh! if they had only smoked – if they had not taken such an unfortunate fancy to spit at the leg of a crank distant a few inches from my head, how much misery and apprehension would have been spared me! To make matters worse, they united with this American practice an Eastern one; as they smoked they related little autobiographical anecdotes – so abominable that three or four decent men who lay at the farther end of the shed were so provoked that they threatened, unless the talk abated in filthiness, to get up and stop it by main force. Instantly, the voice of every blackguard in the room was raised against the decent ones. They were accused of loathsome afflictions, stigmatised as 'fighting men out of work' (which must be something very humiliating, I suppose), and invited to 'a round' by boys young enough to be their grandsons. For several minutes there was such a storm of oaths, threats, and taunts – such a deluge of foul words raged in the room – that I could not help thinking of the fate of Sodom; as, indeed I did, several times during the night. Little by little the riot died out, without any the slightest interference on the part of the officers.

Soon afterwards the ruffian majority was strengthened by the arrival of a lanky boy of about fifteen, who evidently recognised many acquaintances, and was recognised by them as 'Kay', or perhaps I should write it 'K'. He was a very remarkable-looking lad, and his appearance pleased me much. Short as his hair was cropped, it still looked soft and silky; he had large blue eyes set wide apart, and a mouth that would have been faultless but for its great width; and his voice was as soft and sweet as any woman's. Lightly as a woman, too, he picked his way over the stones towards the place where the beds lay, carefully hugging his cap beneath his arm.

Kay showed himself a pleasant companion; what in a higher grade of society is called 'quite an acquisition'.

'Tell us a "rummy" story, Kay,' said somebody: and Kay did. He told stories of so 'rummy' a character that the decent men at the farther end of the room (some of whom had their little boys sleeping with them) must have lain in a sweat of horror as they listened. Indeed, when Kay broke into a 'rummy' song with a roaring chorus, one of the decent men rose in his bed and swore that he would smash Kay's head if he didn't desist. But Kay sang on till he and his admirers were tired of the entertainment. 'Now,' said he, 'let's have a swearing club! You'll all be in it.'

The principle of this game seemed to rest on the impossibility of either of the young gentlemen making half-a-dozen observations without introducing a blasphemous or obscene word; and either the basis is a very sound one, or for the sake of keeping the 'club' alive the members purposely made slips. The penalty for 'swearing' was a punch on any part of the body, except a few which the club rules protected. The game was highly successful. Warming with the sport, and indifferent to punches, the members vied with each other in audacity, and in a few minutes Bedlam in its prime could scarcely have produced such a spectacle as was to be seen on the beds behind me. One rule of the club was that any word to be found in the Bible might be used with impunity, and if one member 'punched' another for using such a word, the error was to be visited upon him with a double punching all round. This naturally led to much argument, for in vindicating the Bible as his authority, a member became sometimes so much heated as to launch into a flood of 'real swearing', which brought the fists of the club upon his naked carcase as thick as hail.

These and other pastimes beguiled the time until, to my delight, the church chimes audibly tolled twelve. After this the noise gradually subsided, and it seemed as though everybody was going to sleep at last. I should have mentioned that during the story-telling and song-singing a few 'casuals' had dropped in, but they were not habitués, and cuddled down with their rugs over their heads without a word to any one.

In a little while all was quiet – save for the flapping of the canvas curtain in the night breeze, the snoring, and the horrible, indescribable sound of impatient hands scratching skins that itched. There was another sound of very frequent occurrence, and that was the clanking of the tin pannikin against the water pail. Whether it is in the nature of workhouse bread or skilley to provoke thirst is more than my limited experience entitles me to say, but it may be truthfully asserted that once at least in the course of five minutes might be heard a rustling of straw, a pattering of feet, and then the noise of water-dipping; and then was to be seen at the pail the figure of a man (sometimes stark naked), gulping down the icy water as he stood upon the icy stones.

At half-past two, every one being asleep, or at least lying still, Daddy came in and counted us: one, two, three, four, and so on, in a whisper. Then, finding the pail empty (it was nearly full at half-past nine, when I entered), he considerately went and refilled it, and even took much trouble in searching for the tin pot which served as a drinking cup, and which the last comer had playfully thrown to the farther end of the shed. I ought to have mentioned that the pail stood close to my head, so that I had peculiar opportunities of study as one after another of my comrades came to the fountain to drink: just as the brutes do in those books of African travel. The pail refilled, Daddy returned, and was seen no more till morning.

It still wanted four hours and a half to seven o'clock – the hour of rising – and never before in my life did time appear to creep so slowly. Four o'clock, five o'clock, six o'clock chimed, and then I had news – most welcome – of the world without, and of the real beginning of day. Half a dozen factory bells announced that it was time for working men to go to labour; but my companions were not working men, and so snored on. A little while, and doors were heard to open and shut; yet a little while, and the voice of Daddy was audible in conversation with another early bird; and then I distinctly caught the word 'bundles'. Blessed sound! I longed for my bundle – for my pleasing brown coat – for my warm if unsightly 'jersey' which I adopted as a judicious substitute for a waistcoat – for my corduroys and liberty.

'Clang!' went the workhouse clock. 'Now, then! Wake 'em up!' cried Daddy. I was already up – sitting up, that is – being anxious to witness the resurrection of the ghastly figures rolled in the rugs. But nobody but myself rose at the summons. They knew what it meant well enough, and in sleepy voices cursed the bell and wished it in several dreadful places; but they did not move until there came in at the hole in the canvas, two of the pauper inhabitants of the house, bearing bundles. 'Thirty two, Twenty eight!' they bawled, but not *my* number, which was thirty-four. Neither thirty-two nor twenty eight, however, seemed eager to accept his good fortune in being first called. They were called upon three several times before they would answer; and then they replied with a savage 'Chuck it here, can't you!' 'Not before you chucks over your shirt and ticket,' the bundle-holder answered, whereupon 'Twenty eight' sat up, and, divesting himself of his borrowed shirt, flung it with his wooden ticket, and his bundle was flung back in return.

It was some time before bundle No. 34 turned up, so that I had fair opportunity to observe my neighbours. The decent men slipped into their rags as soon as they got them, but the blackguards were in no hurry. Some indulged in a morning pipe to prepare themselves for the fatigue of dressing, while others, loosening their bundles as they squatted naked, commenced an investigation for certain little animals which shall be nameless.

At last my turn came, and 'chucking over' my shirt and ticket, I quickly attired myself in clothes which, ragged as they were, were cleaner than they looked. In less than two minutes I was out of the shed, and in the yard; where a few of the more decent poor fellows were crowding round a pail of water, and scrambling after something that might pass for a 'wash' – finding their own soap, as far as I could observe, and drying their faces on any bit of rag they might happen to have about them, or upon the canvas curtain of the shed.

By this time it was about half-past seven, and the majority of the casuals were up and dressed. I observed, however, that none of the younger boys were as yet up, and it presently appeared that there existed some rule against their dressing in the shed; for Daddy came out of the bath-room, where the bundles were deposited, and called out, 'Now four boys!' and instantly four poor little wretches, some with their rugs trailing about their shoulders and some quite bare, came shivering over the stones and across the bleak yard, and were admitted to the bath-room to dress. 'Now four more boys,' cried Daddy; and so on.

When all were up and dressed, the boys carried the bed rugs into Daddy's room, and the pauper inmates made a heap of the 'beds', stacking them against the wall. As before mentioned, the shed served the treble purpose of bed-chamber, workroom, and breakfast-room; it was impossible to get fairly at the cranks and set them going until the bedding was stowed away.

Breakfast before work, however, but it was a weary while to some of us before it made its appearance. For my own part, I had little appetite, but about me were a dozen poor wretches who obviously had a very great one: they had come in overnight too late for bread, and perhaps may not have broken fast since the morning of the previous day. Full three quarters of an hour of loitering and shivering, and then came the taskmaster: a soldierly-looking man, over six feet high, with quick grey eyes, in which 'No trifling' appeared as distinctly as a notice against trespassing on a wayside board. He came in amongst us, and the grey eyes made out our number in a moment. 'Out into the yard, all of you!' he cried; and we went out in a mob. There we shivered for some twenty minutes longer, and then a baker's man appeared with a great wooden tray piled up with just such slices of bread as we had received overnight. The tray was consigned to an able-bodied casual, who took his place with the taskmaster at

A reconstruction of the tramps' bathroom in the former Guildford workhouse 'spike', now renovated as a workhouse museum, complete with original stone-breaking cells.

the shed door, and then in single file we re-entered the shed, each man and boy receiving a slice as he passed in. Pitying, as I suppose, my unaccustomed look, Mr Taskmaster gave me a slice and a large piece over.

The bread devoured, a clamour for 'skilley' began. The rumour had got abroad that this morning, and on all future mornings, there would be skilley at breakfast, and 'Skilley! Skilley!' resounded through the shed. No one had hinted that it was not forthcoming, but skilley seems to be thought an extraordinary concession. There was a loud 'hooray!' when the longed for skilley appeared in two pails, in one of which floated a small tin saucepan, with a stick thrust into its handle, by way of a ladle. Yellow pint basins were provided for our use, and large iron spoons. 'Range round the walls!' the taskmaster shouted. We obeyed with the utmost alacrity; and then what I should judge to be about three-fourths of a pint of gruel was handed to each of us as we stood. I was glad to get mine, because the basin that contained it was warm and my hands were numb with cold. I tasted a spoonful, as in duty bound, and wondered more than ever at the esteem in which it was held by my *confrères*. It was a weak decoction of oatmeal and water, bitter, and without even a pinch of salt to flavour – that I could discover. But it was hot; and on that account, perhaps, was so highly relished, that I had no difficulty in persuading one of the decent men to accept my share.

It was now past eight o'clock, and, as I knew that a certain quantity of labour had to be performed by each man before he was allowed to go his way, I was anxious to begin. The labour was to be 'crank' labour. The 'cranks' are a series of iron bars extending across the width of the shed, penetrating through the wall, and working a flour mill on the other side. Turning the 'crank' is like turning a windlass. The task is not a severe one. Four measures of corn (bushels they were called – but that is doubtful) have to be ground every morning by the night's batch of casuals. Close up by the ceiling hangs a bell connected with the machinery, and as each measure is ground the bell rings, so that the grinders may know how they are going on. But the grinders are as lazy as obscene. We were no sooner set to work than the taskmaster left us to our own sweet will, with nothing to restrain its exercise but an occasional visit from the miller, a weakly expostulating man. Once or twice he came in and said mildly, 'Now then, my men, why *don't* you stick to it?' – and so went out again.

The result of this laxity of overseeing would have disgusted me at any time, and was intensely disgusting then. At least one half of the gang kept their hands from the crank whenever the miller was absent, and betook themselves to their private amusements and pursuits. Some sprawled upon the beds and smoked; some engaged themselves and their friends in tailoring, and one turned hair-cutter for the benefit of a gentleman who, unlike Kay, had *not* just come out of prison. There were three tailors, two of them on the beds mending their own coats, and the other operating on a recumbent friend in the rearward part of his clothing. Where the needles came from I do not know; but for thread they used a strand of the oakum (evidently easy to deal with) which the boys were picking in the corners. Other loungers strolled about with their hands in their pockets, discussing the topics of the day, and playing practical jokes on the industrious few: a favourite joke being to take a bit of rag, anoint it with grease from the crank axles, and clap it unexpectedly over somebody's eye.

The consequence of all this was that the cranks went round at a very slow rate and now and then stopped altogether. Then the miller came in; the loungers rose from their couches, the tailors ceased stitching, the smokers dropped their pipes, and every fellow was at his post. The cranks spun round furiously again, the miller's expostulation being drowned amidst a shout of 'Slap bang, here we are again!' or this extemporised chorus:

We'll hang up the miller on a sour apple tree,
We'll hang up the miller on a sour apple tree,
We'll hang up the miller on a sour apple tree,
And then go grinding on.
Glory, glory, Hallelujah, &c., &c.

By such ditties the ruffians enlivened their short spell of work. Short indeed! The miller departed, and within a minute afterwards beds were reoccupied, pipes lit, and tailoring resumed. So the game continued – the honest fellows sweating at the cranks, and anxious to get the work done and go out to look for more profitable labour, and the paupers by profession taking matters quite easy. I am convinced that had the work been properly superintended the four measures of corn might have been ground in the space of an hour and a half. As it was, when the little bell tinkled for the fourth time, and the yard gate was opened and we were free to depart, the clock had struck eleven.[101]

The day after the first instalment of Greenwood's story appeared, the Poor Law Board Inspector for the Metropolitan District, Henry Farnall, visited the Lambeth Workhouse to view conditions for himself. Farnall later stated that the 'pump shed' in which Greenwood had slept was not a regular casual ward but used only when the other wards were full, a practice which he had asked should cease forthwith. Greenwood's response was that 'an irregularity which consigned some *forty men* to such a den on the night when somebody happened to be there to see, is probably a frequent one; and it certainly is infamous.'[102]

J.H. Stallard
The Female Casual and her Lodging

In September 1866, less than eight months after Greenwood's revelations, the medical reformer J.H. Stallard published the experiences of 'Ellen Stanley', a working woman he had hired to make undercover visits to four of London's female casual wards – Lambeth, Newington, Whitechapel and St George-in-the-East. Her account was no less shocking than Greenwood's, as illustrated here by her description of a night spent at Whitechapel.

On the evening of Friday I again set out for a visit to the female casuals, and having ascertained that the police are not employed either at Whitechapel or St George's-in-the-East, I selected the former, being glad enough to escape the ordeal of the station, which is enough to deter any one who is respectable from seeking a night's lodging in the places provided for the destitute. I again dressed myself in my worn-out and dirty clothes, and after a long and fatiguing walk I arrived at the gate of the Whitechapel workhouse about half-past nine. Having asked for a night's lodging, I was told to go to the stone-yard, which is at the back of the Pavilion Theatre, in the Whitechapel Road. Passing up a wide entry the gates are on the left-hand, and near it there are many stables and a number of empty carts, which seemed to be employed by contractors who mend the roads.

I had great difficulty in finding the place, and when I had found it could not make known my wants, because the knocker was tied down, and could not be raised so as to make any noise. After kicking at the door I succeeded in bringing out a little grey-headed old man, clad in the workhouse clothes, who had a kindly expression, which he tried to disguise by a very stern manner. He asked me shortly what I wanted. I told him a night's lodging. He replied, 'You cannot have it; we are full.'

I said, 'I must have a night's shelter somewhere'; and looking through the gate at a wooden lodge which appeared to be his room, I added, 'I can sit down there, if you please.'

'Oh, no, indeed,' said he, 'you will get me into fine trouble if you go there; you had better go somewhere else, for we cannot take you in here.'

I pretended to be greatly distressed, but he said, 'You must be off, I have no room,' and he slammed the gate, taking good care however to leave it a little open, that he might see what I did.

I said, 'I shall go and sleep in one of those carts, and then the police will come, and lock me up, for I cannot go any further; and if they find me there, you will catch it.'

All this time he watched me through the nick of the door, which he held ajar, and seeing that I still remained, he said, 'Well, there, come along; I got one bed left, and you seem a decent sort of woman. I don't think you were ever here before'; and looking at me very hard, but very kindly, he added, 'Poor soul, I hope you will not want to come again, for there is a rough lot here'; and, thinking that I was still crying, he said, 'There, come along in, and you shall have a bed.'

I was then shown into a little square office, just inside the gate, and was asked my name, which was on this occasion Ellen Smith. He asked me where I slept last, I told him Dockhead. My trade? I told him, a tailoress, but not a regular hand. My age? I said forty-two; and he then dismissed me with a ticket, upon which my name was written, and with a man's blue and white calico shirt to sleep in.

I asked him if I was to undress and give him all my clothes, and he said, 'Yes, everything I had, as there was a very rum lot.'

Looking at the shirt, I said, 'But this is not clean, and if I put it on and get disease what would become of me?'

He then whispered in my ear, and said, 'Well, you don't look like one of the roughs, and if I was you, I wouldn't put it on; I can't answer for it, they are a dirty lot. But mind what you are about, and put it under your pillow, and don't let the nurse see you in your own shift in the morning, or I shall catch it; and now put your clothes together, and pin them in a bundle, and put the ticket on them, that they may be safe.'

He then led me across the yard to a wooden building; which seemed to have been built for a waggon-shed, the sides having been boarded up to make it habitable. He unlocked the door, and showed me in. The place was already well filled; it was nearly square, two sides being occupied by shallow trough beds inclined from the wall. It was about eighteen feet long, and there were nine beds on the one side and seven on the other. There was a tap of water on the right-hand side of the door, and a gaslight hanging from the ceiling. At one corner there was an opening into a second ward, which was about eight feet wide, and held also nine beds, similar to the rest. In the first compartment all the beds were occupied except two, and I took one of those vacant next the door. They were altogether eleven women and five children, and they all lay without speaking whilst the old man went into the other ward, and brought out a bundle of clothes. He told me to undress, and when he came out I was obliged to screen myself with the shirt he gave me.

As soon as he was gone three of the women rose up in their beds and began to talk. It was fearfully hot, and there was not a breath of air. 'Oh dear,' said one, 'what a dreadful night, and what a dreadful place!' 'It is enough to kill us,' said another; and the third observed 'that she would be eaten alive.' Indeed the place was swarming with vermin. The walls were all of wood, whitewashed, but very old, and the vermin ran in and out of the cracks like bees at the entrance of their hive on a summer's morning. It is no exaggeration to say that there were myriads; indeed, it is difficult to conceive so many in so small a place.

A woman now said, 'Have you got your pannum, old girl?' I did not understand, and another said, 'Don't you know, your toke?' and a third then put in, 'Why the **** don't you speak plain? Don't you see the woman ain't up to your flash talk?'

'No,' said I, 'I've got nothing.'

'Then, why,' said she, 'don't you ask him?'

Presently the old man came in and asked me for my clothes. I was sitting up on the bed, with a cotton apron over my shoulders, which I had taken on purpose to put over me. Fearing to betray myself I said, 'I could eat a piece of bread, for I am very hungry.' He went and got it for me, and said, 'There, there! I am sure I forgot you, but here it is.' I put it under my head, for it was impossible to eat; and very soon afterwards I saw it absolutely covered with black vermin. At the same time one of the women asked for some water, and he went for a can and drew some from the tap. He then took away my clothes, and after some time he brought in another woman, and passed her through into the other ward. About two o'clock he again came in, smoking his pipe. He went into both compartments to see that all was quiet, and at four he brought in a ladder and turned the gas off.

It was utterly impossible to lie down: the beds were alive with vermin, and the rugs with lice. The walls and woodwork were all spotted over with marks where they had been killed. On the opposite side of the ward the women lay quiet for some time, but on my side they were up and down the whole night. Here, as elsewhere, there was no rest until daylight. The principal subject of conversation was the filthiness of the place, which they all agreed to be the worst in London. One asked me from what part of the world I came, and I said, Dockhead. She asked me what I worked at, and I told her my needle. 'That is hard lines,' said she; 'you had better do anything than that, it is so – badly paid for.' She recommended me to try the road, where I might do much better; and she wanted me to join her, as she was herself getting too well known. She was evidently a cadger and beggar, and she seemed to think that I might do well under her guidance.

At this time the night was indescribably dreadful. There lay the women, naked and restless, tossing about in the dim gaslight, and getting up from time to time in order to shake off their disgusting tormentors, which speckled their naked limbs with huge black spots. When the old man came in, he motioned to me to lie down and go to sleep, but I told him I dared not, for the vermin were so bad. 'Ah,' said he, 'you are not used to it.' About twelve o'clock the closeness and heat of the room became intolerable, and every one began to feel ill and to suffer from diarrhoea. Several were drawn double with cramp, and I felt sick and ill myself. The children began to cry constantly, and seemed extremely ill. From this time the closet was constantly occupied by one or another, and the stench became dreadful. 'So help me God,' said one, 'I will never come here again. I would rather go to prison a hundred times.' Another said, 'Hold your tongue, you ★★★★ fool, or he will hear you.' Another groaned for a little brandy, with language too dreadful to repeat; and someone else added, 'If you were dying, you would get none here.' For myself, I suffered more than I can say, and as long as I live I shall never forget the horrors of that dreadful night. No wonder there is cholera at the East of London, for it is generated every night in the Whitechapel casual ward.

About seven o'clock in the morning a big, stout woman came in and said 'All up!' and she was followed by a man who brought the clothes. 'Here,' said she, throwing them towards us, 'make haste.' She stood by watching us dress, and urging them to get on and be quick. If anyone lingered for a moment to pick vermin from her clothes, she immediately stopped them, saying 'that she would not have it done there,' and she seemed determined to get over her disagreeable duty with the utmost speed. She stared particularly at me, and seemed to wonder what business I had there, and appeared to be only satisfied when she saw my boots. Outside the door there was a pail of water, but neither soap nor towels. Several attempted to wash, and particularly a woman with three children, who was more decent than the rest. The majority never washed at all, for they had no time, the big, fat woman continually driving them on by saying 'be quick,' 'be off,' 'get on,' etc. etc. Those who succeeded in wetting their faces dried them on their own rags.

When all were ready, we were conducted across the yard to the office before mentioned, and skilly and bread were there served out. The former was horrible stuff; it was black, and totally unfit to eat. At the former places I ate some of it, but I could not touch it here, and many others also left the greater part. It was served partly in tin cans, and partly in white earthenware mugs. We had to carry it across the stone-yard to the oakum-room, which is also a filthy place. It is a wooden building covered with tar, and whitewashed inside, the walls being covered with slang writing and directions for the road. Some now began to undress, and three of them stripped naked to look over their clothes to destroy the vermin. Two of them commenced smoking. Altogether there were sixteen women and five children. One child asked a woman for a block to sit upon, and she refused it. The mother said, 'You know it is not allowed to sit on the oakum-block,' and a row commenced, in which the language used cannot he repeated; it ended in a fight, which was interrupted by the entrance of the old man. The woman again sat down on the block, and the other appealed to him, saying, 'You know me before to-day'; and he said, 'Yes, you are always kicking up a row,' and he then ordered the woman to get off the block; but as she did not move he pulled her off, and he said, 'I won't have this talk, and if you are not quiet I'll turn you out.' She said, 'I wish you would.' He replied, 'If you do, it will not be at the door you want to go out of.'

When the breakfast was over, the pots were put on the floor, and we had to go again to the lodge to fetch the oakum. Everyone had a pound. It was very old and hard, and quite unfit for women to pick. I was nearly four hours doing mine, although I worked very hard, and my hands were quite sore when I had finished. There were four women who, after doing a little bit, refused to go on. I observed that none of them troubled themselves to do it; and when I had nearly finished mine I said to a woman, 'Why don't you get on? You will never be let out to-day.' 'Oh no,' said she, 'they cannot keep you in after twelve o'clock.' I said if I had known that I would not have done mine. She said, 'Ah! I thought you were a **** fool, but we don't hurt ourselves with work.' In the meantime there was a general conversation, chiefly about the road and the workhouse, conducted in flash language.

There were now four smoking, and some appeared very contented and happy. One asked another when she tore up last. She said, 'it was a long time since, for she got seven days for it,' and another said, 'she would tear up every day rather than go lousy, as she had done.' Nevertheless, tearing up did not seem so popular as it had been, for they said the magistrates now gave it so **** stiff. 'Such places as this,' said another, 'ought to be set fire to, and a woman had better do anything than come to it.'

One poor old woman, who had evidently been more respectable, sat in silence, but in great agony; she was sixty years of age, and quite grey. She said to me, 'I feel very faint; I could not touch that muck of stuff, and it is a shame to make a woman do such work as this.' She worked very hard, and got done ten minutes before me.

The woman and her boy continued quarrelling with someone or other the whole time, and one of the women told her that 'she ought to be ashamed of herself coming there, the money she made on the road.' All her clothes had the workhouse marks upon them, and she was evidently a regular beggar. She said, 'How do I get more than you?' and the other replied, 'Because you are so **** impudent, and can go where we dare not.' There appeared to be a great difference amongst the women, a few being more cleanly and respectable. Twelve out of the sixteen had a yellow look, as if they had been jaundiced, and six or eight had short hair, either from having had the fever or from having been in prison. There was none except the old widow who was not able to do a good day's work.

When I had finished I was in no hurry to leave, wishing to observe what was going on, and to read the writing upon the walls, but I was immediately taken to task. 'What the **** are you waiting for?' said one. 'You seem **** modest over it,' said another; and a third thought that I would be glad to get out of it. It was half-past eleven when I had done, and I left five women amusing themselves, and making no attempt to finish their task. I asked them what the man would say. They said they did not care; they supposed they would get a good blowing up, but they did not mind that.

Bad as the night was at Newington, it was a palace compared with this, which was enough to kill any one, and ought to be at once closed.

The queue waiting for admission to the Whitechapel casual ward on Thomas Street. Female casuals queued separately to the right of the entrance.

An illustration of trough beds of the type used by 'Ellen Stanley'. Those shown here are at the St Marylebone casual ward, opened in 1867, with scriptural texts printed in large red letters on the blue walls.

Perhaps not unexpectedly, a review of 'The Female Casual' in the *Pall Mall Gazette* was scathing about Stallard's publication:

WOMEN IN WORKHOUSES

A woman who undertakes such a task as the 'Female Casual' imposed upon herself may be, as this poor pauper widow no doubt was, of the most conscientious character, and animated by the best intentions, but if she has neither education, superior intelligence, nor knowledge of life, no human being will be the better for her visit. She will not know what to observe, on what points the public are ignorant and desire information, or what evils could be and ought to be remedied, and what are in the nature of things inevitable. And it is very improbable that a clever, well-educated woman could be found to volunteer her services for such a purpose. Therefore, the experiences recorded are to the last degree vague and unedifying, and we feel no surprise to learn that the 'Female Casual' cries in one ward, faints in another, and is very ill in a third.[103]

Jack London
The People of the Abyss

In the summer of 1902, the American writer Jack London visited England and
spent time in the capital's East End, staying undercover in dosshouses and spending
a night in the Whitechapel workhouse casual ward. Like James Greenwood,
London encountered the unedifying tramps' bath and the rock-hard bread. After
the next morning's labour – disinfecting the workhouse mortuary and dealing
with the waste from the sick wards – he could take no more and made his escape:

At six o'clock the line moved up, and we were admitted in groups of three.
Name, age, occupation, place of birth, condition of destitution, and the previous
night's 'doss' were taken with lightning-like rapidity by the superintendent; and
as I turned I was startled by a man's thrusting into my hand something that
felt like a brick, and shouting into my ear, 'Any knives, matches, or tobacco?'
'No, sir,' I lied, as lied every man who entered. As I passed downstairs to the
cellar, I looked at the brick in my hand, and saw that by doing violence to the
language it might be called 'bread'. By its weight and hardness it certainly must
have been unleavened.

The light was very dim down in the cellar, and before I knew it some other
man had thrust a pannikin into my other hand. Then I stumbled on to a still
darker room, where were benches and tables and men. The place smelled vilely,
and the sombre gloom, and the mumble of voices from out of the obscurity,
made it seem more like some anteroom to the infernal regions.

Most of the men were suffering from tired feet, and they prefaced the meal
by removing their shoes and unbinding the filthy rags with which their feet
were wrapped. This added to the general noisomeness, while it took away from
my appetite.

In fact, I found that I had made a mistake. I had eaten a hearty dinner five
hours before, and to have done justice to the fare before me I should have fasted
for a couple of days. The pannikin contained skilly, three-quarters of a pint, a
mixture of Indian corn and hot water. The men were dipping their bread into
heaps of salt scattered over the dirty tables. I attempted the same, but the bread
seemed to stick in my mouth, and I remembered the words of the Carpenter:
'You need a pint of water to eat the bread nicely.'

I went over into a dark corner where I had observed other men going, and
found the water. Then I returned and attacked the skilly. It was coarse of texture,
unseasoned, gross, and bitter. This bitterness which lingered persistently in the
mouth after the skilly had passed on, I found especially repulsive. I struggled
manfully, but was mastered by my qualms, and half a dozen mouthfuls of skilly
and bread was the measure of my success. The man beside me ate his own share,
and mine to boot, scraped the pannikins, and looked hungrily for more.

'I met a "towny", and he stood me too good a dinner,' I explained.

'An' I 'aven't 'ad a bite since yesterday mornin',' he replied.

'How about tobacco?' I asked. 'Will the bloke bother with a fellow now?'

'Oh, no,' he answered me. 'No bloody fear. This is the easiest spike goin'. Y'oughto see some of them. Search you to the skin.'

The pannikins scraped clean, conversation began to spring up. 'This super'tendent 'ere is always writin' to the papers 'bout us mugs,' said the man on the other side of me.

'What does he say?' I asked.

'Oh, 'e sez we're no good, a lot o' blackguards an' scoundrels as won't work. Tells all the ole tricks I've bin 'earin' for twenty years an' which I never seen a mug ever do. Las' thing of 'is I see, 'e was tellin' 'ow a mug gets out o' the spike, wi' a crust in 'is pockit. An' w'en 'e sees a nice ole gentleman comin' along the street 'e chucks the crust into the drain, an' borrows the old gent's stick to poke it out. An' then the ole gent gi'es 'im a tanner'.

The majority of these men, nay, all of them, I found, do not like the spike, and only come to it when driven in. After the 'rest up' they are good for two or three days and nights on the streets, when they are driven in again for another rest. Of course, this continuous hardship quickly breaks their constitutions, and they realise it, though only in a vague way; while it is so much the common run of things that they do not worry about it.

'On the doss,' they call vagabondage here, which corresponds to 'on the road' in the United States. The agreement is that kipping, or dossing, or sleeping, is the hardest problem they have to face, harder even than that of food. The inclement weather and the harsh laws are mainly responsible for this, while the men themselves ascribe their homelessness to foreign immigration, especially of Polish and Russian Jews, who take their places at lower wages and establish the sweating system.

By seven o'clock we were called away to bathe and go to bed. We stripped our clothes, wrapping them up in our coats and buckling our belts about them, and deposited them in a heaped rack and on the floor – a beautiful scheme for the spread of vermin. Then, two by two, we entered the bathroom. There were two ordinary tubs, and this I know: the two men preceding had washed in that water, we washed in the same water, and it was not changed for the two men that followed us. This I know; but I am quite certain that the twenty-two of us washed in the same water.

I did no more than make a show of splashing some of this dubious liquid at myself, while I hastily brushed it off with a towel wet from the bodies of other men. My equanimity was not restored by seeing the back of one poor wretch a mass of blood from attacks of vermin and retaliatory scratching.

A shirt was handed me – which I could not help but wonder how many other men had worn; and with a couple of blankets under my arm I trudged off to the sleeping apartment. This was a long, narrow room, traversed by two low iron rails. Between these rails were stretched, not hammocks, but pieces of canvas, six feet long and less than two feet wide. These were the beds, and they were six inches apart and about eight inches above the floor. The chief difficulty was that the head was somewhat higher than the feet, which caused the body constantly to slip down. Being slung to the same rails, when one man moved, no matter how slightly, the rest were set rocking; and whenever I dozed somebody was sure to struggle back to the position from which he had slipped, and arouse me again.

Many hours passed before I won to sleep. It was only seven in the evening, and the voices of children, in shrill outcry, playing in the street, continued till nearly midnight. The smell was frightful and sickening, while my imagination broke loose, and my skin crept and crawled till I was nearly frantic. Grunting, groaning, and snoring arose like the sounds emitted by some sea monster, and several times, afflicted by nightmare, one or another, by his shrieks and yells, aroused the lot of us. Toward morning I was awakened by a rat or some similar animal on my breast. In the quick transition from sleep to waking, before I was completely myself, I raised a shout to wake the dead. At any rate, I woke the living, and they cursed me roundly for my lack of manners.

But morning came, with a six o'clock breakfast of bread and skilly, which I gave away; and we were told off to our various tasks. Some were set to scrubbing and cleaning, others to picking oakum, and eight of us were convoyed across the street to the Whitechapel Infirmary, where we were set at scavenger work. This was the method by which we paid for our skilly and canvas, and I, for one, know that I paid in full many times over.

Though we had most revolting tasks to perform, our allotment was considered the best, and the other men deemed themselves lucky in being chosen to perform it.

'Don't touch it, mate, the nurse sez it's deadly,' warned my working partner, as I held open a sack into which he was emptying a garbage can.

It came from the sick wards, and I told him that I purposed neither to touch it, nor to allow it to touch me. Nevertheless, I had to carry the sack, and other sacks, down five flights of stairs and empty them in a receptacle where the corruption was speedily sprinkled with strong disinfectant.

Perhaps there is a wise mercy in all this. These men of the spike, the peg, and the street, are encumbrances. They are of no good or use to any one, nor to themselves. They clutter the earth with their presence, and are better out of the way. Broken by hardship, ill fed, and worse nourished, they are always the first to be struck down by disease, as they are likewise the quickest to die.

They feel, themselves, that the forces of society tend to hurl them out of existence. We were sprinkling disinfectant by the mortuary, when the dead wagon drove up and five bodies were packed into it. The conversation turned

The interior of the Whitechapel casual ward on Thomas Street. The men slept in hammock-style beds which were slung on rails, placing their head nearest the wall and feet at the centre of the room.

to the 'white potion' and 'black jack', and I found they were all agreed that the poor person, man or woman, who in the Infirmary gave too much trouble or was in a bad way, was 'polished off'. That is to say, the incurables and the obstreperous were given a dose of 'black jack' or the 'white potion', and sent over the divide. It does not matter in the least whether this be actually so or not. The point is they have the feeling that it is so, and they have created the language with which to express that feeling – 'black jack', 'white potion', 'polishing off'.

At eight o'clock we went down into a cellar under the Infirmary, where tea was brought to us, and the hospital scraps. These were heaped high on a huge platter in an indescribable mess – pieces of bread, chunks of grease and fat pork, the burnt skin from the outside of roasted joints, bones, in short, all the leavings from the fingers and mouths of the sick ones suffering from all manner of diseases. Into this mess the men plunged their hands, digging, pawing, turning over, examining, rejecting, and scrambling for. It wasn't pretty. Pigs couldn't have done worse. But the poor devils were hungry, and they ate ravenously of the swill, and when they could eat no more they bundled what was left into their handkerchiefs and thrust it inside their shirts.

The Whitechapel workhouse infirmary where Jack London 'scavenged' after his night in the casual ward.

It is the rule of the casual ward that a man who enters must stay two nights and a day; but I had seen sufficient for my purpose, had paid for my skilly and canvas, and was preparing to run for it.

'Come on, let's sling it,' I said to one of my mates, pointing toward the open gate through which the dead wagon had come.

'An' get fourteen days?'

'No; get away.'

'Aw, I come 'ere for a rest,' he said complacently. 'An' another night's kip won't 'urt me none.'

They were all of this opinion, so I was forced to 'sling it' alone.

'You cawn't ever come back 'ere again for a doss,' they warned me.

'No bloody fear,' said I, with an enthusiasm they could not comprehend; and, dodging out the gate, I sped down the street.

Straight to my room I hurried, changed my clothes, and less than an hour from my escape, in a Turkish bath, I was sweating out whatever germs and other things had penetrated my epidermis, and wishing that I could stand a temperature of three hundred and twenty rather than two hundred and twenty.[104]

Mary Higgs
A First Night in the Workhouse Tramp Ward

Mary Higgs was born in 1854 at Devizes in Wiltshire, the daughter of
Congregational minister William Kingsland. In 1862, the family moved to
Bradford where her father became minister at College Chapel. She was educated
at a local private school, and at Girton College in Cambridge where she was the
first woman to study for the Natural Science Tripos. In 1879, she married the
Revd Thomas Kilpin Higgs. She later settled in Oldham and, amongst many other
religious and philanthropic activities, became Secretary of the Ladies Committee
visiting the Oldham Union workhouse.

An interest in vagrancy reform led her to discover first hand what conditions
were like, particularly for women, in accommodation such as casual wards and
common lodging houses. Her experiences revealed the squalid conditions often
to be found, and how vulnerable female vagrants could be. Her 1904 pamphlet,
Five Days and Five Nights as a Tramp Among Tramps, was published under the pen
name 'A Lady'. It described her visits to five different lodging houses, shelters
and casual wards in West Yorkshire which, for safety, she undertook accompanied
by her friend Annie Lee. Her initiation into the casual ward was at Dewsbury
workhouse, on the third night of her travels:

We arrived, alone, a few minutes before six, at the workhouse lodge, which
stood all by itself down a long lane which ended in iron gates. This lodge was
very small, and was occupied by a man, the workhouse buildings being a little
way off. There were a good many trees around, and it was a pretty spot, but
lonely. The man was a male pauper, and no one else was in sight. We had to
enter his hut to answer questions, which he recorded in a book, and we were
then out of sight of the house. The nearest building was the tramp ward, the
door of which stood open; but there was no one in it, as we afterwards found. A
single woman would be completely at the mercy of this man. If our pilgrimage
has had no other result, I shall be glad to be able to expose the positive wrong
of allowing a male pauper, in a lonely office, to admit the female tramps. When
we first arrived at the gate he told us to wait a few minutes, as we were before
time. Some male tramps came up, and we saw him send away one poor, utterly
ragged man, who begged pitifully to be admitted. The lodge-keeper told him
he could not claim because he had been in that workhouse within the month.
So he limped away. He could not possibly reach another workhouse that night.
The man admitted three others, and sent them on to the male quarters. He let
us in at five minutes to six. We thought this was kind, as he might have kept
us waiting, and it had begun to rain. He took my friend's name, occupation,
age, where she came from, and her destination, and then sent her on, rather
imperatively, to the tramp ward. She stood at the door, some way off, waiting

for me. He kept me inside his lodge, and began to take the details. He talked to me in what I suppose he thought a very agreeable manner, telling me he wished I had come alone earlier, and he would have given me a cup of tea. I thanked him, wondering if this was usual, and then he took my age, and finding I was a married woman (I must use his exact words), he said, 'Just the right age for a bit of funning; come down to me later in the evening.' I was too horror-struck to reply; besides, I was in his power, with no one within call but my friend, and all the conditions unknown and strange. Probably silence was best; he took it for consent, and, as other tramps were coming, let me pass on. I made a mental vow to expose him before I left the place. He took my bundle, and asked if I had any money. I gave him my last penny. I received a wooden token for the bundle. I then joined my friend, and told her she had better give up her umbrella and her penny. She went to do so after some tramps had passed, and though I stood and waited, and she was only gone a moment, he tried to kiss her as she gave him the things!

When she joined me, very indignant, we went forward into an oblong room containing six bedsteads with wire mattresses and filthy straw pillows. A wooden table and bench and 'Regulations for Tramps' were the remaining articles of furniture. There were big, rather low, windows on three sides; the bottom panes were frosted, except one, which had been broken and mended with plain glass, and overlooked the yard where the male tramps worked. Presently our wayfaring friend arrived, and we all three sat and waited a considerable time. A solitary woman might have been at the mercy of the man at the gate some time. No one was in sight, or came near us, till at last a motherly-looking woman entered by a door leading to a room beyond. She asked us if we were clean. Our fellow traveller (whose garments were at any rate *not* clean) was let off, as she had spent the last night in a workhouse tramp ward. We said we should like a bath, and were shown into a bath-room and allowed to bathe ourselves. Our clothes were taken from us, and we were given blue nightgowns. These looked fairly clean, but had been worn before. They were dirty round the neck, and stained in places; we *hoped* they had been stoved![105] The old woman dressed in one without bathing. We found in the morning that both blankets and nightgowns were folded up and put away on shelves, just as we found them, apparently, and left for new corners. We were told that the blankets were 'often stoved', but I have since ascertained that they are not stoved at all workhouses every day. All kinds of personal vermin might be left in them by a tramp who went straight out of dirty clothes to bed, and even a bath might leave them open to suspicion. We saw several bugs on the ceiling in this ward. Perhaps the using of others' dirty nightgowns was the most revolting feature in our tramp. At neither workhouse were the garments handed to us *clean*. We found afterwards that by Government regulation clean bath water and a clean garment can be *demanded*, but this we did not know.

It should be *supplied*. After the bath we were each given four blankets and told to make our beds and get into them. The art of bed-making on a wire mattress, without any other mattress to cover it, is a difficult one, even with four blankets. The regulation number is two, and with these I fancy the best plan would be to roll yourself round and lie on the mattress. For the wire abstracts beat from the body, and *one* is an insufficient protection. Even with one spread all over and another doubled under the body and two above I woke many times cold. In winter the ward is warmed by hot-water pipes, but the blankets are the same. A plank bed, such as is given in some workhouses, would probably be warmer, though harder. Put to bed, like babies, at about half-past six, the kind woman in charge brought us our food. We felt rather more cheerful after our bath, with the large, airy room, instead of the foul, common lodging-house; only one thing had exercised my mind – 'What did that pauper mean by my going to him later?' However, I told the portress all about what he said. She was very indignant, and said I must tell the superintendent of the tramp ward next morning, that she had to leave us, but would take good care to lock us in, and I need not be afraid, he could not get at us. We were very hungry, having had nothing to eat since about twelve o'clock. Anything eatable would be welcome, and we were also thirsty. We were given a small lading-can three parts full of hot gruel and a thick crust of bread. The latter we were *quite* hungry enough to eat, but when we tasted the gruel it was *perfectly saltless*. A salt-box on the table, into which many fingers had been dipped was brought us; the old woman said we were 'lucky to get that.' But we had no *spoons*; it was impossible to mix the salt properly into the ocean of nauseous food. I am fond of gruel, and in my hunger and thirst could easily have taken it if fairly palatable. But I could only cast in a few grains of salt and drink a little to moisten the dry bread; my companion could not stomach it at all, and the old woman, being accustomed to workhouse ways, had a little tea in her pocket, and got the kind attendant to pour the gruel down the w.c. and infuse her tea with hot water from the bath tap. We were then left locked in alone, at eight o'clock, when no more tramps would be admitted. The bath-room, containing our clothes, was locked; the closet was left unlocked; a pail was also given us for sanitary purposes. We had no means of assuaging the thirst which grew upon us as the night went on; for dry bread, even if washed down with thin gruel, is very provocative of thirst. I no longer wonder that tramps beg twopence for a drink and make for the nearest public-house. Left alone, we could hear outside the voice of the porter. I wondered if he expected us to open a window. However, we stayed quiet, but had one 'scare'. Suddenly a door at the end of the room was unlocked, and a *man* put his head in! He only asked, 'how many?' and when we answered 'Three,' he locked us in speedily. I could not, however, get to sleep for a long time after finding that a *man* had the key of our room, especially as our elderly friend had told us of another workhouse where the portress left the care of the female tramps to a man almost entirely, and she added that 'he did what he liked with them.' I expressed horror at such a state of things, but she assured me it was so, and warned us not on any account to go into that workhouse. She said, however, that it was some time since she had been there, and 'things might be different'.

At last my companions slept the sleep of weariness. Sounds outside had ceased; within, my friend coughed and the old woman groaned and shifted. The trees waved without the windows, and two bugs slowly crawled on the ceiling. I measured distances with my eye. They would not drop on my bed! I pity the tramp who has only two blankets on a wire mattress. I could not get thoroughly warm with four; some part of me seemed constantly to feel the cold wire meshes through the thin covering. The floor would be preferable. I have been told since at one workhouse, with considerable surprise on the part of the portress, that the male tramps prefer the floor to their plank bed! I do not wonder. The pillow was too dirty to put one's face on, so I covered it with a blanket.

In this workhouse the management was lax – too lax to ensure cleanliness; clothes and towels appeared to have been used, and blankets were probably unstoved. As our own clothes are taken away and locked up, it would be impossible for a tramp to wash any article of personal clothing. Consequently she must tramp on, growing day by day more dirty, in spite of baths, especially as really dirty work is required of her in return for 'board and lodging!' There was no comb for the hair; fortunately we had one in our pocket. In the morning we were roused about seven o'clock and told to dress. Our clothes were in the bath-room. We had the luxury of a morning wash. Our garments had been left on the floor just as we took them off, and so were our companion's, which looked decidedly unclean by daylight. The kind attendant said she had to go, but waited till I had told the portress (who arrived to set us our task) the conduct of the man at the gate, and I claimed her protection, as I should have to pass him when going out. Both exclaimed when I told his words, and one said, 'Plenty of cups of tea I expect he's given, the villain!' The portress assured me she would watch me out, and that I need not fear him, as he daren't touch me when she was there, and she said that after I had gone she should report him.

Before this happened, however, we had our breakfast given us, which was exactly a repetition of supper – saltless gruel and dry bread. We ate as much as we could and were very thirsty. I had drunk some water with my hand from the bath-room tap as soon as I got up. We put what bread we could not eat into our pocket as a supply for the day, and were told to empty the rest of our gruel down the w.c. It thus disappeared; but what waste! A mug of coffee or tea would at least have washed down the dry bread; or a quarter of the quantity of gruel, properly made, would have been acceptable, with a mug of cold water for a proper drink.

The remarkable Mary Higgs who, in her fifties, underwent the privations experienced by women in casual wards, hostels and dosshouses. Her experiences enabled her to provide important evidence to the Local Government Board's Departmental Committee on Vagrancy in 1904.

The portress told us when we had done our work we might go out at eleven o'clock. We thanked her – we had expected to stay another night, and perhaps pick oakum, but we should have almost starved on the food, as our sugar was in our bundle, so we were relieved to find we had only to clean the tramp ward and go. We were told to 'sweep the ward and make all clean.' We did not think of scrubbing the room, which, as it was large, would have been a big task, but the portress afterwards scolded us for not doing so. It was not dirty, so we swept it, cleaned the taps, bath, and wash-basins, washed up the pots, dusted, and, having made all tidy (except that we could find nowhere to empty our dust-pan, unless it was the w.c.), we waited for release. We sat on the form, and when the portress came in and saw us sitting down she spoke to us very sharply. I suppose she did not like to see us idle. We told her we would have scrubbed the floor if we had known we ought; but we did not know, as we had never been in a workhouse before. She was somewhat mollified, and let us off with a mild scolding some time before eleven o'clock. She stood at the door and watched us receive our things from the male pauper and leave the gates. He hastened to give us them without a word, and also restored our two pennies.[106]

Frank Gray: The Tramp
His Meaning and Being

In the late 1920s, former Oxford MP Frank Gray recorded his undercover experiences in the casual wards of Oxfordshire workhouses which he visited disguised as a tramp. Gray was a strong advocate of helping young tramps to escape the downward slope of life on the road and regularly provided accommodation for such men at his own home, Shipton Manor. Gray was particularly struck by the dire conditions in the Headington 'spike', which were in strong contrast to its much more well-appointed neighbour a mere two miles away in Oxford. However, Headington was still popular with tramps because there was virtually no supervision during their stay:

> I reach the gates of Headington; so do about twenty others. We loaf around the gates. Two boys in a milk float jeer at us as they pass. A casual snarls: 'You ****, your turn may come!' Another says: 'Why do the **** exhibit us out here?'
>
> The doors open, the 'tramp major' in charge lets us in; we push to get front places, to answer questions hurriedly, and snatch our piece of bread. Then we go into the casual ward without any suggestion of a search or a bath, or indeed a wash. We are locked and bolted in. How curious it is that any one should be afraid that we may abscond from the hospitality given us!
>
> The ward is a narrow building, perhaps eleven feet wide and eighteen yards long, four feet of the width being passageway till this stone passage becomes sleeping accommodation under pressure for space. On the right, as you enter, is a sloping platform, starting nine inches from the stone floor and rising to a height of eighteen inches against the wall. This platform is broken up by nine-inch upright boards, fourteen inches apart.
>
> It looks in the gloom like a row of coffins, and each tramp who is quick enough to get in claims one. He thinks himself lucky in getting it. Everyone else sleeps on the floor, under this erection or in the passageway.
>
> At the end of this ward – a cold outbuilding – and only partly partitioned off, is a foul lavatory and bath, unused and unusable for washing. This was all we were given at Headington, however great or small the number requiring accommodation.
>
> Nobody has to sleep under the raised boards to-night, in the dirty, high-windowed, elongated cell, with the almost uncovered combination of bath and cesspool at the end. The young tramp and I sleep in our clothes, for there is neither search, baths, nor handing over of raiment in this hell, where all men are at least equal.
>
> In society we all believe we have our inferiors, if not our superiors. This first belief fades in the Headington casual ward. Reproduce this casual ward in any gaol in England and the nation would cry 'Shame!'

There is one candle to light the fifteen yards of humanity, and two Irish tramps arriving late and in drink quarrel with the rest of us locked in this cell as to the exact position where this candle shall stand. Why do we quarrel in this black hole – in this horror of filth and indecency? Why, in truth, do we want this candle at all to cast shadows in this hole of shame?

Morning has come; the dirt-laden grills of our cell say so. There is a shout from the porter for the production of unemployment cards by those who can produce them. There is not one, for none of us here is a genuine worker. Had we cards we should produce them, for by doing so we gain our immediate release, without task or work. Like the rest I have no card, so I perforce do three hours' sawing.

The task is over. I am again on the 'open road', on the outskirts of Oxford, and less than two miles from the Oxford workhouse, where I intend to stay to-night. I have passed through Headington Union. I might have passed in an advanced stage of carrying smallpox, at death's door, or mad, and yet have remained uncared for and unnoticed.

I reach the grounds of the Oxford workhouse, pass through the long foregrounds, and track out the casual ward. I sit on the ground outside. The concourse of tramps here gathers by twos and threes.

It must want many minutes to six o'clock when a permanent inmate passes and says: 'Why don't you go in? It's been open for a long while.' We enter a brightly lighted room with spotlessly clean tables and forms, and to these are brought bread, margarine, and cocoa, before any inquisition, search, or inquiry is held; for this is an institution which has not lost its soul.

'Dad'[107] is of the gathering. He sits next to me. He pours a little sugar into my mug of cocoa – the widow's mite – a much greater act from a tramp to a tramp than it may appear.

The meal at the Oxford casual ward is over. The porter calls first for those who have come from Woodstock. A lot get up – so do I – and the porter says: 'You are as deaf as I am.' In a later class I get up again. I am searched. How well I know the porter and how well he knows me! But he does not recognise me. I am passed on to a permanent inmate, who is lending a hand – and he superintends me while I strip with others, pile my bundle of rags on theirs, and take my bath. There is certainly more ceremonial about the bath at Oxford, and no man is entitled to complain if he uses the water after another – some use it without complaining. You see this consideration becomes a mere unnoticeable detail in the general horror of life as a tramp.

I get a workhouse shirt, go into a spacious, healthy, and clean department, and, best of all, to a spring bedstead, straw mattress, and straw pillow. There is sufficient space, too, between the bedsteads. We are treated like decent men.

The former Oxford MP Frank Gray. Before going undercover to explore the casual wards of Oxfordshire, he gave tramps lifts in his car in order to hear about life on the road.

Frank Gray in his tramp's garb. Despite the considerable alteration in his appearance, he was once recognised by a friend while walking through Oxford in the outfit.

Some of us are, and all have got a great deal of good in them. If men's hearts could be searched it would be found that this better treatment has more than once stirred that latent better spirit to rise from the level of the tramp and the outcast.

And so to sleep.

On the morrow my task before release is to scrub the floors of two large outhouse dormitories, apparently overflow casual wards.

We are now about to parade for our departure. I see 'Dad' at the parade. I watch a young official go up to him and hear him say: 'Why don't you stop here with us, Dad? You are too old for this game now. You will be getting knocked down on the road.' At this act of kindness a tear comes to the old man's eye – he is still capable of responding – and then he passes out, passes out to pick up the trail of death.

As I walked from the Oxford workhouse, released, I reflected that there were two 'spikes' within two miles of each other conducted on very different lines. It might fairly be supposed that if my description of the two be correct, Headington would be deserted by tramps and Oxford overcrowded. This is not so, and there are good reasons why – reasons taking you to the heart of the problem of vagrancy.

Seven out of ten tramps stayed at both Headington and Oxford on the same journey. A tramp said to me: 'I hate to be ★★★★ and ★★★★ about,' and when he has said this he has expressed the terms in which many tramps think. They like to be left to their own devices, and to gain this they will put up with a lot of filth and beastliness.

We tramps are all the same just under the skin. We prefer a dung heap and a cigarette to a clean prison cell and fifty questions. Do not think, late Guardians, that by locking dirty men with hunks of bread in a dirty, insanitary hole without interference, question, or inquiry, you could have emptied your casual wards.

FIVE

VISITORS

WORKHOUSE INMATES WERE allowed to receive visitors, subject to whatever conditions and restrictions each Board of Guardians decided to impose. For the sick, there were usually fixed visiting times each week for which a ticket had to be obtained beforehand, while for the seriously ill, access would generally be allowed at more or less any time. Other inmates could receive visitors, by permission of the workhouse Master, in a separate room and in the presence of the Master, Matron, or porter. Access restrictions, especially for those visiting elderly inmates, were gradually relaxed, partly as a result of the efforts of the Workhouse Visiting Society founded in 1858 by Louisa Twining.

Although there was no formal requirement for them to do so, workhouses were generally ready to open their doors to anyone making a reasonable request to view the institution. This could include local people of standing – the workhouse was, after all, funded by the rate-payers – as well as journalists from local or national publications, or even just the plain curious visitor to the area.

J.G. Kohl
The North Dublin Workhouse

In 1844, German traveller J.G. Kohl published accounts of his travels through England, Scotland and Ireland. On his visit to Ireland, he stopped off to visit the North Dublin workhouse. The workhouse system had been introduced into Ireland in 1838, broadly along the lines of that operating in England, with the creation of 130 Poor Law Unions, each providing a workhouse for its paupers. Kohl's account is particularly interesting for its descriptions of the inmates' diet – just two meals a day for adults – and of the cooking and serving of potatoes:

The food and clothing within an Irish workhouse is certainly better than the pauper could enjoy out of it, for of course the inmates of such a house are not allowed to go about half-naked and half-starved, the usual condition of the poor in Ireland. The food consists generally of potatoes, oatmeal, and milk, particularly buttermilk. Bread is given only to the children and the sick. The diet tables and other regulations of public institutions are of interest to the inquiring traveller, for they often afford him a convenient insight into the manner of life of a whole nation. When, therefore, I detail to my readers the fare of a pauper in an Irish workhouse, I give them a picture of the style of living of the great mass of the Irish people, of those at least among them who have it in their power to eat their daily fill.

As among most classes in Ireland and England, the day is divided into three acts or meals, breakfast, lunch, and dinner. By the last is not to be understood the noonday meal, but the chief meal of the day. The lunch is participated in only by the children and invalids. The healthy and full-grown are excluded from it. The hours at which these meals are taken are later than with us in Germany. Nine o'clock is the hour for breakfast, and four in the afternoon for dinner. The breakfast, as in most parts of Ireland, among those who have the means of decent maintenance, consists of new milk and stirabout, a kind of porridge of oatmeal; the dinner is composed of potatoes and buttermilk. The children, for their lunch, receive bread and milk. On Sundays, holidays, and on every Thursday, a little 'brose', or soup, is given, in addition to the customary diet. An adult receives seven ounces of oatmeal and half a pint of new milk for breakfast, and four pounds of potatoes and a pint of buttermilk for dinner. The board of an adult is calculated to cost one shilling and fourpence three-farthings weekly. That of the children is more expensive, on account of the bread, and the more liberal supply of milk. The most costly of all is the board of the children under two years old, who cost one shilling and sixpence three-farthings a week, for which they receive one pint of new milk and a pound of bread daily. There is therefore a potato diet for adults, a bread diet for children, a rice and meat diet for the sick, and lastly, a fever diet for the class of patients always most numerous in an Irish workhouse.

The clothing of each pauper has been calculated at a halfpenny a day, or threepence-halfpenny a week, so that the food and clothing amount to somewhat under two shillings a week. With the cost of the house, the salaries of officers, and incidental expenses, the maintenance of each pauper may entail on the community an outlay of three shillings weekly, or seven pounds sixteen shillings a year. The expenses have been on the decline for the last few years, in consequence of the decline in the prices of provisions. In some workhouses, also, the cost may differ from others, but these calculations I have given may be taken as a fair average.

I was astonished by the appearance of the potato-kettle at this house. No less than 1,670 pounds of potatoes are boiled at once. This enormous quantity is all divided into portions of three and a half and four pounds, and each portion is enclosed in a small net. All these nets are laid together in a large basket, and this basket, with its nets and potatoes, is deposited in the boiler. When the potatoes are supposed to have been sufficiently boiled, the basket is wound up again by a machinery, constructed for the purpose, and the poor are then marched up in military order, when each receives his net and marches away with it.

In the school, belonging to this house, the Chinese-Russian calculating board, or numerical frame, had already been introduced, but only a fortnight before my arrival.

Most of the people were employed picking oakum, the occupation assigned to the inmates of most of the prisons and workhouses of England, who are thus made to prepare lint for the wounds of the British men of war. This article is indispensable in the dockyards, where it is used for caulking ships. Hundreds of thousands of hands are daily occupied in the workhouses, and houses of correction, in untwining old rope ends for this purpose.

One of the most interesting parts of the establishment is the old clothes store, in which the variegated rags that the paupers bring with them are carefully preserved, to be returned to them on their departure. A pauper, on entering the house, receives in exchange for his motley drapery, the grey uniform of the house, with N.D.U.W.H. (North Dublin Union Work House) embroidered upon it in large letters. His liberty rags, together with hat, stockings, shoes, &c., are first carefully fumigated, and then, having been folded together, are marked with the name of their owner, and deposited in the old clothes store. The pauper may at any time have his discharge, by simply intimating a wish to that effect to the governor, but to allow him to take with him the clothes worn in the workhouse would never do, or many would enter one day and go away again the next, merely for the sake of a new suit of apparel. Their old rags are therefore restored to them, and their ingenuity is again taxed to discover the right entrance to their distorted sleeves. It happens almost every day that among the 2,000 inmates of the house, one or other, weary of discipline and confinement, and longing for his former liberty, gives the governor notice to quit, and demands the restitution of his wardrobe. It so happened that, at the period of my visit, such an application had just been made, and the clothes store was, in consequence, open. All the theatres in Europe could not have matched, in point of variety, the wardrobe here displayed to me. It must cost the poor a painful struggle when they waver between the servile N.D.U.W.H. costume, and the ragged *sans-culotte* drapery of freedom. Most of them prefer the latter, with all the privations that accompany it. [108]

Louisa Twining
Recollections of Life and Work

Louisa Twining (1820–1912) was a granddaughter of Richard Twining, the head of the long-established firm of tea merchants. Her experiences visiting an inmate at the Strand Union's Cleveland Street workhouse led to a lifetime of campaigning to improve conditions for workhouse inmates. Her activities included lectures, books and pamphlets, letters to the press, and the founding in 1858 of the Workhouse Visiting Society. In 1879, she set up the Workhouse Infirmary Nursing Association to promote the use of trained nurses in workhouses. Two years later, she helped finance the Association for Promoting the Return of Women as Poor Law Guardians and herself became one of the first female Guardians at Kensington in 1884:

In 1853 my first visit to a workhouse was made to the Strand Union, then situated in Cleveland Street, containing five hundred inmates, the good old woman whom I had known in Clare Market being the one inmate who attracted me, and had begged me not to forget her; but my acquaintance soon extended to others, and the Master and Matron encouraged me to continue my visits, I saw at once how much good could be done by many more than I could make, and, therefore, applied to the chairman of the board to allow me to take other visitors with me; but when this was, brought forward, they replied that 'unpaid and voluntary efforts were not sanctioned by the Poor Law Board', and the offer was declined. In 1854, as the difficulty seemed to rest with the central board, I determined to ask for an interview, which was granted. The Rt. Hon. Matthew Talbot Baines was president, and Lord Courtenay, secretary. I thought it would be a most alarming interview, and as I drove down to Whitehall, I conjured up all sorts of fears as to the results of my audacious attempt. I suppose these fears were apparent, for, as I entered, the attendant said to me, 'You need not be afraid, ma'am, you will find them very nice gentlemen indeed.' And so it proved, for the president in particular was most agreeable and encouraged conversation. My idea had been that I should meet an array of formidable officials, forming the board, but I saw only these two. Lord Courtenay said that if I could get the sanction of one board to my proposal, they would not refuse permission, which was something gained; and Mr Baines admitted that good might be done by it. It was clear, however, that the Guardians had no intention of granting my request; for on a further application it was again declined. So I continued to go on alone, notwithstanding many hindrances and disagreeables, especially from more than one of the gate porters, who were so rude and insolent that I quite dreaded to encounter them. The climax came when one of these officials was appointed to be Master, when the good homely couple whom I had first known retired; his wife being equally unsuitable, a reign of terror then began which can hardly be

As well as her involvement with workhouse visiting, Louisa Twining also took an interest in pauper schools, the training of workhouse nurses, and the election of women as union guardians.

believed at the present time. The memoirs of Dr Joseph Rogers, who became medical officer during this year, will give further information as to the terrible condition of this workhouse during some following years. I have often thought since then that it was fortunate such an extreme case of mismanagement should have been the one brought to my notice, showing in such strong colours the evils to which the system was exposed by incompetent Guardians and the lowest class of officers, whose deeds of despotism and cruelty were sanctioned or perhaps ignored by those who appointed and upheld them; for they reported, even of such as these – tyrannical, passionate, and ignorant as they were – that 'They kept order and were economical.'

In 1855 I was induced to publish some of my experiences in a small pamphlet, 'A Few Words about the Inmates of our Union Workhouses'. I consulted Mrs Jameson about this, and she advised me to do so, as she had already noticed the subject in her lecture on 'Sisters of Charity', saying, 'Strike while the iron is hot.' The following year I took her to see the Strand Union, as she was preparing her second lecture on the 'Communion of Labour'. She agreed that it was a most depressing sight, more so than any prison, for no effort seemed to be made to do any good or to combat the evil. In 1856 I made acquaintance with another London workhouse, St Giles's, which in some bad respects exceeded even the Strand Union. My visits were to a poor old crossing-sweeper who had sat and swept for years in Bloomsbury Square, and was well known to us. He was in the basement ward, nearly dark, and with a stone floor; beds, sheets, and shirts were all equally grey with dirt. To get in, I had to wait with a crowd at the office door to obtain a ticket, visitors being allowed only for one hour once a week. The sick in the so-called infirmary, a miserable building, long since destroyed, were indeed a sad sight, with their wretched pauper nurses in black caps and workhouse dress. One poor young man there, who had lain on a miserable flock bed for fourteen years with a spine complaint, was blind, and his case would have moved a heart of stone; yet no alleviation of food or comforts were ever granted him, his sole consolation being the visits of a good woman, an inmate, who had been a ratepayer, and attended upon him daily, reading to him to while away the dreary hours.

I must name one more friend in the Strand Union Workhouse who truly valued the Sunday services and reading which I was able to hold there. She was a middle-aged woman, always seated upon a low stool for which there was just room, between two turned-up bedsteads, under a window. She was quite unable to walk from some cause, and I never saw her in any other position. I shall never forget her first greeting to the only visitor she had ever had, and the joyful welcome of the Church Service, which she had not heard for years but knew well, as she used to go to St Paul's Cathedral; she joined in everything, and was able to read the Psalms with me. I can truly say that this was the only ray of light in her dark and dreary life, and she cherished the flowers I took, during the next week. I made her promise to send a message to me if she were to become worse, for I would go to her at any time; but this was not possible, for she died, with short warning, during my absence from home, and when I went the next Sunday her place was vacant. Though she was not 'aged', she was surely one of the 'poor' who are being now considered as deserving of some better fate than the distasteful food and utter want of all comfortable surroundings, which were her portion in that sad abode. Nowhere can such genuine gratitude be shown and given as in a workhouse.[109]

W.H. Wills and Philip Taylor
A Day in a Pauper Palace

In 1850, the magazine *All The Year Round*, which was edited by Charles Dickens, included an account of a visit to the Manchester Union's 'industrial schools' at Swinton. Although not credited, the piece was written by William Henry Wills and Philip Taylor. Despite Dickens being a frequent critic of the Poor Law system, the article found much to praise at Swinton:

At the easy distance of five miles from the great Cotton Capital, on the road to the great Cotton Port, through shady lanes and across verdant meadows, is

the village of Swinton. At its entrance, on a pleasing elevation, stands a building
which is generally mistaken for a wealthy nobleman's residence. The structure
is not only elegant but extensive; it is in the Tudor style of architecture, with a
frontage of four-hundred and fifty feet. It is studded with more than a hundred
windows, each tier so differing in shape and size from the others as to prevent
monotonous uniformity. Two winding flights of steps in the centre lead to a
handsome entrance hall, above which rise two lofty turrets to break the outline
of the extensive roof. The depth of the edifice is great – its whole proportions
massive. Pleasure-gardens and playgrounds surround it. In front an acre and a
half of flower-beds and grass-plots are intersected by broad gravel-walks and
a carriage-drive. Some more of the land is laid out for vegetables. Beyond is
a meadow, and the whole domain is about twenty-two acres in extent; all in
good, some in picturesque, cultivation.

The stranger gazing upon the splendid brick edifice, with its surrounding
territory, is surprised when he is told that it is not the seat of an ancient
Dukedom; but that it is a modern palace for pauper children. He is not surprised
when he hears that it cost £60,000.

Having passed through the entrance hall, we chatted for a time with the
chaplain, -who is at the head of the establishment. From him we learnt that
there are in the institution six hundred and thirty children, of whom three
hundred and five are orphans, and one hundred and twenty-four deserted by
their parents. Besides the chaplain there is a head Master, a medical officer, a
Roman Catholic priest, a governor and Matron, six schoolmasters and four
schoolmistresses, with a numerous staff of subordinate officials, male and female,
including six nurses, and teachers of diverse trades. The salaries and wages of the
various officers and servants amount to about £1,800 a year, exclusive of the
cost of their board which the greater number enjoy also.

We went into the playground of the junior department, where more than
a hundred and fifty children were assembled. Some were enjoying themselves
in the sunshine, some were playing at marbles, others were frisking cheerfully.
These children ranged from four to seven years of age. There are some as young
as a year and a half in the school. The greater number were congregated at one
end of the yard, earnestly watching the proceedings of the Master who was
giving fresh water to three starlings in cages that stood on the ground. One very
young bird was enjoying an airing on the gravel. Two others were perched on a
cask. The Master informed us it was a part of his system to instruct his charges
in kindness to animals by example.

The play-ground is a training school in another particular. On two sides
grew several currant trees, on which the fruit is allowed to ripen without any
protection. Though some of the scholars are very young, there do not occur
above two or three cases of unlawful plucking per annum. The appropriate
punishment of delinquents is for them to sit and see the rest of their school-

fellows enjoy, on a day appointed, a treat of fresh ripe fruit, whilst they are debarred from all participation.

The personal appearance of the pupils was not prepossessing. Close cropping of the hair may be necessary at the first admission of a boy, but surely is not needed after children have been for some time trained in the establishment, in habits of cleanliness. The tailors of the establishment (its elder inmates), are evidently no respecters of persons. Measuring is utterly repudiated, and the style in vogue is the comic or incongruous. The backs of the boys seemed to be Dutch-built; their legs seemed cased after Turkish patterns; white the front view was of Falstaffian proportions, some of the trousers are too short for the legs, and some of the legs too short for the trousers. The girls are better dressed. Amongst them are some of prepossessing faces, intelligent appearance, and pleasing manners. Here and there may be discerned however, vacancy of look, and inaptness to learn. Among the boys, sometimes, occurs a face not quite clean enough, and a shirt collar that seems to have suffered too long a divorce from the wash-tub.

During the time we spent in the playground, sundry chubby urchins came to the Master with small articles which they had found; it being the practice to impress on each that nothing found belongs to the finder unless, after due inquiry, no owner can be discovered. One brought something looking like liquorice; another produced a halfpenny, which the Master appropriated. Perhaps, the Master had dropped the halfpenny to test the honesty of some of his pupils. One little fellow was made happy by permission to keep a marble which he had picked up.

The children obeyed the summons to school with pleasing alacrity. This is owing partly to the agreeable mode of tuition adopted, and in some measure to the fact that the lessons are not allowed to become tedious and oppressive. As soon as any parties give unequivocal signs of weariness, either there is some playful relaxation introduced, or such children are sent into the play-ground. On the present occasion, as soon as the Master applied his mouth to a whistle, away trouped the children in glad groups to an ante-room. Here, arranged in five or six rows, boys and girls intermixed stood with eyes fixed on the Master, awaiting his signals. At the word of command, each alternate row faced to the right, the others to the left, and filed off, accompanying their march with a suitable tune; their young voices blending in cheerful harmony, while they kept time by clapping their hands, and by an occasional enthusiastic stamp of the foot.

The teaching of the juniors is conducted mainly *viva voce*; for the mass of them are under six years of age. The class was opened thus:

'What day is this?'

'Monday.'

'What sort of a day is it?'

'Very fine.'

'Why is it a fine day?'

'Because the sun shines, and it does not rain.'

'Is rain a bad thing, then?'

'No.'

'What is it useful for?'

'To make the flowers and the fruit grow.'

'Who sends rain and sunshine?'

'God.'

'What ought we to do in return for his goodness?'

'Praise him!'

'Let us praise him, then,' added the Master. And the children, all together, repeated and then sung a part of the 149th Psalm. A lesson on morals succeeded, which evidently interested the children. It was partly in the form of a tale told by the Master. A gentleman who was kind to the poor, went to visit in gaol a boy imprisoned for crime. The restraint of the gaol, and the shame of the boy, were so described, as to impress the children with strong interest. Then the boy's crime was traced to disobedience, and the excellence of obedience to teachers and parents was shown. The fact that punishment comes out of, and follows our own actions, was enforced by another little story.

By this time some of the very young children showed symptoms of lassitude. One fat little mortal had fallen asleep; and this class was consequently marshalled for dismissal, and as usual marched out singing, to play for a quarter of an hour.

A lesson in reading was now administered to a class of older children. For facilitating this achievement, generally so difficult, the Master has introduced the phonic system, in some degree according to a mode of his own, by which means even the youngest children make remarkable progress.

The scene the schoolroom, during the reading lesson, presented, was remarkable. Groups of four or five little fellows were gathered in various parts of the room before a reading-card, one acting as monitor; who was sometimes a girl. It was a pleasing sight to see half-a-dozen children seated or kneeling in a circle round the sane book, their heads almost meeting in the centre, in their earnestness to see and hear, while the monitor pointed quickly with the finger to the word which each in succession was to pronounce. All seemed alert, and the eyes of the monitors kindled with intelligence. Meanwhile the Master wan busied in passing from one class to another, listening to the manner in which the pronunciation was caught, or the correctness with which the rapid combination of letters and syllables was made. Sometimes he stayed a few minutes with a class to give aid, then proceeded to another; and occasionally, on finding by a few trials, that a boy was quite familiar with the work of his class, he would remove him to another more advanced. These transfers were frequent.

In an adjoining room were assembled, under the care of the schoolmaster's wife, some of the more advanced scholars. One class in this room was particularly

The Manchester Union School at Swinton in about 1905. The Swinton School was one of the first separate institutions to be set up to house pauper children away from what was often viewed as the 'taint' of the union workhouse.

interesting – a class composed of the monitors who receive extra instruction in order to fit them for their duties.

After an interval the whole attended a class for general knowledge: in this the mutual instruction system was adopted. A pupil stood out on a platform – the observed of all observers – to be questioned and cross-questioned by his or her schoolfellow, like a witness in a difficult law case, until supplanted by a pupil who could answer better. A degree of piquancy was thus imparted to the proceeding, which caused the attention of the pupils not to flag for a moment. One girl, with red hair and bright eyes, weathered a storm of questions bravely. A sample of the queries put by these young inquisitors will show the range of subjects necessary to be known about. What are the months of spring? What animal cuts down a tree, and where does it live? Which are the Cinque Ports? What planet is nearest the sun? What is the distance from Manchester to Lancaster? How high is St Paul's Cathedral? What are the names of the common metals? What causes water to rise and become clouds?

Meanwhile, the education of the elder children was proceeding in other parts of the building. The lessons of the senior sections are conducted in a much quieter manner than those of the junior classes; even in a way which some persons would consider tame and uninteresting. This quietude was, however, more than balanced by another department. As we passed to the elder boys' court-yard, the chaplain threw open the door of a room, where a small music class was practising the fife and the drum. The class consisted of eight youths, who had not learnt long, but performed the 'Troubadour' in creditable style. When they marched out, they headed about two hundred boys, who were drawn up in line; the music-master acting as drill-sergeant and commander-in-chief. After passing through some drill-exercises, they marched off, drums beating and colours flying, to dinner.

We need say no more of this pleasing ceremony than that it was heartily performed. The viands were relished in strong illustration of Dr Johnson's emphatic remark, 'Sir, I like to dine.'

After dinner, we visited the workshops – a very active scene. The living tableaux were formed chiefly by young tailors and cobblers. A strict account is kept of all manufactured articles and of their cost; and we learnt that a boy's suit of fustian (labour included) costs 4s 10½d; a girl's petticoat 12¾d; and that the average weekly cost of clothing worn by the children was estimated at 3½d per head – making 15s 2d for the wearing apparel of each child per year.

In all the industrial sections, the children are occupied alternately at their work and in school – labouring for one afternoon and next morning, and then attending their classes in school for the next afternoon and morning. There is, however, something defective in the Swinton plan, as applicable to advanced pupils; perhaps they are not stimulated sufficiently; but it happens that no pupil-teacher had ever passed a government examination; although last year the grant of money, by the Committee of Privy Council for the educational departments of the Swinton school, amounted to £531. Those among the scholars who have gone into other lines of life, have generally conducted themselves well; and when absorbed into the masses of society, have become a help and a credit instead of a bane to it. Indeed, having been brought up at the Pauper Palace appears a safe certificate with the public, who are eager for the girls of this school as domestic servants. Both boys and girls, on leaving the institution, are furnished with two complete sets of clothes, and their subsequent behaviour is repeatedly inquired into.

The Swinton Institution is a practical illustration of what can be done with even the humblest section of the community; and if it have a disadvantage, that is precisely because it succeeds too well. It places the child-pauper above the child of the industrious. Narrow minds advocate the levelling of the two, by withdrawing the advantage from the former. Let us, however, hope that no effort will relax to bring out, in addition to Pauper Palaces, Educational Palaces for all classes and denominations.[110]

Charles Dickens
Wapping Workhouse

The writer most closely associated with the workhouse is undoubtedly Charles Dickens. Beginning with *Oliver Twist*, which began publication in serialised form in 1837, the workhouse and other aspects of the Poor Law system regularly featured in both Dickens' fiction and journalism, and in other articles he commissioned for the two magazines he later edited, *Household Words* (1850–1859) and *All The Year Round* (1858–1870).

'Wapping Workhouse', first published in February 1860 in *All The Year Round*, was one of a series of literary sketches from Dickens' own pen, subsequently collected together under the title of *The Uncommercial Traveller*. Despite being infused with his characteristic larger-than-life style, the piece was based on a recent visit the author had paid to the workhouse at Wapping after reading a Thames Police Court Magistrate's severe criticisms of the establishment in *The Times*.[1]

Dickens' tour of the institution, which housed only female paupers, began in the 'foul wards' where those suffering from venereal conditions were housed:

I made bold to ring at the workhouse gate, where I was wholly unexpected and quite unknown.

A very bright and nimble little Matron, with a bunch of keys in her hand, responded to my request to see the House. I began to doubt whether the police magistrate was quite right in his facts, when I noticed her quick, active little figure and her intelligent eyes.

The Traveller (the Matron intimated) should see the worst first. He was welcome to see everything. Such as it was, there it all was.

This was the only preparation for our entering 'the Foul wards'. They were in an old building squeezed away in a corner of a paved yard, quite detached from the more modern and spacious main body of the workhouse. They were in a building most monstrously behind the time – a mere series of garrets or lofts, with every inconvenient and objectionable circumstance in their construction, and only accessible by steep and narrow staircases, infamously ill-adapted for the passage up-stairs of the sick or down-stairs of the dead.

A-bed in these miserable rooms, here on bedsteads, there (for a change, as I understood it) on the floor, were women in every stage of distress and disease. None but those who have attentively observed such scenes can conceive the extraordinary variety of expression still latent under the general monotony and uniformity of colour, attitude, and condition. The form a little coiled up and turned away, as though it had turned its back on this world for ever; the uninterested face at once lead-coloured and yellow, looking passively upward from the pillow; the haggard mouth a little dropped, the hand outside the coverlet, so dull and indifferent, so light, and yet so heavy; these were on every pallet; but when I stopped beside a bed, and said ever so slight a word to the figure lying there, the ghost of the old character came into the face, and made the Foul ward as various as the fair world. No one appeared to care to live, but no one complained; all who could speak said that as much was done for them as could be done there, that the attendance was kind and patient, that their suffering was very heavy, but they had nothing to ask for. The wretched rooms were as clean and sweet as it is possible for such rooms to be; they would become a pest-house in a single week, if they were ill-kept.

I accompanied the brisk Matron up another barbarous staircase, into a better kind of loft devoted to the idiotic and imbecile. There was at least light in it, whereas the windows in the former wards had been like sides of schoolboys' bird-cages. There was a strong grating over the fire here, and, holding a kind of state on either side of the hearth, separated by the breadth of this grating, were two old ladies in a condition of feeble dignity, which was surely the very last and lowest reduction of self-complacency to be found in this wonderful humanity of ours. They were evidently jealous of each other, and passed their whole time (as some people do, whose fires are not grated) in mentally disparaging each other, and contemptuously watching their neighbours. One of these parodies on provincial gentlewomen was extremely talkative, and expressed a strong desire to attend the service on Sundays, from which she represented herself to have derived the greatest interest and consolation when allowed that privilege. She gossiped so well, and looked altogether so cheery and harmless, that I began to think this a case for the Eastern magistrate, until I found that on the last occasion of her attending chapel she had secreted a small stick, and had caused some confusion in the responses by suddenly producing it and belabouring the congregation.

So, these two old ladies, separated by the breadth of the grating – otherwise they would fly at one another's caps – sat all day long, suspecting one another, and contemplating a world of fits. For everybody else in the room had fits, except the wards-woman; an elderly, able-bodied pauperess, with a large upper lip, and an air of repressing and saving her strength, as she stood with her hands folded before her, and her eyes slowly rolling, biding her time for catching or holding somebody. This civil personage (in whom I regretted to identify a reduced member of my honourable friend Mrs Gamp's family) said, 'They has 'em continiwal, sir. They drops without no more notice than if they was coach-horses dropped from the moon, sir. And when one drops, another drops, and sometimes there'll be as many as four or five on 'em at once, dear me, a rolling and a tearin', bless you! – this young woman, now, has 'em dreadful bad.'

She turned up this young woman's face with her hand as she said it. This young woman was seated on the floor, pondering in the foreground of the afflicted. There was nothing repellent either in her face or head. Many, apparently worse, varieties of epilepsy and hysteria were about her, but she was said to be the worst here. When I had spoken to her a little, she still sat with her face turned up, pondering, and a gleam of the mid-day sun shone in upon her.

Whether this young woman, and the rest of these so sorely troubled, as they sit or lie pondering in their confused dull way, ever get mental glimpses among the motes in the sunlight, of healthy people and healthy things? Whether this young woman, brooding like this in the summer season, ever thinks that somewhere there are trees and flowers, even mountains and the great sea? Whether, not to go so far, this young woman ever has any dim revelation of that young woman – that young woman who is not here and never will come here; who is courted, and caressed, and loved, and has a husband, and bears children, and lives in a home, and who never knows what it is to have this lashing and tearing coming upon her? And whether this young woman, God help her, gives herself up then and drops like a coach-horse from the moon?

I hardly knew whether the voices of infant children, penetrating into so hopeless a place, made a sound that was pleasant or painful to me. It was something to be reminded that the weary world was not all aweary, and was ever renewing itself; but, this young woman was a child not long ago, and a child not long hence might be such as she. Howbeit, the active step and eye of the vigilant Matron conducted me past the two provincial gentlewomen (whose dignity was ruffled by the children), and into the adjacent nursery.

There were many babies here, and more than one handsome young mother. There were ugly young mothers also, and sullen young mothers, and callous young mothers. But, the babies had not appropriated to themselves any bad expression yet, and might have been, for anything that appeared to the contrary in their soft faces, Princes Imperial, and Princesses Royal. I had the pleasure of giving a poetical commission to the baker's man to make a cake with all despatch and toss it into the oven for one red-headed young pauper and myself, and felt much the better for it. Without that refreshment, I doubt if I should have been in a condition for 'the Refractories', towards whom my quick little Matron – for whose adaptation to her office I had by this time conceived a genuine respect – drew me next, and marshalled me the way that I was going.

The Refractories[112] were picking oakum, in a small room giving on a yard. They sat in line on a form, with their backs to a window; before them, a table, and their work. The oldest Refractory was, say twenty; youngest Refractory, say sixteen. I have never yet ascertained in the course of my uncommercial travels, why a Refractory habit should affect the tonsils and uvula; but, I have always observed that Refractories of both sexes and every grade, between a Ragged School and the Old Bailey, have one voice, in which the tonsils and uvula gain a diseased ascendency.

'Five pound indeed! I hain't a going fur to pick five pound,' said the Chief of the Refractories, keeping time to herself with her head and chin. 'More than enough to pick what we picks now, in sich a place as this, and on wot we gets here!'

'A pretty 'ouse this is, Matron, ain't it?' said Refractory Two, 'where a pleeseman's called in, if a gal says a word!'

'And when you're sent to prison for nothink or less!' said the Chief, tugging at her oakum as if it were the Matron's hair. 'But any place is better than this; that's one thing, and be thankful!'[113]

<hr />

Anonymous
London Pauper Burials

The fear of a pauper burial – in an unmarked mass grave – was one that drove many of the elderly poor to try and survive outside the workhouse, no matter how great their state of misery. The terror of the pauper's grave was explored in an 1878 article following the inquest of an elderly man who had died after a period of barely surviving on parish relief in preference to entering the workhouse. The judge had commented that this was tantamount to the heinous crime of suicide and that such a person would be consigned to an 'ignominious grave'. The deceased's widow, on learning that such an interment would be in a single grave, perhaps with an elm coffin, was however delighted that her husband might receive such treatment compared to dying as a workhouse inmate.

The widow herself subsequently entered a workhouse, where she was visited by the article's author:

SIGHS FROM A LONDON WORKHOUSE
I took advantage of my three or four visits to the workhouse in question to 'sound' a few of the aged inmates concerning the delicate question on which my old woman held such extreme views, and I am bound to say that her prejudice against pauper burial could hardly be called exceptional. One or two there were amongst the men with whom I gossiped on the subject who affected to treat it as one that was not worthwhile wasting a thought on, and who recklessly declared that they didn't care a button what became of their bodies when they had no further use for them; but it almost invariably happened that those who so expressed themselves were fellows in robust health, and not so old but that they might, with good luck, by and by get out of the 'house', and become eligible for the good offices of the paid undertaker. Others there were who professed not to care very much 'how it went'; but these were generally found to be men who had friends or relatives 'outside', and who clung desperately to the hope that 'for their own sake' they would avoid the disgrace of having it said that their father, or their uncle, or their poor old brother, was buried 'with his

name chalked on his coffin-lid'. As one aged gentleman put it, 'A man does not like the idea of being wrongly described even to his coffin, and he is very likely to be here, I do assure you, sir. It is a dreadfully ignorant man they have got to look after the coffins now. The shameful mistakes he makes ought to be brought before the Board. I've seen 'im with my own eyes, so I know. Why, it ain't a long while since when there was quite a respectable old gentleman died broken-hearted here after a stay of six weeks. His name was Job Manistre. Well, sir, you'd hardly believe it, when the coffins were being brought out ready to be carried to the cemetery, there was wrote on his coffin-lid "Joe Banister", with no more respect for the poor man than though he had been part of an old staircase.'

But it was those who had outlived or been discarded by relatives and children, and who in their extreme age and abject poverty were without a friend in the world, who seemed to take most sorely to heart the inevitable end. Over and over again, and in almost the same words, did I hear the objections of the starved old man's widow repeated, 'It isn't that living here is so bad; it is the thought of dying here, and being buried as they bury 'em all.'

I found that the yearning after an 'el-lum' [elm] coffin was universal; but this is an extreme of fastidiousness that cannot be entertained. The ordinary parish coffin is shaped out of pine-wood of decent substance, and made sombre by a coating of lamp-black. I was given to understand, however, that it was the actual burial – the way in which deceased paupers were consigned to mother earth – that made the subject such a sad one to reflect on. There was no other way of satisfying myself on this score than by being present at some burying-place when the last funeral rites were being performed under poor-law auspices. This might be easily accomplished, and it ought to be taken for granted that the melancholy business as transacted at one cemetery was pretty much what it would be found at another.

On the northern road, in which direction lie the united cemeteries of St Pancras and St Mary's Islington, I had frequently observed on certain days of the week an odd-looking black carriage of the composite order. A respectable vehicle enough, and drawn by a pair of stout handsome horses. That it was a mourning-coach I was of course aware; that it was a hearse as well was evident from the fact that the great square space in front, and above which the driver sat, was not unfrequently so very full of coffins, little and big, that the overhanging hammercloth revealed bluntly the shape of the ends of the boxes in which the mortal remains were deposited; but I did not discover that it was a parochial conveyance until one morning, while out walking Highgateward, I espied the black coach in question at a roadside inn, with the horses partaking of necessary refreshment from their nose-bags. The compartment in which the coffins are bestowed was empty; the coach portion in which mourners were bestowed was tenantless. Curiosity led me to step into the tavern to discover what had become of the bluff coachman, with his ruddy visage and his blacktop-boots,

An illustration depicting philanthropist Lord Shaftesbury as a youth and being moved by the sight of a pauper funeral while he was resident at Harrow School in about 1816.

I had so often seen urging his sable team at a brisk trot towards the cemetery. I found the individual in question at the bar partaking of a pint of ale, and in a kind of tap-room near at hand, there were the mourners. I regret to relate, however, that although the coachman was in a position to regale on bread-and-cheese and ale, his unlucky 'passengers' were by their poverty denied the poorest refreshment the tavern professed to supply.

I ascertained that the next batch of paupers would be brought down for burial on the following Tuesday, and that it was due at the cemetery about ten o'clock. It was a bitterly cold morning, snow was on the ground to a depth of half a foot, and the roadway and the hedges were sparkling with hoar frost. Being at the cemetery in good time, I made my way to the place of parochial sepulture to see what preparation had been made. There can be no question that a parish grave of modern construction is not an affair the contemplation of which is calculated to favourably impress a person inevitably doomed thereto. It may not unreasonably be urged that burial-ground is precious – worth more per foot perhaps as regards many of our fashionable cemeteries than the precious earth at London's heart's core on which they build banks and insurance offices. But this does not alter the fact that the parish pit-hole is an ugly thing to see, especially when the mounds of raw clay thrown up from the chasm are covered with snow, and the ironbound boards that temporarily cover the great hole are so thickly coated with the white of frost that the sparrows who have been hopping there have left the imprint of their busy feet. The way it is managed seems to be to bury a dozen paupers, more or less, in one grave, and after it is filled in to raise one gigantic mound of clay above the spot. Only the clay, however. In a line with the newly dug trenches were many of these small hills; but though they were overgrown with rank weeds and grass it was evident that no verdant mantle of green turf had been spared for any one of them – no stone, no flowers; nothing but an iron ticket of the size and shape of a working man's shoe-sole, and with a letter and a number on it to denote, I suppose, when the short lease of the land granted to its occupiers would expire, so that new tenants might come in. I lingered at the frosty spot until the parish hearse arrived, and the bodies, having been first carried into the church, were decently lifted out by the grave-diggers There were not so many mourners that day – not so many as there were coffins, if my counting was correct; but three of them were women, and as they stood there in a melancholy row while the blackened boxes were being lowered, it seemed easier to be sorry for those who were going back to the 'house', taking with them this grim haunting of what, after all, the end must be, than for those who, though consigned to the humblest of beds, were happily out of the world and its worries.

But I cannot help repeating that since it could be done so cheaply something might be done to make the pauper's grave a little more like that of other folks. It seemed to me that the poor workhouse mourners, as they looked around them from the frosty mound that edged the black hole, thought so too. They are only graves of the poorest class that are to be found in the vicinity of the patch hired by the Poor-law Board, but there was scarcely one that was not adorned by some token of affection – crosses, vases, pictures, and images under glass shades, with bright bunches and bouquets of everlasting dyed grass and flowers.

'In God's acre, i.e. the churchyard, pride has no place,' is a favourite theme with moralists and pulpit preachers. But come to regard the matter practically, and it is soon discovered that there is a deal of fudge in this kind of holding forth – from a worldly point of view, that is to say. No social distinctions in a place of public burial! Ask any undertaker what he has to say on this head. Why, he has as many 'classes' on his funeral price-list as the draper has in his silk department. There is the 'extra superfine', the 'superfine', the 'very good', the 'ordinary', and the 'common'. The undertaker has the greatest contempt for the 'common', as indeed have the cemetery authorities. Commercially speaking, they don't pay house-room. It has been my experience to be assured of this from the lips of a cemetery functionary with whom I had sad dealing.

'You see,' he explained, 'the site you have chosen will in a short time be much improved, and consequently will increase in value.'

'How improved?' I asked him.

'Well, you see, sir, it is in the plan of the cemetery to have a broad path from where we stand straight to the church-door.'

'But,' said I, pointing towards a long array of recently made mounds, 'what as to those?'

'Those?' he repeated, as though not catching my meaning; and then it suddenly struck him, and he replied, with a shrug of his shoulders, 'Those are merely common interments, sir; they don't interfere with the ultimate plan in the least.'

From which I could draw but one inference, namely, that when the time for the path was come nothing would be easier than to shovel off the mounds, run the heavy roller over the ground, and make all ready for the gravel.[114]

R.J. Pye-Smith
The Sheffield Union Workhouse

In 1896, the Sheffield workhouse at Fir Vale was visited by Mr Rutherford Pye-Smith, Emeritus Professor of Surgery at Sheffield University, and consultant at the city's Royal Hospital. While in the workhouse kitchen he was rash enough to sample the institution's dinner for the day, something which he was soon to regret:

It was a bright morning, and the beautiful situation of the establishment, and its long avenues of poplars, bright with nasturtium borders, and the well-timbered wood beyond, were quite refreshing. A few men were at work, wheeling earth, in the field, where were also a crop of oats and large quantities of vegetables. But then the 'Great House!', a block of buildings close on a quarter of a mile long, with isolated blocks springing up all over the estate. Some of these are the 'Cottage Homes', large houses one might call them, but cottages, indeed, compared with this great pauper palace. The date on the foundation stone is September, 1878, and the house has been in use for 15 or 16 years. It has accommodation for 1,748 inmates.

On asking to see the Master, I found that he was away, but the Matron very kindly offered to take me over the institution. In a bright-looking grass-yard a few old women were walking about, their ugly uniform spoiling what might otherwise have been a pleasant picture. The first room we entered was the sewing room, where some 60 or more old women were busily engaged making the same ugly garments that they are forced to wear. Passing through one of the day-rooms, where a few books seemed to be the only source of recreation, we came to the Nursery, where in their quaint little cage-like cradles, infants were being attended by infirm old women. How unlike the bright young nursemaids one sees in ordinary life! We have recently been told why the babies are considerately removed from such influences when they arrive at three years of age! The poor little mites have only a dreary asphalted yard to take their out-door exercise in.

The next was, indeed, a dismal room, but happily it was empty. It is for able-bodied women who misconduct themselves in the house, or who are constantly returning after their discharge. On an average there are half-a-dozen here every day. They sit here, with no outlook through the windows, and pick two pounds of unbeaten oakum a day. The work makes their fingers sore at first, but not to the extent of blistering them.

We then passed through several dormitories, on the doors of which is marked the cubic space of each room, and the number of occupants. About 440 cubic feet of air per person seems to be generally allowed. It is none too much, though well over the minimum allowed by the Local Government Board.

I was glad to find that the pauper wards-women have no authority over the inmates, their duties being cleaning only. The doors of the dormitories are locked from outside at night, and, indeed, locked doors during the day time seem almost universal throughout the building, but, inside a glass case, which can be broken in case of fire or other need, a key hangs near the door in almost every room.

The next department seen was the laundry, where about 20,000 articles are washed every week! A dozen women, out-workers, get 1s 6d a day and their three meals for working here. Besides these, about 30 of the able-bodied inmates assist the two paid laundry women. In other parts of the house out-workers receive 1s 3d a day and their meals for scrubbing. These are women without children. The extra 3d a day earned by the women in the laundry is for the support of their children! There is apparently plenty of work in the house to occupy all the able-bodied women. It is with the able-bodied men, in times of bad trade, and when most outside work is stopped by frost, that the Guardians seem to experience the greatest difficulty.

After a glance at the dining hall, we went to the kitchen, and I was invited to taste the dinner of the day, which happened to be soup. I was rash enough to take a breakfast cupful, with a piece of their excellent bread, and I paid the penalty of a severe attack of indigestion. A professional cook and five bakers are employed here, and have half-a-dozen inmates to assist them. Black beetles are a great nuisance, and occasionally get into the food, but vigorous steps are being taken to decimate them.

In the stores I saw specimens of the milk, which is tested daily, and is on the whole very satisfactory, 145 gallons are consumed every day! It might be well to have the margarine and other provisions analysed occasionally. Large quantities of clothing were seen in another part of the stores. Exactly the same articles of underclothing are given to every inmate according to sex and age – an arrangement I have known to act harshly and injuriously in individual instances.

The Lunatic Asylum was next visited. Both male and female day rooms are provided with a piano, which, when a good performer is obtainable, must

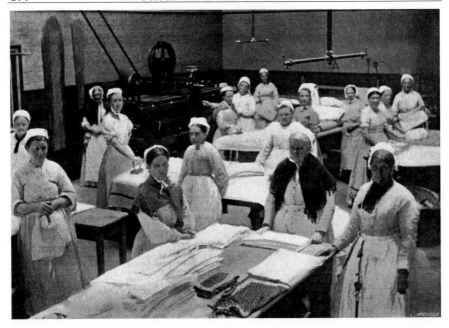

The workhouse laundry at Mitcham in 1896. The number of items of clothing and bedding washed and ironed each week in a large establishment could run into tens of thousands.

exercise a most beneficial influence. In the male ward, a poor old scripture reader was pathetically singing hymns to the tune of 'Auld Lang Syne'! The hospital wards are, most of them, very bright, the decoration of the walls and the fine show of flowers giving an aspect of cheerfulness which forms a pleasing contrast to the rest of the institution. Previous to the introduction of trained nursing, six years ago, the nursing, I was told, was done by a staff of seven untrained women. Now, there are as many as 36 nurses. Much of their time is, however, occupied in attending to the bed-linen and clothing of the patients.

Passing through the dispensary and operation room, we were shown the manufacture of aerated waters, which, by means of a machine lately purchased, are supplied to the hospital and other parts of the institution at a surprisingly cheap and rapid rate.

The married people's quarters were not on view, in consequence of classification alterations. There are at present four such couples in the institution, but provision is being made for nine old couples near the old site, and for about 20 more at Goddard Hall. They are to have a day-room and a bath-room to every nine persons.

Taking leave of the Matron, who had so courteously devoted three or four hours to showing me over the main building, and finding that I should not have time to visit the Children's Homes, I was now conducted to the casuals' quarters.

The Tramp Master has two paid assistants under him. The porter's wife looks after the women and children. The numbers of late have considerably exceeded 6,000 a year, giving a weekly average of 120. No stone-breaking has been done here for the last three months, the Corporation not requiring it; 13 cwt of granite is the quantity given for a day's task. The casuals present at the time of my visit were all engaged in cutting wood. I was told that, perhaps, three-quarters of the casuals are chronic tramps, and that drink is the main cause of their falling out of the ranks of honest labour, into which their very appearance must make it well nigh impossible for them ever again to enter.[115]

Anonymous
A Phonograph at the Haslingden Workhouse

The description of a visit to a union workhouse was occasionally the subject of a 'human interest' feature in a local newspaper. Such articles were invariably complimentary, often commenting on the concern demonstrated by the staff for their charges, the cleanliness of the premises and inmates, the happy faces of the children, and the colourful old 'characters' encountered by their visitor. Nonetheless, interesting detail of the institution and its inmates is also often included. The Haslingden Union workhouse in East Lancashire was the subject of an 1898 report in which the then novel invention of the phonograph played a prominent part:

When visiting [the workhouse] last week the afternoon was fine, but very much overcast, and the inmates received quite an unexpected and to them marvellous treat. Mr John Duckworth, one of the now Accrington Guardians, and his wife, and Mr and Mrs Fawbert, also of Accrington, were on a tour of inspection. Mr Duckworth had brought with him his phonograph, and I attached myself to him to see how the inmates received an entertainment from Edison's wonderful invention. It was Mr Duckworth's idea to give an entertainment in every room, but I suggested the advisability of trying the instrument in the dining room so that if acted the inmates in bulk, young and old, could have the entertainment after tea, or supper, as they call it, which is served at a quarter to six. We went into the room to try the experiment, and placed the phonograph on the harmonium. There were two old men in the room, one placing the bread, another who seemed to be deafish, doing ditto with spoons and knives. On Mr Duckworth starting the machine the man with the bread, who was about the middle of the room, stopped short, with astonishment, and seemed for a moment literally transfixed with the slice of bread in his hand. As the song proceeded I went towards him, and was astonished to find that the phonograph

Haslingden's imposing union workhouse at Higher Pikelaw, on the west side of the Rossendale valley, stood a lofty 900ft above sea level.

was heard to better advantage than I had ever heard the instrument in any other place. The sound was even better at the far end of the room, and Mr Duckworth was greatly pleased. I asked the old man what he thought of it, and he replied, 'Do you want to mek all the lunies leet?' (Do you want to make all the lunatics light in their heads?) Jack and I laughed, and the old man asked whose invention is was. When he was told Edison, the American, he remarked that those Americans were wonderfully sharp fellows. This old man said he had been in the house seven years, as he was unable longer to work in a cotton mill.

More than pleased with the experiment the instrument was conveyed to the old women's room which overlooks the front grounds, and is well lighted, with numerous windows, each containing flowering plants or shrubs, grown in the workhouse greenhouses. As you enter here you cannot fail to be struck with the neatness of everything. The floors are as well scrubbed as a kitchen table top; the twelve cots are neatly tucked up, with a blue coverlet on the top with the name of the Haslingden Union and year thrown up in white. There were eleven old women here, and as the little instrument was carried into the room and placed on a table near the fireplace, curiosity was aroused. Some wanted to know if it was a new-fangled clock, and when the funnel came to view, they said it was suggestive of beer brewing, and spiced ale at Xmas time. When the funnel was fixed on the phonograph, one said it was a coffee mill. A band selection happened to be on the roller, and the sensation it caused the old people is not likely to be soon forgotten by those who witnessed it. The old lady, who was darning stockings in the other corner of the room, put them down, and the eleven old women in the adjoining room also came trouping in to learn where the music was coming from. One was reading, but dropped her book. How they all smiled and laughed and wondered. Some even said they could dance to it. Next came a comic song; and then a song with a chorus 'Waste not, want not', seemed to please immensely. One old lady, pointed out to me as the oldest in the room, and who had been sitting on her chair, and chuckling right merrily to herself, now rose and examined the 'thing', as they called it, and pronounced it wonderful. Another old lady pulled off her white cap and bent her ear over the trumpet to catch every sound. The old woman comes from Accrington, and is 86, and the youngest in this room was 64. If this group could only have been photographed in the positions they assumed the photo would have been worth treasuring. 'Nothing too good for the Irish' brought a clapping of hands by an Irish woman, and 'Shure it's moighty wonderful.' These old women seemed quite content, and looked very neat in their striped gowns, which were not all of one pattern, white caps, and grey woollen shoulder shawls.

The instrument was introduced to the inmates in the general dining room immediately after tea. The phonograph was placed on the pulpit, and the wonder, the laughing of the old and young as George Emms's comic song, 'I'm a funny little man' broke on their ears, and the clapping of hands of the boys and girls, showed what a success the 'marvel' was going to be with them. Mr Duckworth changed about a dozen tunes, and then having two new cylinders there was a roar as John Henry, a very comic-looking lad, was called to sing

Although workhouses are often depicted as cheerless places, the inmates occasionally enjoyed concerts or other entertainments. This 1901 illustration shows the National Sunday League at London's City Road workhouse. Some of the audience (and band) appear less than attentive.

into the trumpet. He sang most comically the song 'One more polka', and then a little girl piped in a clear soprano voice a song about 'Gathering shells on the seashore'. A whistler was asked for but none was forthcoming, and then 'John Henry' was in requisition again. A sheet of music was handed to him, which he rolled up for a trumpet and performed a singular melody which they called 'Ding-dong'. His singing was so funny that he was asked to repeat it, with his usual accompaniment of a few steps. The lad bends both knees together, and throws out his legs as if skating, and dances his steps on the edge of his clogs. A whistler was now forthcoming in a boy named Forrest, who whistled 'I'll stick to the ship lad' very nicely. When Mr Duckworth reproduced these songs the joy of the inmates was very great and they applauded heartily, evidently convinced that there were 'no boggarts or witches of Pendle', as one old woman remarked. Mr Brown [the workhouse Master] briefly and plainly explained how the sounds of the lads and lasses' voices produced impressions on the wax cylinder so fine that he could not see them, and then when the instrument was set going it reproduced the tones of the voice. He expressed his own gratification and those of the nurses and inmates for what had been to them all a marvellous treat, and his call on them to give three hearty cheers for Mr Duckworth was responded to with huzzahs, which showed that they were very heartfelt and came from good lungs.[116]

REFERENCES AND NOTES

Abbreviations:

LMA – London Metropolitan Archives

BPP – British Parliamentary Papers

1 e.g. Longmate, N., 1974, *The Workhouse*; Crowther, M.A., 1981, *The Workhouse System*.

2 e.g. Brundage, A., 1978, *The Making of the New Poor Law 1832–39*; Gray, P., 2009, *The Making of the Irish Poor Law 1815–1843*.

3 e.g. Digby, A., 1978, *Pauper Palaces*; Green, D.R., 2010, *Pauper Capital*.

4 e.g. Morrison, K., 1999, *The Workhouse*; Higginbotham, P., 2008, *The Workhouse Cookbook*.

5 Anonymous, 1653, *Poor Out-Cast Children's Song and Cry*.

6 Strype, J., 1720, *A Survey of the Cities of London and Westminster*, Vol. 1, p.19.9

7 A rough woollen cloth, reddish-brown in colour.

8 *Ibid.*, pp.201–202.

9 The settlement laws determined the parish to which a person legally 'belonged' and from which they were thus able to claim poor relief.

10 LMA MS11280C St Dionis Backchurch, papers relating to a Poor Law appeal from Paul Patrick Kearney, 1771, No.1.

11 *Ibid.*, No.3.

12 *Ibid.*

13 Candler, A., 1803, *Poetical Efforts*, pp.2–3.

14 Dame schools, usually run by a lone woman, took in children from poor families who paid a small weekly fee. The schools were little more than child-minding establishments, with only the most rudimentary education being provided.

15 A 'muffin' was a small plate made on a mould. The 'runner' carried freshly made plates, still on their moulds, from the maker into a drying oven.

16 Shaw's memoirs first appeared as a series of anonymous articles in the *Staffordshire Sentinel* in 1892–93.

17 Shaw, C., 1903, *When I Was a Child*, pp.96–114.

18 Withers, J.R., 1854, *Poems Upon Various Subjects*, Vol. 1, pp.140–142.

19 National Archives, MH 12/14019/195, Folios 285–289. (Spelling and punctuation as in original.)

20 *Ibid.*, Folios 294–296.

21 Mayhew, H., Labour and the Poor. Letter LXII, *Morning Chronicle*, 25 July 1850, p.5.

22 Oakum picking was a common labour task given to workhouse inmates. It involved teasing apart the fibres of old ropes.

23 Stanley, H.M. (ed. Stanley D.), 1909, *The Autobiography of Sir Henry Morton Stanley*, pp.10–11.

24 *Ibid.*, pp.32–33.

25 *Evening Standard*, 16 February 1865.

26 BPP 1866, *Reports on Vagrancy Made to the President of the Poor Law Board by Poor Law Inspectors*, pp.62–67.

27 BPP 1874, *Third Annual Report of the Local Government Board 1873 74*, pp.249–255.

28 *Law Times*, Vol. 80, p.340.

29 A union official who assessed poor relief applicants and what relief they should be offered.

30 Anonymous [Rutherford, J.], 1885, *Indoor Paupers*, pp.13–14.

31 Rutherford's rather over-embroidered description of the departed wife is an occasional example where the veracity of his writing seems questionable.

32 *Ibid.*, pp.16–23.

33 *Ibid.*, pp.49–53.

34 *Ibid.*, pp.53–55.

35 *Ibid.*, pp.32–38.

36 John Sims Reeves (1821–1900) was the foremost tenor vocalist of the mid-Victorian period, noted for his performances of ballads as well as the operatic and oratorio repertoire.

37 John Braham (1774–1856) was a noted English tenor, best known for his stirring renditions of songs such as 'The Death of Nelson'.

38 *Ibid.*, pp.61–67.

39 *Ibid.*, pp.24–29.

40 *Ibid.*, pp. 67–73.

41 Chaplin, C., 1979, *My Early Years*, p.19. Chaplin actually returned to the Newington Workhouse rather than Lambeth.

42 *Ibid.*, pp.20–21.

43 *Ibid.*, pp.22–23.

44 From 1904, to prevent stigma in later life, birth certificates of children born in workhouse infirmaries disguised the place of birth by giving a euphemistic street address such as 'North View, High Street'.

45 Transcribed from a conversation with the author recorded in January 2005.

46 Aronovitch, B., 1974, *Give It Time*, pp.63–67.

47 Workhouse institutions could punish miscreants by a spell of solitary confinement in a 'refractory cell' which might be located in a cellar.

48 Transcribed from a conversation with the author recorded in July 2005.

49 From 1601, parishes had between two and four overseers, appointed annually and without salary.

50 Gilbert's Act of 1782 allowed groups of parishes to administer poor relief jointly and to share a workhouse.

51 Local Acts of Parliament allowed a parish or town to adopt special local legislation. The procedure for obtaining a local Act was expensive, however.

52 Becher, J.T., 1834, *The Anti-Pauper System* (2nd edition), pp.8–19.

53 Gear, G. (ed.), 2010 *The Diary of Benjamin Woodcock Master of the Barnet Union Workhouse 1836–1838.*

54 The so-called 'body-snatchers' who stole corpses to sell to medical training schools.

55 In the year of the *Diary*'s publication, a change in regulations permitted elderly couples to request a shared room. Relatively little accommodation of the type was ever provided, with Boards of Guardians arguing – apparently with some justification – that elderly couples often preferred to be separated.

56 Houses of Correction, originally set up to punish those who infringed the Poor Laws, had by the 1840s often become common gaols housing a variety of petty offenders.

57 Cousins, D.L., 1847, *Extracts from the Diary of a Workhouse Chaplain*, pp.5–23.

58 A valley to the south of Jerusalem where, in biblical times, children were sacrificed by fire to the god Moloch. Gehenna thus became a synonym for 'hell'.

59 In December 1831, 'London Burkers' John Bishop and Thomas Williams were hanged for the murder of the 'Italian Boy' – their victim actually hailed from Lincolnshire.

60 Rogers, M.D., 1889, *Reminiscences of a Workhouse Medical Officer*, pp.3–22.

61 Workhouse reformer Louisa Twining.

62 Bailward, W.A., 1899, *Poor Law Conferences Held in the Year 1898 99*, pp.508–530.

63 Haw, G., 1907, *From Workhouse to Westminster – the Life Story of Will Crooks M.P.*, p.11.

64 BPP 1906, *Transcript of shorthand notes taken at the public inquiry held by J.S. Davy, C.B., Chief General Inspector of the Local Government Board, into the general conditions of the Poplar Union, its pauperism, and the administration of the Guardians and their officers*, p. 317.

65 Wells-Gardner, M.J., 1959, 'Ring in the Old' – *Growing up in the Lexden and Winstree Workhouse* (unpublished typescript held at Essex Record Office, reference T/Z 219/1).

66 Ira Sankey and Dwight Moody were American evangelists and publishers of collections of Christian hymns. They visited Britain several times in the 1870s and 1880s.

67 Anonymous [but probably by E.V. Jones], 1985, 'Before It's Forgotten – Workhouse Days Remembered', *The Carmarthenshire Historian*, Vol. 15, pp. 81–86. (Also online at http://carmarthenshirehistorian.org/cgi-bin/twiki/view/Historian/BeforeItsForgottenVol15.)

68 A pudding usually made by boiling up milk and flour.

69 Christmas Day, Easter Sunday, and Pentecost (Whit Sunday).

70 Anonymous, 1725, *An Account of Several Work-houses for Employing and Maintaining the Poor*, pp.51–52.

71 The 1697 Poor Act required poor relief recipients to wear a badge on their shoulder bearing the initial letter of their parish followed by the letter 'P', e.g. 'AP' for Ampthill Parish. Badging was abolished in 1810.

72 Eden, Sir F.M., 1797, *The State of the Poor*, Vol. II, pp.570–572.

73 *Ibid.*, Vol. III, pp.900–901.

74 BPP 1834, *Report of Royal Commission on the Poor Laws*, Appendix A, Part III, pp.114–115.

75 BPP 1835, *First Annual Report of the Poor Law Commissioners*, pp.108–109.

76 BPP 1846, *Report from the Select Committee on Andover Union*, pp.1336–1337.

77 Until 1867, the 1834 Poor Law Amendment Act did not apply to parishes which prior to 1834 had obtained special local parliamentary Acts covering their administration of poor relief.

78 'Clerkenwell Infirmary', *The Lancet*, 9 September 1865.

79 BPP 1867, *Poor Law (Workhouse Inspection)*, pp.390–391.

80 *Ibid.*, pp.346–347.

81 *Ibid.*, pp.380–381.

82 *Ibid.*, p.382.

83 'Haverfordwest, South Wales', *British Medical Journal*, 30 June 1894, pp.1422–1423.

84 BPP 1839, *Fifth Annual Report of the Poor Law Commissioners*, p.35.

85 'Cootehill Union, Co. Cavan', *British Medical Journal*, 12 October 1895, pp.923–925.

86 BPP 1910, *Royal Commission on the Poor Laws and Relief of Distress*, Appendix vol. XXVIII, pp.44–47.

87 *Ibid.*, pp.133–135.

88 *Ibid.*, p.287.

89 *Ibid.*, p.251.

90 Henry Fowler, President of the Local Government Board 1892–94.

91 Preston-Thomas, H., 1909, *The Work and Play of a Government Inspector*, pp.223–233.

92 *Ibid.*, pp.238–239.

93 Wallace-Goodbody, F.G., 1883, 'The Tramp's Haven', *Gentleman's Magazine*, Vol. 254, pp.176–192.

94 Craven, C.W., 1887, 'A Night in the Workhouse', *The Keighley Series of Poems, Tales and Sketches, No. 1*.

95 Sherard, R.H., 1901, *The Cry of the Poor*.

96 Flynt, J., 1899, *Tramping with Tramps: Studies and Sketches of Vagabond Life*.

97 Crane, D., 1910, *A Vicarious Vagabond*.

98 Edwards, G.Z., 1910, *A Vicar as Vagrant*.

99 Malvery, O., 1907, *The Soul Market*.

100 Scott, J.W.R., 1950, *The Story of the Pall Mall Gazette*, pp.166–167.

101 Greenwood, 1866, 'A Night in a Workhouse', *Pall Mall Gazette*, 12–15 January.

102 *Pall Mall Gazette*, 15 January 1866, p.5.

103 *Ibid.*, 5 October 1866, p.10.

104 London, J., 1903, *The People of the Abyss*, chapter IX.

105 'Stoving' was a form of disinfection carried out in an oven, sometimes employing sulphur fumes.

106 Higgs, M., 1904, *Five Days and Five Nights as a Tramp Among Tramps*, pp.16–22.

107 'Dad' was an elderly tramp previously encountered by Gray.

108 Kohl, J.G., 1844, *Travels in Ireland*, pp.287–291.

109 Twining, L., 1893, *Recollections of Life and Work*, pp.112–117.

110 Anonymous [Wills, W.H., and Taylor, P.], 1850, *Household Words*, Vol. 1, pp.361–364.

111 Slater, M. and Drew, J. (eds.), 2000, *Dickens' Journalism – The Uncommercial Traveller and Other Papers 1859–70*, p.41.

112 Inmates who committed any of the workhouse's more serious misdemeanours, such as disobeying or insulting the Master or Matron, were deemed 'refractory'. Punishments included a period in solitary confinement or on a bread and water diet.

113 Dickens, C., 1860, 'The Uncommercial Traveller', *All The Year Round*, pp.392–396.

114 Anonymous, 1878, 'Sighs from a London Workhouse', *London Society*, pp.561–567.

115 Pye-Smith, R.J., 1896, *Sheffield Daily Star*, 24 August 1896.

116 'The Union Workhouse', *Rossendale Divisional Gazette*, 25 June 1898.

INDEX